Praise for
IT STARTS WITH ONE

"Linkin Park is a rock story like no other—the band that fused hip-hop bravado, emo vulnerability, and classic-rock grandeur. Jason Lipshutz finally does justice to their one-of-a-kind history. *It Starts with One* is a brilliant chronicle of how a band of kids with so many contradictions—musical and emotional—managed to conquer the world."

> —**Rob Sheffield**, author and *Rolling Stone* contributing editor

"At the towering peaks of their success, Linkin Park's music was adamantly beloved by fans and mostly shrugged off by then-too-cool critics. Jason Lipshutz's *It Starts with One* stands as a heartfelt amendment, reappraising the band's artistic legacy and contextualizing its enduring fame. He looks at the members' individual and polymathic contributions to an always-evolving discography, reflects on the tough experiences that fed cathartic lyricism, and sheds light on the kindness and intentionality that left a lasting impression on the band's friends and peers. Lipshutz tells this detailed story much the same way Linkin Park crafted their songs—with sincerity and with passion."

> —**Sadie Dupuis**, Speedy Ortiz singer-songwriter, guitarist, and author

"Growing up resonating with the down-tuned riffs and raw hurt nu metal mined in the late '90s and '00s meant chafing at its reputation as white male suburban low culture, a stigma maintained by a noisy contingent valuing aggression over expression. *It Starts with One* is refreshing as an honest exploration of the unlikely arc of Linkin Park and the overarching scene the band occupied and ultimately departed. Avoiding rap-rock apologia but upending a long-standing critical apathy that followed lyricists like Chester Bennington and Mike Shinoda—who spoke to a generation in pain—Lipshutz surveys the thousand chance meetings, studio epiphanies, classic concerts, and lingering sorrows uniting Linkin Park and their millions of admirers."

> —**Craig Jenkins**, music critic, *New York* Magazine and *Vulture*

IT STARTS WITH ONE

IT STARTS WITH ONE

THE LEGEND AND LEGACY OF **LINKIN PARK**

JASON LIPSHUTZ

hachette
BOOKS
NEW YORK

Hachette Books
Hachette Book Group
1290 Avenue of the Americas
New York, NY 10104
HachetteBooks.com
Twitter.com/HachetteBooks
Instagram.com/HachetteBooks

First Edition: October 2024

Published by Hachette Books, an imprint of Hachette Book Group, Inc. The Hachette Books name and logo are trademarks of the Hachette Book Group.

The Hachette Speakers Bureau provides a wide range of authors for speaking events. To find out more, go to hachettespeakersbureau.com or email HachetteSpeakers@hbgusa.com.

Books by Hachette Books may be purchased in bulk for business, educational, or promotional use. For information, please contact your local bookseller or email the Hachette Book Group Special Markets Department at Special.Markets@hbgusa.com.

The publisher is not responsible for websites (or their content) that are not owned by the publisher.

Print book interior design by Bart Dawson

Library of Congress Cataloging-in-Publication Data
Name: Lipshutz, Jason, author.
Title: It starts with one: the legend and legacy of Linkin Park / Jason Lipshutz.
Description: First edition. | New York, NY: Hachette Books, 2024. | Includes
    bibliographical references and index.
Identifiers: LCCN 2024003752 | ISBN 9780306832505 (hardcover) | ISBN
    9780306832512 (trade paperback) | ISBN 9780306832529 (ebook)
Subjects: LCSH: Linkin Park (Musical group) | Rock musicians—United
    States—Biography.
Classification: LCC ML421.L558 L56 2024 | DDC 782.42166092/2[B]—dc23/
    eng/20240126
LC record available at https://lccn.loc.gov/2024003752

ISBNs: 9780306832505 (hardcover); 9780306832529 (ebook)

Printed in the United States of America

LSC-C

Printing 1, 2024

For Chester and Phoebe

CONTENTS

INTERLUDE • 282
"I Will Never Forget That Experience"
by Ryan Key (Yellowcard)

INTRODUCTION

I WAS THIRTEEN IN the year 2000, an awkward middle schooler clutching a Discman in the back of the school bus. My favorite mixtape was a cherry-red Memorex disc that I had paid a friend five dollars to burn, and I spun that CD endlessly as the bus bounced around the South Jersey suburbs on brisk fall mornings.

In the middle of a track list that included Green Day's "Minority," Outkast's "Ms. Jackson," and Incubus's "Drive," Linkin Park's "Crawling" represented that compilation's cathartic high for my teenage psyche. With cheap plastic headphones snapped around my ears, I'd clench my teeth and whisper-scream the chorus; the sound of Chester Bennington's voice surely bled through, and my sing-along would no doubt rise too high, reaching whatever unfortunate soul was seated next to me. I was a dorky, insecure kid—but on those bus rides when I heard Chester sing "I've felt this way before / SO IN-SE-CUUUUUUURE," that lack of confidence gave way to brash instinct. Headbanging was committed on multiple occasions. My oversized glasses fell off my pimpled face during one of them.

Fast-forward a few decades: having worked as a writer and editor at *Billboard* for more than twelve years, I've spent the majority of my career nerding out about chart stats and music-biz data as much as huge hits and roaring hooks. Numbers can tell a story of music success both past (like 4.8 million—the number of copies Linkin Park's debut album *Hybrid Theory* sold in 2001) and present (like 34.2 million—Linkin Park's average monthly Spotify listeners total). I've been spotlighting those stories for readers, often to see where they might lead in the future, while also jamming to the songs behind the digits.

So, when I started thinking about writing this book, my personal fandom of Linkin Park's music naturally intertwined with my professional curiosity about how their numbers became, and stayed, so damn huge. The stature of their songs could be simultaneously heard in verse and chorus and seen in numerical evidence. For years, my job has been to listen to the biggest hits of yesterday, today, and tomorrow and help clarify their statistical importance, like a baseball fanatic underlining the most meaningful data on the back of a trading card. I knew some of Linkin Park's gaudy stat lines, was sure there would be plenty more to uncover with enough research, and couldn't wait to start highlighting.

Yet the more time I spent watching, listening, and learning about Linkin Park's career, the less the numbers seemed to matter. That's because the more I immersed myself in their world—the more closely I studied this universally beloved group that has personally impacted countless individuals, who hear their own struggle in the music—the less useful those numbers started to feel.

Ultimately, my adult chart geekery mattered far less than those angsty, flailing bus rides.

Linkin Park's story is one of human spirit being translated into emotional power—six guys, including two leaders from wildly different walks of life, coalescing around the turn of the millennium and becoming the rock band that means the most to the most listeners this century. Chester Bennington was a troubled kid from Arizona who was just about to give up on a music career, golden voice be damned; Mike Shinoda was a hip-hop nerd from California with years of bedroom demos and a bottomless well of ideas. Along with Brad Delson, Rob Bourdon, Dave "Phoenix" Farrell, and Joseph Hahn, they came together offering a different vision at a time when post-grunge mainstream rock had splintered into sanded-down alternative and ultra-aggro nu metal.

When Linkin Park found their balance, the world was quickly put on notice. To me, *Hybrid Theory* remains one of the greatest debut albums of all time, and its deep cuts and demo tracks are just as fascinating as its five-star smashes. The singing–rapping interplay between frontmen, the quiet–loud contrasts, the electronic and hip-hop influences of their production, the subtle pop sheen of the heaviest moments—it all elevated Linkin Park above their contemporaries, and *Hybrid Theory* erased genre lines more than a decade before streaming playlists were blurring those boundaries.

From there, commercial dominance: huge hits across multiple projects, six-figure album debuts, ubiquitous music videos, audiences that required stadium settings. Linkin Park became big enough to score pop hits with side projects and have the biggest rapper in the world calling for an extended collaboration. And yet, although their songs were accessible enough to travel far and wide, their combined message was just as important as their sound. Long before mental health discussions were foregrounded in popular music, Linkin Park addressed internal struggle within and outside of their music, and always in thoughtful and dynamic ways. The vulnerability never wore thin; it resonates even more clearly today, all these years later.

I realized that, more than any pile of statistics, Linkin Park's legacy is defined by an indescribable sensation that millions of listeners have felt in their gut. It's made countless people feel a little bit more understood and a little bit less alone.

An emotional reaction like that is impossible to quantify, but as a fan, of course I understand. I was seventeen when Linkin Park's "Breaking the Habit" became my favorite song to catch on Philadelphia alt-rock radio station Y100, and I was twenty-three when I got to see the band lay waste to Madison Square Garden on their 2011 world tour. I was a few weeks away from my thirtieth birthday when Chester passed away—an editor at *Billboard*, tasked with memorializing a lost legend—and thirty-three when Mike and Joe told me the backstory of every song on *Hybrid Theory* for a feature on its twentieth anniversary.

I've been fortunate enough to write about Linkin Park and chat with the band members multiple times over the course of my career at *Billboard*, and I remain grateful to the band and their team for their encouragement on this project. This book features a mix of original reporting from interviews that I conducted—including never-before-published passages—and archived quotes from previously published interviews.

And though this project combines my biographical exploration, critical analysis, and overall appreciation of Linkin Park, I never wanted my voice to be the be-all and end-all. That's why I've asked a handful of other artists—touring partners, studio collaborators, musicians who exist in the extended Linkin Park universe—to share some of their memories and insights, which are sprinkled in between chapters.

When you dive deep into the story and discography of Linkin Park, their musical impact—and cultural impact beyond that—becomes a lot more undeniable. Absorbing the richness of their catalog has been one of the highlights of my career as a writer and life as a music fan, and I hope that passion comes across in my words.

Linkin Park's full story has never been properly amplified. It's time to press play.

IT STARTS
WITH
ONE

THE IDENTITY

CHAPTER 1

I**T STARTS WITH** one performance at one of the most famous music venues in the United States, a haphazard opening set now frozen in rock lore. The show that changes a band's trajectory doesn't need to be perfect. It doesn't even need to be *good*. But when the group that would become Linkin Park strolled onstage at Whisky a Go Go in Los Angeles on November 14, 1997, to play their first show together, a great performance was never in the cards.

For one: Mike Shinoda, the band's rapper and one of its de facto leaders, looked absolutely absurd.

As the rest of the group plugged in their instruments and let the lights wash over them, Mike prowled the stage with a white beanie hat pulled down over his jet-black hair, blue goggles shielding his dark brown eyes, and his mic gripped in a pair of white gloves. It was a fashion crime of a getup, even in the cargo-pants heyday of the late nineties, and dry laughs wafted up from the audience members who hadn't ditched the pit to grab another beer.

Mike took a breath. He had been thinking about setting foot on this stage—hallowed ground, in his eyes—for a long time, and his band was fortunate enough to make its live debut here. Whisky a Go Go is the sticky-floored mecca of the Sunset Strip, the same lovably sweat-stained five-hundred-cap venue that Led Zeppelin, The Doors, Blondie, and Soundgarden had all graced while careening across West Hollywood.

The audience wasn't there to see Mike or his band, Xero, that November evening. A fast-rising rock group out of Glendale called System of a Down was headlining, and SX-10, the alt-metal side project from Cypress Hill's Sen Dog, was playing before System. On this bill, Xero was an opener—and more or less an afterthought. But Mike had spent countless hours writing songs, streamlining beats, and hustling with his bandmates to figure out how to turn this very moment into a reality.

And when that moment finally arrived, he decided to greet it while essentially cosplaying as a Smurf.

"I was wearing the most ridiculous thing ever," Mike recalled years later. "I think because it made me feel more like a performer, and not the normal dude that I knew I was. So I had to get into costume in order to get psyched up and get into character."

It made sense that Mike didn't really understand how to present himself onstage at that point: he was just a twenty-year-old graphic design college student, not a rock star. Meticulous and down-to-earth instead of brash and rowdy, Mike was used to playing music with his friends, making beats in his bedroom, and writing controlled rhymes seared by emotion, with the hope of someday making his own demos and sharing them with a wide audience.

He was, indeed, a "normal dude"—cerebral and talented, but also one of thousands of aspiring California musicians chipping away at a brighter tomorrow. His band Xero was still a rap-rock rough sketch, with their brittle guitar lines, warbled hooks, and nebulous rhymes constituting loose contours and half-drawn ideas. As part of the third band on a three-band bill, how was he supposed to get anyone to pay attention? Who was he supposed to be up there?

So: white beanie, blue goggles, white gloves. When you're an ordinary guy a few months shy of your twenty-first birthday and tasked with briefly taking over the same famous platform where Plant, Morrison, Harry, and Cornell had previously conjured magic, sometimes a costume can help cover up some of that imposter syndrome—however misguided that costume may be.

Six years before that night, Mike was a kid on the other side of the threshold, a spectator at his first concert, which happened to be one of the more unlikely co-headlining tours of the early nineties.

In 1991, Anthrax recorded a new version of Public Enemy's "Bring the Noise," reinventing the hip-hop collective's 1988 single through a thrash-metal lens. The remix was a sign of mutual appreciation: Anthrax guitarist Scott Ian wore Public Enemy tees onstage during the band's pummeling shows in the eighties, and Public Enemy leader Chuck D shouted out the cult rock group in the lyrics to "Bring the Noise" ("Beat is for Eric B. and LL as well, hell / Wax is for Anthrax, still it can rock bells").

Three years after "Bring the Noise" became the urgent opening salvo of Public Enemy's 1988 hip-hop classic *It Takes a Nation of Millions to Hold Us Back*, Anthrax reconfigured the song, flattening its funk samples and record-scratching with blunt-force guitar work, cymbal rides, and air sirens. The remixed "Bring the Noise" became an improbable hit, particularly overseas—the Anthrax version of "Bring the Noise" reached the top 10 in New Zealand, and reached No. 14 in the UK—and Public Enemy and Anthrax decided to hit the road as a joint bill. The two groups ended each show of their 1991 trek onstage together, their headbang-ready take on the years-old song ringing in thousands of ears.

A fourteen-year-old Mike was among those onlookers, giddy with excitement, dizzied by the scene around him. Even though he had already been immersed in music for more than half his life, Mike had never experienced anything like *this*.

Michael Kenji Shinoda was born on February 11, 1977, and grew up across the eighties in Agoura Hills, a small, sun-kissed suburb on the outskirts of Los Angeles, the type of idyllic setting for a sweeping film sequence (the opening scene of *Gone with the Wind*, in fact, was shot not too far from the Shinoda household). His parents, Muto and Donna, didn't listen to a lot of music around the house, other than the occasional show tune or country song, but Mike was still encouraged to master classical music and make use of the family's upright piano. Lessons and recitals started when Mike was six, followed by performances in a local youth group, where he'd belt out songs from *West Side Story*.

He didn't love any of it. Mike would have much rather been playing video games or watching medieval-times adventure movies. But he had a creative mind—he particularly enjoyed drawing and painting—and musical instincts; plus, he was making friends during rehearsals.

A few weeks before Shinoda turned eight years old, however, Run-D.M.C. released their second album, *King of Rock*. A friend played him a couple tracks from the cassette tape one day, and Mike was instantly hooked.

Although Run-D.M.C. is arguably the most impactful hip-hop group of all time, *King of Rock*, released a little less than a year after their 1984 debut album, was actually a moment of transition. The Queens trio's first album foresaw a future in which rapping constituted the basis of a mainstream genre, and their third album, 1986's *Raising Hell*, would become the group's stone-cold classic—the one with "It's Tricky," "My Adidas," and their version of "Walk This Way"—the record that elevated them to real stardom. In between, *King of Rock* augmented the rapping-over-guitars proposition hinted at in parts of Run-D.M.C.'s debut.

The album leaned into rock-based production, acknowledged the ascension of hair metal, and attempted to bring the group's brand of call-and-response hip-hop to the masses. But for every effective guitar squeal and lyrical jab ("I'm the king of ROCK, there is none HIGHER / Sucker MC's should call me SIRE," which kicks off the title track, remains the most quotable), *King of Rock* had thudding stomp-claps that didn't really land and one-liners too mushy to be considered menacing. The album sounds like a dress rehearsal for *Raising Hell*, and specifically that album's "Walk This Way," on which Run-D.M.C. resuscitated a decade-old Aerosmith song by supplementing its funky riff and hook with some slick new rapping. "Walk This Way" made Run-D.M.C. a household name and basically became the commercial apotheosis of the *King of Rock* blueprint.

Mike grew up absorbing rap when it was still a few years away from bubbling over and topping the pop charts—a bold, rapidly developing, predominantly Black form of underground music that members of the record industry were either dismissing as a fad or angling to unlock as a mega-seller. The fusion of rhyming and hard-rock production made sense as an avenue to widen rap's appeal in the second half of the eighties, and songs like "Walk This Way" and Tone Lōc's "Wild Thing," which turned a Van Halen sample into a smash, streaked into the top 10 of the Hot 100 chart.

Stylistic mash-ups would continue to evolve in more problematic directions as rap grew bigger; digestible pop-rap hits by artists like Vanilla Ice and Marky Mark and the Funky Bunch would be prioritized on Top 40 radio in the early 1990s, co-opting the sound of an established Black culture for a wider (read: whiter) audience to enjoy. But a preteen Mike was always more interested in digging deeper into the DNA of rap music than consuming its sanitized versions, and he started inhaling as much hip-hop as he could find.

Beastie Boys, a trio of white kids from New York, made their debut a year after *King of Rock*, and as a punk-rock group positioning themselves toward hip-hop, they represented the inverse of the Run-D.M.C. arc, with catchy songs and a rap credibility that could serve as a gateway to adolescent listeners like Mike. The Beasties' first album, 1986's *Licensed to Ill*, was the first record that Mike purchased with his own money, followed by LPs from LL Cool J and Ice-T. After that, he began exploring blues, jazz, and funk music, as if stripping down the influences of rap music and inspecting its disassembled parts.

When he was around thirteen years old, Mike told his longtime piano teacher that he wanted to start playing other types of music, including hip-hop. "She said she couldn't help me out with that because that wasn't her training," he recalled. "She said, 'Maybe you just wanna get a keyboard and start learning those things on your own.' I thought that was really big of her to say, and definitely led to an important point in my life where I bought a keyboard. Then I got a sampler, started making beats and playing around with MIDI [an electronic music format] and digital-based music."

Mike quit his piano lessons but was able to rely upon those years of understanding music theory to make mathematically legible beats. In those hours of tinkering with bedroom productions, he used his technical knowledge and personal taste to mix sounds in methods that excited him: Mike would take old jazz and rock songs, decipher the ingredients that made them what they were, and reimagine those ingredients as the backbone of a hip-hop beat.

He worshiped Dr. Dre—as in, sought out every piece of music that he touched—at a time when the future superstar mogul was still grinding out beats for his group N.W.A and their West Coast cohorts. And part of that adoration came from Dre's gift of recontextualization. Dre had the ability to contort existing musical elements into new shapes, and in a way he couldn't quite specify yet, Mike wanted that for himself, too.

To be clear, Mike didn't think he was the *next Dr. Dre*—he was a nerdy kid, from a very different part of Southern California. When he entered an original piano song contest as a preteen, he did so with a song about Dungeons & Dragons. But he was *good*. That D&D song came in first place in the contest and won him fifty bucks.

So by the time he went to that Public Enemy and Anthrax show in 1991—chaperoned by his friend's dad, bellowing "Turn it up, *BRING THE NOISE!*," watching Anthrax deconstruct a rap song into a rock song in the way that he wanted to deconstruct rock songs into rap songs, marveling at the mashed-up tenacity and moshing bodies and velocity of the words being hurled from the groups onstage and back at them—Mike already knew he could make music. But that was the night he started thinking about becoming a musician.

BRAD DELSON HAD BEEN FRIENDS with Mike since they were kids and balanced him out in many ways. He was louder than his producer friend, plucky where Mike was precise. They grew up together in Agoura Hills and ended up alongside each other on that Whisky a Go Go stage. But Brad's route there couldn't have been more different.

Unlike Mike, who was more of a rap kid, Brad played Metallica non-stop growing up, . . . *And Justice for All* constantly rattling his bedroom windows. As a preteen, he traded his trumpet in the elementary school orchestra for a six-string, taking guitar lessons before teaching his own. And while Mike spent the first few years of high school holed away with his sampler, mashing up Depeche Mode and Wu-Tang Clan, Brad was playing in band after band, basement shows bleeding into one another.

He treated performing in those groups like a social activity instead of a lifelong goal. "I did it as a hobby," Brad explained. "Something that I loved, but I never thought I would pursue it professionally."

Brad played guitar in a rap-rock band called The Pricks, and Mark Wakefield, Mike's neighbor and friend, was their lead singer. The members of The Pricks palled around with another Agoura Hills band a few years older than them called Hoobastank; Brad and Mark were even there for Hoobastank's first show ever, the opening act at a June 1995 gig in singer Doug Robb's backyard. Both bands "borrowed" stage equipment from Agoura High School in the middle of the night for the performance, and 150 local kids showed up to support the cause.

The Pricks broke up, and Brad and Mark formed another band—this time with a drummer named Rob Bourdon, from Calabasas High School a few miles away, who hated playing in the jazz band but who sounded sturdy enough behind the kit to recruit for the new group. The new band was named Relative Degree, and although the group preserved The Pricks' general rap-infused rock techniques, they took themselves seriously enough to function more like a proper group than a teenage pastime.

They wrote a dozen songs together, hammered them out during practice sessions at Rob's mom's house, and even scored a gig at the Roxy, a few blocks down from the Whisky on Sunset Boulevard, in May 1996. Some of the members had started college by this point, attending classes in between rehearsals and not considering Relative Degree successful enough to provide as a viable future . . . but they were also letting band life seep into their minds and habits, learning how to compose rock songs with panache and showcase them with discernment.

All the while, Mike watched from the sidelines. He would crash Relative Degree practices to hang out with Brad and Mark and toss the band samples every so often to consider for their songs. Yet Mike was more invested in producing mash-ups and spinning them into beats for local rappers than joining a band. "We always just figured we were in two different worlds," Brad explained.

Mike had also started rapping over his beats by this point—but as a literal joke. He and Mark would write gangsta-rap parody songs, as a dorky-fun alternative to high school parties. One song, "North Coast Killa," spoofed the East Coast–West Coast feud raging in mainstream hip-hop at the time by taking shots at, of all places, Canada. And a demo tape they made titled *Pooch Pound*, a riff on Snoop Doggy Dogg and the Dogg Pound, would have the teen boys doubled over in laughter.

"They were all about smoking weed and being pimps, and those were two things we were totally unfamiliar with," Mike said. "Like with a lot of suburban kids, there was an element of voyeurism there—I had never been down to Long Beach, y'know?"

None of it was serious. By that point, Mark was already enrolled at California State University Long Beach, and Mike was headed to Pasadena's ArtCenter College of Design to study graphic design and illustration. Brad got a scholarship to UCLA and entered as a communications major, weighing his parents' advice of going to law school and his own ideas of figuring out a job in the music-business world.

Relative Degree stopped practicing after the Roxy show and eventually broke up. The core of that group was still hacking around Agoura, but everyone was growing up, expanding toward the next phase of their lives. Maybe playing in a band wasn't going to be part of that.

But then, something funny happened: Mike started writing songs that weren't jokes.

In fact, the words he began furiously scribbling were darn near melodramatic, extreme in their late-teen emotional weight, and declarative in their first-person rhyme schemes. Mike had never viewed himself as a rapper, but once he tried his hand at writing rhymes for himself, he realized that he had both the production knowledge—he could make songs concocted on a four-track recorder in his bedroom sound professional—and the passion. By this point, he had *studied* rap for years and understood how to drill down on the nuances of a delivery.

Mike enlisted Mark's help as a cowriter and sounding board before the two became dueling vocalists on songs hatched in private. Thinking back to that formative moment of Run-D.M.C. rhyming over metal guitars and Anthrax positioning Public Enemy toward thrash, Mike collided styles with abandon, but the sound he was looking for needed more heft. After orbiting his friends' bands for years, it was finally time to form one himself.

Xero came together relatively seamlessly: Brad helped Mike and Mark flesh out a demo after a few writing sessions before officially joining the group, then Mike showed the songs to Rob, who hopped on the project as the drummer. Brad's roommate at UCLA, a biology major named Dave Farrell, happened to play bass, and when he heard the music that Brad was playing with his high school friends, he asked if he could join. And Joe Hahn, a classically trained musician from Glendale who had gotten into DJing in high school, was studying illustration at ArtCenter College of Design at the same time as Mike, and he climbed aboard Xero when they started rehearsing in 1997.

The collective crackled: six not-boys, not-yet-men, who understood the type of genre hybrid they wanted to create and had the personnel to make it happen. Mike would be the rapper and sonic engine, and Mark would provide the rock vocals. Brad and Rob had played guitar and drums, respectively, in Relative Degree and knew each other's sonic cues. Having Joe on board allowed the group to infuse their performances with live samples and scratching—a huge factor in how their songs were assembled.

"There was a goal in the type of song we were writing at the time, and a big part of that was to have songs to play live," Joe later explained. Xero's songs needed to "explode at a certain point," to have the rap and rock elements fuel each other and heighten the intensity of the climax for a hypothetical group of onlookers. "Part of our goal was to get this personal idea that has conflict," Joe continued—then added with a laugh, "and that was easy to do, because of our age at that time and that universal emotion of not fitting in and teen angst."

When the members of Xero felt confident that the songs on their first demo could translate to the stage, they set their sights on Whisky a Go Go for a live debut. Next, they had to figure out: How does an unknown band actually book a spot?

"Basically, with clubs of that magnitude, you pay to play," Rob said of the Whisky show. "If you can sell enough tickets, you can play." So, the six members hustled—most of them were still in school, and each would try to sell fifty to seventy-five tickets to friends and classmates, brandishing swaths of show passes around campus. "We would just go crazy," said Rob, "and try to sell them to everyone; family members, it didn't matter. We had to sell them to everyone just to play there." Fortunately, they hit the target in time and snagged an opening slot on the night of November 14, 1997.

Suddenly, it was showtime, and Xero was on the clock. The band started playing.

Within minutes of Rob's first drum thwacks and Brad's opening riffs, however, most of the baggy-jeans crowd at Whisky shrugged them off. Mike and Mark were trading rapped breakdowns and melodic hooks, Dave was letting his bass notes fly, and Joseph Hahn was interjecting turntable scratches within the pockets of noise . . . but the audience didn't care about the effort and instead turned away to start conversations among themselves.

Mike's outfit, laughable as it may have been, wasn't to blame. Though they wouldn't have been able to recognize it at the time, *no* part of the band—not its lineup, its name, its stage presence, or its sound—was fully formed when they played that night at the Whisky. Their moniker (*Zero* with an *X*, in order to look cooler than just the word *Zero*) was forgettable. Some of the members had known each other for years and cycled in and out of different bands together; others had just recently met. They were full of energy but lacking in chemistry, and they needed more time to figure out how to play off one another. And though some of the songs in their Whisky set sizzled with promise, they also lacked polish and a point of view.

Xero's set concluded with little fanfare, the band and their instruments doused in sweat. At some point, Mike removed his blue goggles, his band's first live performance in the books. The crowd was sparse, but at least they didn't get booed offstage—for the time being, that was enough. And, unbeknownst to him, someone important was watching from the back of the crowd, a vague idea of what this band could become burrowing into their brain.

"We were awful, just horrible," Mike admitted of that first show, "but we survived."

T HERE WAS NO guarantee that the Whisky show would mean anything in the long run. The six members of Xero were still plotting out other career paths and weren't banking on music as a future. After months of writing songs, rehearsing sets, and driving tickets, though, they wanted the Whisky performance to at least signify . . . *something*. They didn't want the show to be a tree falling in the woods—they needed someone, anyone, within earshot.

And thanks to Brad, they made a sound.

A few weeks before the Whisky show, Xero's guitarist had started interning at Zomba/Jive Music under Jeff Blue, a manager of creative at Zomba Music Publishing. Jeff had delivered an inspiring guest lecture at UCLA, and Brad quite literally stumbled into the internship: he crashed Jeff's office unannounced one morning and waited in his desk chair for the publishing rep to arrive at work. Brad swiveled around and caused a freak-out; it was a scene straight out of an angry-dad *Calvin & Hobbes* Sunday strip.

But Jeff liked Brad, appreciated the moxie of the college kid with the floppy head of curly hair and the stones to declare that his own band would be cooler than any of Jeff's recent signees. "I saw a lot of myself in this kid," Blue wrote in the opening pages of his memoir *One Step Closer*. And when Brad passed him a demo tape of his band Xero—in between sessions of helping Jeff deliver a rising R & B singer named Macy Gray to the mainstream—Jeff listened to it. He was impressed by Brad's guitar playing and the kid named Mike who was rapping on top of it.

Brad mentioned the Whisky gig in hopes that his boss would come check out his band's first performance, but Jeff had a date scheduled for that night and said he'd have to catch their next show. On the afternoon of the show, from his office window Jeff saw Brad walking down Sunset toward the Whisky and felt a pang of guilt for not being able to go. "I wanted to support Brad," he wrote, "so I canceled my plans, grabbed a slice of pizza, and walked up to the box office."

A million tiny hypothetical situations have to become reality for a band to be "discovered." Chalk it up to the law of averages: for every one musical act that gets noticed and scooped up by a music-industry power broker, countless others play without being heard and never fulfill their dreams. Sure, some of those voices on the perpetual sidelines don't have the talent or ideas to hack it, but plenty *are* worthy and still can't button-mash a combination to fame and fortune. Breaking through requires a chain reaction of quietly correct decisions, some of which can be controlled, plenty of which cannot, and almost none of which feel significant in the moment.

For the members of Xero, the list of possible detours away from that night at Whisky a Go Go, right turns that could have easily gone left, was endless. What if Mike hadn't attended that Anthrax and Public Enemy concert in 1991 and felt that sharp pang of early-teen inspiration? Or what if Brad had kept playing trombone instead of guitar in middle school, Metallica obsession be damned? If Rob had stuck with drumming in the jazz band instead of joining rock groups . . . if Mark hadn't started writing songs with Mike . . . if Dave had been placed with a different roommate than Brad at UCLA . . . if Joe hadn't overlapped with Mike at art school. But those thoughts, choices, and intersections *did* happen—minor collisions of luck and skill that delivered the band of six onto a major stage that November evening.

And just think: all those bursts of serendipity might have *still* meant nothing if Jeff Blue had decided not to bail on his date that night.

From Jeff's vantage point at the back of the disinterested Whisky crowd, Xero sounded raw, which was natural for a first-ever performance.

Their stage presence was lacking, sure, and the lead vocalist wasn't attacking the notes like he should. Yet their energy onstage masked some of the awkwardness, and the songs themselves were pretty good. Jeff wasn't in the business of breaking his intern's band, but he was intrigued.

Yes, Jeff also noticed that Mike was dressed like a rapping Smurf. No, that didn't dissuade him from hastily jotting down a final word onto a napkin at the end of their set: "*Potential!*"

TIMING IS *EVERYTHING* IN ROCK 'n' roll. The Whisky gig took place at a formative moment for the band—playing their first show together, testing the songs from the Xero demo tape, inching their way toward a congealed identity—with an early configuration of the members and an onlooker who could detect their promise. But beyond that, they started their journey at the exact right moment in rock history.

Put it this way: that same show could have taken place in November 1996 instead of November 1997 and probably wouldn't have had a fraction of the butterfly-effect shockwave it caused. Hell, even a *few months* before that moment, and it's possible—maybe even probable—that it never happens for the guys.

In November 1997, popular rock music was more diverse and exciting than ever or totally lost in the wilderness, depending on who you asked. At the beginning of the 1990s, hair metal was fully usurped as the dominant form of commercial rock music—it was more than time for a change-up from the materialism and casual sexism. Bands like Van Halen, Def Leppard, and Mötley Crüe had become superstars in the eighties by filtering fat guitar riffs through arena-ready choruses and outlandish onstage personalities. Hit songs looked and sounded like the video of Poison's 1988 smash "Nothin' but a Good Time": shimmering blond locks, lime-green guitars, end-of-the-week hedonism, ridiculous slow-motion fireworks displays.

By the early nineties, however, the scene's harder edges had been fully sanded down to yield radio-chasing, yawn-inducing ballads like Extreme's "More Than Words" and Mr. Big's "To Be with You." Both of those songs were chart toppers, but the party was clearly wrapping up. "It became too commercialized," Twisted Sister's Dee Snider said of hair metal in a 2022 interview, "and then it got unplugged and became nothing but power ballads and acoustic songs, and it wasn't metal anymore. It had to go; it had to change."

Grunge—a Pacific Northwest strain of metal with more introspective songwriting, sludgier guitar distortion, churning tempos, and gritty vocal timbres—presented a course correction. It helped that grunge's leaders were actively rooting against hair metal. "I hated it," said Pearl Jam's Eddie Vedder. "I hated how it made the fellas look. I hated how it made the women look. It felt so vacuous." Their music, in turn, was steeped in reality, and reality was grimy. And so it was that a movement built on glam, excess, and artifice naturally gave way to one writhing around in unwashed hair, plain clothes, and gravelly calls to "Come as You Are."

Although hair metal still existed as grunge bands started finding an audience at the start of the nineties, Nirvana's second album, released in September 1991, was an extinction-level event. Once *Nevermind* exploded—quickly accepted as a generation-defining blockbuster, with lead single "Smells Like Teen Spirit" reaching the top 10 of the Hot 100 while frontman Kurt Cobain's call of *Here we are now, entertain us!* sounded like *nothing else* around it on the chart—the tenets of popular rock music shifted, and record labels swiftly traded in leather pants for flannel shirts.

The idea of "grunge" was straightforward enough for the moniker to stick, even if the bands being categorized as grunge didn't love the nickname. But the bleary "Smells Like Teen Spirit" music video, the echoing yowl of Alice in Chains' Layne Staley, the social alienation of Pearl Jam's "Jeremy," the heavy solos of Soundgarden's Kim Thayil—they all seemed to be parts of a larger whole, from the same region of the United States, that rock fans could easily digest and classify.

In truth, however, grunge was only the tip of an iceberg, the most prominent subgenre in the middle of a revolution that was much bigger than a handful of bands breaking out of Seattle. "Alternative," a catch-all for several forms of underground rock loosely defined as left of commercial (alternative to the mainstream, as it were), suddenly *became* the mainstream, thanks to bands like Nirvana and Pearl Jam redefining what rock stars sounded and looked like for the incoming wave.

R.E.M., Red Hot Chili Peppers, Jane's Addiction, Sonic Youth, Nine Inch Nails, Violent Femmes, The Breeders—none of these bands sounded *quite* like grunge, and some of them had found varying degrees of success in their respective scenes in the years leading up to its takeover. But once Cobain and Vedder helped knock down the gates, alternative rock turned into big business. Lollapalooza gathered disparate sounds and ideas into a mega-selling road show, MTV and radio programmers took more chances on insular and unorthodox-looking newcomers, and artists who had started their careers rebelling against the music establishment unwittingly found themselves in the middle of it.

"There is a serious market for a youth counterculture," Perry Farrell, the Jane's Addiction leader and Lollapalooza founder, said in 1992, just as Lolla was starting to turn into a juggernaut. Then he added, "That's the bad news."

Most of the biggest bands in the alternative boom weren't prepared for rock stardom or for the music industry to eagerly position them as such. It was as if the movie *Revenge of the Nerds*, where a bunch of college geeks band together to defeat the jocks and date the bombshells, kept going for years after the triumphant final scene. The nerds were without an opponent and uncertain how to wield their new alpha status.

In late 1993, Vedder was openly rebelling against MTV, swearing off arena shows, and suffering something of an identity crisis. A few months later, Cobain was found dead in his Seattle home.

Grunge lost its greatest leader, and the alternative music scene, already loosely tied together, began to unravel. Popular rock music splintered in several different directions in the mid-nineties: there were the post-grunge bands like Stone Temple Pilots and Bush; snotty pop-punk stars like Green Day and The Offspring; Britpop kings like Oasis and Blur; ska-punk interlopers like No Doubt and Sublime; eighties-bred hard rockers like

Metallica and Pantera; college-rock stalwarts like Sonic Youth and Pavement; pop-loving experimentalists like Beck and Ween; and of course, the grunge torchbearers like Soundgarden and Pearl Jam.

Even as the center of alternative music became too unwieldy to fit onto a single Lollapalooza lineup, some incredible rock records were made—Radiohead's *The Bends*, Björk's *Post*, Hole's *Live Through This*, and Nine Inch Nails' *The Downward Spiral* were all released within a year and a half of Cobain's death, supernovas in their own universes. But just like hair metal's vivacity eventually became watered down, popular alt-rock turned exceedingly safe—and soft—during the second half of the nineties, with bands that flaunted the faintest whiff of grunge's warbled vocals but none of its muddy production or thematic heaviness.

And listeners ate up that family-friendly post-grunge far and wide. Songs like Counting Crows' "Mr. Jones," Matchbox Twenty's "3AM," Goo Goo Dolls' "Name," and The Wallflowers' "One Headlight" turned wails and growls into the catchiest sounds you could hear on pop radio and helped those bands sell millions of albums without ever turning up the volume too loud. Sure, there was great rock to be found on the fringes, and some of the bands innovating within alternative music could play to arenas. But this was an era when Hootie & the Blowfish were getting name-checked on *Friends* and their *Cracked Rear View* outsold any single album by, say, alt-rock leaders like Smashing Pumpkins. Darius Rucker's brawny croon of "I only wanna be with *yooouuu-hoooo*" was more culturally inescapable than Billy Corgan's best pinched wail.

"As a movement, we blew it," Corgan declared following the Pumpkins' international run supporting 1995's ultra-ambitious double album *Mellon Collie and the Infinite Sadness*. "We dropped the ball. It's like all these bands created this thirst in the early nineties for a new era of rock, and then we didn't finish it."

FLASH FORWARD TO 1997. IT was the best of times, it was the worst of times, depending on how closely your CD collection matched what was being played across the FM dial. But even as sanded-down post-grunge dominated the airwaves, another shift was coming: rap-rock was about to explode.

In the twelve years since Run-D.M.C.'s *King of Rock*, rap and rock music continued to prod each other for ideas while coexisting on the same plane of popular music. For years, rappers sampled popular rock tracks— "Rhymin & Stealin," the logically titled first song on the first Beastie Boys album, is built around a Led Zeppelin riff—taking cues from guitar-heavy rap hits like LL Cool J's "Rock the Bells."

Meanwhile, rock bands were starting to incorporate rap cadences into their song structures as a result of a mix of artistic appreciation (like Anthrax reworking a Public Enemy hit in 1991) and, undoubtedly, commercial intrigue. For all intents and purposes, early-nineties hits like Faith No More's "Epic" and Red Hot Chili Peppers' "Give It Away" were built *around* rapping, but because the rhymes were being delivered by white guys in band setups and surrounded by spiraling guitars, both songs received heavy alternative airplay, were played to sprawling crowds at rock festivals, and made those bands a lot of money. Not all bands that dabbled with these sounds were immediately successful, though. An LA quartet called Rage Against the Machine earned critical acclaim and a cult following with their explicitly political rapping over metal noodling, but their self-titled 1992 album took *years* to find a real following—years that Rage spent on the road, proselytizing and proving themselves over and over again.

Rap-rock music rolled on in the background of popular rock as grunge begat the alternative revolution. It may have stayed there in the back forever, a genre experiment too unwieldy for a mainstream happily gulping down Sugar Ray singles. But something else was going on simultaneously during this era of change in rock music: popular rap music had entered its golden age, a full-on outburst of riveting personalities and ideas.

At the beginning of the decade, popular rap was composed of novelty-leaning pop crossovers—think MC Hammer, Vanilla Ice, Sir Mix-a-Lot. Within five years' time, however, performers like The Notorious

B.I.G., Outkast, 2Pac, Nas, Fugees, Lil' Kim, Snoop Doggy Dogg, and Busta Rhymes burst onto the scene, many of whom were scoring real hits, releasing classic albums, soaking up MTV airtime, and becoming brand-name stars across the pop, fashion, and movie worlds.

That renaissance of popularized rap music was crucial to the commercial development of rap-rock, and not just because the music industry recognized an increased demand for all types of rap. The fact was, rap stars *were* the new rock stars—edgy and intoxicating, playing music that was fresh for Gen X teens and loathed by their parents, Tipper Gore, and other authority figures just begging to be rebelled against. The fracturing of alternative music meant fewer rock artists holding the center of the genre, and that vacuum was filled by it-factor rap stars. All of a sudden, Puffy and Snoop were now the ones controlling the direction of popular culture, not Third Eye Blind, no matter how many times "Semi-Charmed Life" was being played on the radio.

Because rap artists were setting the tone, rock bands that incorporated elements of rap music—the rhyme patterns, yes, but also the production, style, and overall magnetism—were starting to play to bigger crowds and get sniffed out by the music industry. Rage Against the Machine's second album, 1996's *Evil Empire*, sold a quarter million copies in its first week, and by the following year, the band was opening for U2. Korn, a metal band from Bakersfield, California, that embraced rap beats and hip-hop fashion while singing about domestic agony, also scored its first top 10 album in 1996 with *Life Is Peachy* and brought a brash new group with their own cult following, Limp Bizkit, out with them on the road.

These bands approached rap-rock differently—Korn's alienated fury was never in conversation with Rage's social righteousness—and there was some overlap with the concurrent "electronica" boom, in which groups like The Prodigy and Chemical Brothers emphasized digitized production and aggressively blended genres. But the impact of popular hip-hop was clear across the board, and by 1997, record labels were hard at work molding them into hybrid stars.

The members of Xero weren't thinking about any of these grand industry machinations, though. They were just pressing play on the music they liked and swapping their favorite tracks with friends.

"It was the differences in what we listened to that informed one another," Mike later explained. He and Mark "both loved a lot of the same groups, but he was introducing me to more guitar-based music. He introduced me to Rage Against the Machine and Red Hot Chili Peppers and Nirvana and Pearl Jam. And I introduced him to Biggie and 2Pac and Mobb Deep and Wu-Tang."

Those disparate influences are evident on Xero's first demos. "Reading My Eyes" begins as a rap showcase for Mike: operating over a sample of the strings from Club Noveau's "Why You Treat Me So Bad," he delivers a laundry list of boasts ("The microphone molester, machete undresser / Stupid-dope-fresh-type shit resurrector / Top gun, Miramar best-of-the-best-er / The leave-an-MC-peace-in-rest-er") that recalls Inspectah Deck's rhyme scheme on Wu-Tang Clan's 1997 classic "Triumph." Then the song turns on a dime into a sludgy rocker, with Mark's voice going full Vedder on the line "Reading my eyes will say it in many ways!"

Songs like "Fuse" and "Stick N Move" move similarly, with Mike's rap swagger pasted onto Mark's angsty singing over bulldozing production. The music wanders around, the lyrics are vague and a little clumsy, and neither vocalist sounds particularly comfortable. But then the blueprint locks into place on the demo's standout song, "Rhinestone."

Over a pulverizing guitar riff from Brad and some nifty turntable work from Joe, Mike and Mark circle around each other on the hook, then clear out to give each other space to emote in separate corners of the song. The rapping flows smoothly, the singing carries weight. "Rhinestone" was Xero's most polished track, the sound of a band clawing at their artistic promise.

Jeff Blue heard it in "Rhinestone," too—it was the song that sold him on the band back when he watched them perform their first-ever show at Whisky a Go Go. Jeff had recently signed Korn and Limp Bizkit to songwriting deals; he understood the direction that popular rock music was headed at that moment. And even though Xero still had plenty of details begging for refinement, they had crossed into the music industry at a moment where the raw energy of their sound was a hot commodity, years of genre twists and turns leading to an alignment in the stars.

After the performance, Brad beckoned Jeff backstage to meet the rest of the band; two days later, Xero was invited up to his office for a meeting. That all-important seed had been planted.

Meanwhile, their lead singer—whom none of them knew or could've ever seen coming—was still one state away.

CHESTER BENNINGTON WAS well beyond the demo phase at that point. By the time his future bandmates had gotten together to debut their first few songs to a thinning crowd, he had already performed for thousands of people across Arizona, released two albums, and prowled the stage for nearly a half decade. In the dry heat of late-nineties Phoenix, Chester had been a glistening hero—not quite a rock star, but close enough that locals regarded him as such.

Chester was ready to move on from it all, though. He didn't *want* to be a hero. He was thinking of selling houses instead.

"I had basically decided to retire from music," Chester explained. "I'd got a job in real estate and thought that while I would probably still make tunes for fun, I would need to find something else to do full-time."

The idea seems impossible now: Chester Bennington forever setting down the microphone that he gripped harder than anyone, trading it for a suit and tie, chitchatting with young couples about neighborhoods with good schools and low taxes. And, keep in mind, Chester was still only twenty-two years old, which, for most people, was too soon to settle for a desk job, to stow away dreams as just-for-fun weekend activities.

But by the end of 1998, Chester was convinced that he wasn't built for the relentless churn of the music world. For five years professionally—and even longer personally—he had experienced barely controlled chaos. At twenty-two, Chester had already overcome far more than what most people experience in a lifetime. He wanted to play music, but more than that, he needed solid ground beneath his feet.

Grey Daze, the band that Chester fronted for the majority of his early days in music, had never represented that stability for him. The Phoenix group brought in a seventeen-year-old Chester as their singer in 1993, thanks to a prior connection with drummer Sean Dowdell, who had briefly played with Chester in the band Sean Dowdell and His Friends? Grey Daze cycled through new members constantly, changing guitarists and bassists seemingly every year before landing on Bobby Benish and Mace Beyers in 1995. And whenever they *did* lock in a lineup, Grey Daze performed nonstop: they played bars, restaurants, private events, and warehouse gigs, kicking up dust in the desert and trying to conjure invested listeners across scorching days and bleary nights.

Eventually, the grind paid off—but only partially. Grey Daze gradually developed into a popular band within their city's limits but produced zero buzz outside of it. Still, if you breathed the Phoenix rock scene in the mid-nineties, you knew Chester's voice, had maybe heard his songs on KUPD-FM, had probably caught one of his sets opening for a bigger act at the Electric Ballroom in Scottsdale. Even when they weren't headlining, Grey Daze would beguile audience members, and the bandmates would "sign autographs from the minute we finished playing until they closed the venue," Chester said.

Unfortunately for them, those shows never resulted in the major-label recruitment that would have introduced the band to listeners outside of the greater metropolitan area—no Jeff Blue character waiting in the back of a Grey Daze gig, scribbling "Potential!" onto a napkin. And so, the grind went on and on and on.

Grey Daze independently recorded and released two albums, 1994's *Wake Me* and 1997's . . . *No Sun Today*. Both CD covers showcased Photoshopped surrealism—a blackened slug on a beach at night! A woman in overalls walking through a field at night!—with sludgy overlaid text. Chester was the main writer on nearly every song. "We had a grungy sound," Chester recalled years later, "and though I'm proud of the songs, there wasn't anything super original about most of them."

It was a fair assessment: the two albums that Grey Daze released were full of competent, faceless grunge music, the type of pretty good yet generic songs that could have inspired an ample mosh pit on most nights, but never begged to linger in a stereo system for too long. The formula was clear on songs like "What's in the Eye," "Sometimes," and "Soul Song": the track would begin with a contemplative guitar riff, Chester would demonstrate vulnerability on the opening verse ("Sometimes, things just seem to fall apart / When you least expect them to," he glumly concludes on "Sometimes"), then a gaudy chorus full of roiling guitar and vein-bulge scream-singing would come crashing in.

Effective enough for a casual listener, especially if you were digging through crates to find bands that weren't Soundgarden and Stone Temple Pilots but sounded a lot like them. The problem was that Grey Daze didn't have the hooks or personality of those bands, so they couldn't distinguish themselves as more than a local photocopy of a national movement. And whenever the band *did* try to widen their aesthetic—"She Shines" nods toward industrial with a listless rhythm; "B12" aims for political urgency but sounds closer to a conspiracy-theory message board covering "We Didn't Start the Fire"—the results were either rough and fragmented or downright unappealing.

If Grey Daze had debuted a few years earlier, they might have been able to hitch a ride on the rocket ship of early-nineties grunge music and become national stars. But when the band played its first show—a January 1994 gig at Thunder & Lightning Bar & Grill in Scottsdale—Kurt Cobain's death, a tragedy that effectively disintegrated grunge's grip on popular rock music, was just a few months away. Grey Daze instead had to fend for themselves during the alternative-rock revolution in their five-year run through 1998, a grunge band muddling through a post-grunge world. They ended up getting outmoded during that time by groups who could market their singles to pop audiences and alternative artists who were pushing the boundaries of popular rock outward.

In the same way that Xero had unwittingly showed up to the rap-rock roll call right on time, Grey Daze had arrived to the grunge party a couple years too late. It was the difference between the rock 'n' roll fantasy—multistate tours, radio smashes, magazine covers—and the reality of Chester working at a Burger King in 1996 as a means of earning enough money to live on in between Grey Daze's two albums.

Chester, who was also younger than twenty-one for the majority of his time in Grey Daze, hadn't quite been ready to lead a band toward outsized goals or pen songs that resonated after the final riff. If you listened closely enough, however, you could hear that he possessed natural ability.

"Sickness," a song on . . . *No Sun Today* that Chester cowrote with Dowdell, boasts a vocal performance that sounds like the prototype of a five-tool rock legend: melodic singing on the verses, a maelstrom of intensity on the hook, jab-step interplay with the percussion, syllables elongated into a soaring effect, and all parts recorded cleanly for maximum impact. Chester's voice curls into a wounded snarl on "Sickness," then rattles the walls; the song is fine, but the person singing it—his range and rock-star aptitude—is special and clearly in distress.

"*I need more,*" Chester pleads on the chorus. "*Can you help me?*"

WHEN HE WAS IN FOURTH grade, Chester Charles Bennington would daydream about a jet plane touching down in his schoolyard. A crowd would gather around, the plane door would open, and out would step the members of one of his favorite bands: Depeche Mode.

Once they touched the ground, the British synth-rock pioneers would search for him in the mob of children, point him out, and announce to the rest of the school that they needed Chester, and only Chester, to be the fifth member of their band. "I think the dream for me," Chester admitted as an adult, "was really joining the band of a bunch of singers."

It's a fantasy that any young music fan might have—your favorite band beams into your life, because they need your help rocking out! It's also, of course, the type of fantasy that prioritizes escape.

On the surface, Chester's adolescence wasn't dissimilar to that of Mike Shinoda, who was one year younger and four hundred miles away.

A lanky kid with a pointed chin, slightly curling hair, and round oversized glasses, Chester started singing in his school's musical theater around the same time that Mike was performing show tunes in youth group. Chester thought he had an okay voice, but what he really loved was acting; he had been performing since he was four years old, singing and acting out the entirety of the *Popeye* film for his family or whoever was over their house at the time. Theater was "what I actually thought I was going to be doing professionally," he said later—disappearing into roles, pretending to be someone else.

Even though drama was his first love, he was also a budding lyricist at heart, and up in his bedroom he would write songs and poems. Around the same age that Mike started consuming any and all popular hip-hop, Chester fell in love with The Doors, learning their entire catalog and slowly transitioning from hanging with the theater kids to circling around the local music scene. In Agoura Hills, Mike's friends and future bandmates broke into their high school to steal stage equipment for a backyard gig; meanwhile, in Phoenix, Chester broke into a church and stole a microphone so that he could jam with a friend who had a guitar. He didn't consider it theft; he thought he was committing divine intervention.

That's where the parallels end, however. Chester's parents, a detective named Lee and a nurse named Susan, divorced when he was eleven years old, and although Chester was the youngest of four siblings, his older brother and oldest sister had already left home, and his other sister was seldom around. Chester lived with his dad, who investigated child-sex crimes in the greater Phoenix area and frequently pulled double shifts. As he entered his teens, Chester was often home alone or else trying to diffuse tension with his father. "He was hardened by dealing with the shit of the world every day," Chester explained. "So, he brought a lot of that home."

Chester was never harmed by anyone in his family. But, as he was candid about in his first major interviews, he was abused for years—and during some of the most formative years of his life.

"I started getting molested when I was about seven or eight," he said. "It was by a friend who was a few years older than me. It escalated from a touchy, curious, 'what does this thing do' into full-on, crazy violations. I was getting beaten up and being forced to do things I didn't want to do. It destroyed my self-confidence."

Chester never said anything to anyone until years later, too afraid to admit what was happening to him. The sexual assaults continued until Chester was thirteen. By then, he hated everyone in his family: his mother for the divorce, his father for being emotionally unavailable, his siblings for never being around. Music helped Chester cope—he was comforted by the voices of Dave Gahan, Morrissey, Robert Smith, and Al Jourgensen, outsiders who proudly sang about their detachments from modern society—but it wasn't enough to truly heal him. His spirit had been ripped in half, and he needed something to feel whole.

And so, with no one around enough to tell him not to, Chester sank into an abyss of drugs and alcohol, at a time when most kids his age were focused on algebra tests and extracurriculars. "I was a lot more confident when I was high," he admitted, looking back. "I felt like I had more control over my environment when I was on hallucinogens or drinking."

When asked what type of drugs he had been taking in his early teenage years, Chester said, "Everything." It was mostly acid, but when he and his friends couldn't scrounge any up, he turned to speed, which was relatively cheap and effective. Chester also had dalliances with cocaine, mushrooms, and pills, in addition to pot and alcohol, but on a typical day, he and his friends would pack a bong full of meth and rip through an eight-ball, then use opium to come down.

While high out of his mind, Chester still thought about music; he and his friend Jason Abner would shamble into local parties with a beat-up guitar and stolen microphone, slur through Doors songs like "Crystal Ship" and "L.A. Woman," barely able to remember a detail, so naturally they assumed they sounded amazing. Lost in substances at this point, Chester was hoping that his own reckless abandon would evoke Jim Morrison's, the foggy nights bleeding together to produce raw, unvarnished artistry. The reality was that Chester's drugged-out performances sucked—he could barely function, let alone put on a good show—but the sinewy nerves of his voice did ring out, even in that state.

In 1992, Sean Dowdell, the older brother of a kid named Scotty who often jammed in garages with Chester and Jason, invited Chester to audition for a band he was putting together. Even though Chester was sixteen and close to three years younger than everyone else in the band, a few seconds of singing Pearl Jam's "Alive" was enough to convince Sean and his bandmates that they had found their frontman.

Sean Dowdell and His Friends? bounced around the Phoenix area in 1993, playing covers of the Ramones' "I Wanna Be Sedated" and Alice in Chains' "Would?," in addition to a handful of original songs, at frat parties and warehouses. The band eventually recorded a three-song demo of their own songs and printed two hundred cassette tapes, half of which made it into the hands of local supporters, half of which were destroyed in the Arizona heat. But that was as far as Sean Dowdell and His Friends? ever made it, in no small part because its lead singer was constantly showing up late to practice and getting in trouble at school for his drug habits. Ultimately, Chester was kicked out of the first band he had ever joined, and the rest of Sean Dowdell and His Friends? broke up soon after.

By the time he was seventeen, the drugs had thoroughly ravaged Chester, a wiry kid whose body had shed any semblance of heft. One day, he showed up, emaciated, to his mother's house, and she banned him from stepping foot outside until he got clean. Quitting meth cold turkey produced howling pain for Chester, an agonizing physical phenomenon that he used weed and alcohol to subside. "In later years," he said, "the drinking would come to take over my life." Recovery is never a straight line. Even as the harrowing effects of hard drugs fell away from his life, addiction would shape-shift, return, gnaw at him, ever present.

But even in these pitch-black moments, Chester could still hear the siren call of performing. When Sean Dowdell and His Friends? dissolved, Sean helped form another band, and took another chance on auditioning Chester's talent, only a few months after his last one had flamed out. After months of searching for a singer, the members of the newly formed Grey Daze still needed an emotive voice at their center; Chester, in turn, still needed to hoist himself out of the hell he had been wading around in for far too long. The stage would be his escape.

CONSIDERING WHAT HE HAD LIVED through in his early years, Chester could have been unrelentingly resentful about the hand he had been dealt, a bitter old man in the body of an eighteen-year-old. The fact that he made it through that tumultuous childhood with his good humor and grace intact is a minor miracle.

During his first few years performing in bands, Chester was often described as quiet and kind, passionate yet egoless, a good kid and a team player who could quickly get into trouble (like, say, stealing a microphone from a church) and just as quickly be forgiven. His voice was also becoming sharper and more refined as Grey Daze developed a loyal following. He was off drugs, holding down a job at Burger King during off days, piecing together how to reside on the stage at nights, and constantly exploring the singular contours of his scream.

"Nobody ever heard anything like him," said Rob Rogers, who had coproduced the Sean Dowdell and His Friends? demo. In addition to the vocal technique, Rogers added, "He also had a natural ability to perform."

Chester was onstage when he met his future wife, Samantha Olit, in January 1996, finding her face in the crowd of a Grey Daze show at Club Rio in Tempe and refusing to unlock eyes with her. "Almost the entire time, every song he sang, it was as if he was singing directly to me," Samantha recalled in her memoir, *Falling Love Notes*. Two months later, Chester proposed to Samantha from the stage: while performing at Electric Ballroom, Grey Daze launched into a cover of Dramarama's power-punk anthem "Anything, Anything," and Chester gazed at his future wife and lingered on the song's line "Because you married me, married me, married me."

There was a magnetism to Chester's early stage persona, all tattoos and bone in front of a mic stand: his craft may have been unpolished, but the way he could harness his personal issues and channel them into a set provided a natural feeling of release, and that power resonated with audiences. Yet as the years with Grey Daze wore on, the audiences never expanded to a point of forward momentum beyond the local scene.

Chester loved his bandmates and would stay close with them in the coming years, but by 1998, a year after the release of Grey Daze's second album. . . *No Sun Today*, the squabbling had dialed up. Chester felt like the rest of the band wasn't including him in business decisions, still treating him as the oblivious youngest member. A third album was planned, but never recorded. Meanwhile, the band's grunge sound, a genre that had been waning on a national level when they formed in 1994, was now completely out of vogue. One day, Chester gave Samantha a heads-up that he was driving over to Grey Daze's garage studio with his father, packing up his equipment, and quitting the band.

When Grey Daze was finally behind him, Chester tinkered around on some electronic music with a friend in Phoenix, but conflicting schedules made it difficult to get anything meaningful accomplished. His frustration grew. "He was screaming and yelling, 'I'm not doing music anymore!'" said Samantha. She convinced her husband to practice at least one hour each day and be prepared if an opportunity came his way—like a free-agent athlete staying fresh and in shape while awaiting a call from a team in need.

Chester was gifted, still young but already stage-seasoned, having put in five years of performance reps; all things considered, it made sense for him to continue plugging away in music and hope that something would break his way. But he was also married, in need of a steady job, healing from trauma, and exhausted. Prior to his wedding to Samantha, Chester learned that he was the biological father of Jaime, the son of his high school girlfriend Elka Brand; although Elka would remain the boy's primary caretaker, unexpected fatherhood spawned a new set of responsibilities for Chester. He was hired as an assistant at a digital services firm—normal work for the normal life he had been craving—and mentally began packing away his rock-star dreams.

On March 20, 1999, Chester woke up on his twenty-third birthday believing that he had retired from music. He was at peace with that decision; he and Samantha had just returned to Phoenix from a trip to Mexico with a group of friends—there had been rented houses on the water, bonfires, dirt bikes, and grilled lobster—and she decided to invite some friends over to their place for a mini surprise party for her husband.

The phone rang three times. Samantha answered, cupping her hand over her ear to block out the party music. After a minute, she passed the receiver to Chester, the music still blaring between them. The voice on the other end told Chester about a band based in Los Angeles called Xero. They were looking for a new singer.

CHAPTER 4

FOR AN OVERWHELMING majority of music groups, the lead singer represents the head—the face at the front of the stage, the voice on the radio, the persona delivering the words that will resonate with listeners—and the rest of the band is the body, supporting their message and enabling their movement. Therefore, swapping out a lead singer runs the high risk of altering the entire substance that makes a band special. It's an irreversible, and possibly perilous, change.

And though Xero wasn't built around a lead singer like most bands, by the end of 1998, that was the change they needed to make.

On paper, Mark Wakefield was the perfect lead singer for Xero. For starters, he had a lot of history with his bandmates. He had lived across the street from Brad in Agoura Hills and had been friends with Mike since they were preteens, schooling him on "guitar-based music," as he had described it, from bands like Deftones and Rage Against the Machine, while Mike in turn passed Mark his favorite hip-hop records.

Along with his years of reps as a frontman prior to Xero—plowing through shows with The Pricks and Relative Degree, and forming chemistry with Brad and Rob under stage lights—Mark was also writing songs with Mike behind-the-scenes. He encouraged Mike to develop his mechanics on a refurbished mixing board in the corner of his bedroom, until one day, they were suddenly co-fronting a band, merging their respective influences into one sound.

And Mark wasn't just in the right place at the right time: he also possessed an intrinsic understanding of hard-rock dynamics (which would, in

34

fact, define the rest of his career). You can hear his knowledge at work on demos like "Rhinestone," "Stick N Move," and "Reading My Eyes"—all of which he cowrote with Mike—with their crisp rock hooks indebted to grunge (Mark was a huge Nirvana and Pearl Jam fan) that created an equilibrium with Mike's rapping. There's a reason why multiple Xero demos with Mark's name in the credits would go on to become Linkin Park songs, streamed tens of millions of times. They just *worked*.

If you saw Mark strutting toward a microphone, you'd also assume that this guy could play the part. He was tall and handsome, often sporting a disarming smile and a bit of stubble. Mark exuded a confidence that convinced Xero's early supporters, as well as his bandmates, that he could be a rock star.

But then, too often, Mark would open his mouth and that fantasy would evaporate. As Mike succinctly put it many years later: "He wasn't a singer."

The problem involved both technical skill and singularity. As Xero's frontman, Mark served as an adequate grunge singer in front of a special band in the same way that Grey Daze was an okay grunge band dressed around Chester's exceptional voice. Mark was able to sink into the hooks of Xero songs, relying on his musical know-how to make clipped lines ring out ("From the TOP! To the BOTTOM!" he punches to open "Rhinestone") and elongate words with a scuzzy croon ("In a minute, you'll find *meeeeee . . . / Eyes burn me uuuuuuup*," he wails on the post-chorus). Listen closely, however, and you could hear the strain—a thin vocal foundation and brittleness of delivery, as if Mark had to sing as loud as possible to cover up his lack of physical ability.

Sure, plenty of rock legends weren't technically trained vocalists, including some of Mark's grunge heroes, such as Kurt Cobain and Eddie Vedder, but were able to supplement their lack of classical technique with unique styles that brought listeners closer. Yet Mark never found that special element. As a frontman, you can coast for a while if you have a compelling enough image and understand sonic nuance, but the higher up the ladder you climb, the more you need real, distinctive power to keep on climbing. And once Xero entered the high-pressure music-industry ecosystem, it didn't take long for Mark's shortcomings to become painfully clear.

"I never pretended I could carry the vocals on my own," Mark later admitted. "I had these great melodies in my head, and I couldn't get them across."

Following the showcase at the Whisky in November 1997, Jeff Blue pushed to get Xero a development deal at Zomba Music Publishing. As he noted in *One Step Closer*, Jeff roped in his surfing buddy, Danny Hayes, to act as the attorney on the deal and warded off raised eyebrows about the idea of signing his intern's band (especially as he was still trying to break Macy Gray out as a mainstream artist). The publishing deal took months to sign—allegedly, the Xero members were quietly shopping for other offers, even poking around for label deals, despite only playing one show together—but eventually, the band agreed to join Zomba. Soon after, Jeff arranged a studio session with Darryl Swann, who had already been producing and writing with Macy.

On August 25, 1998, Mark entered Paramount Recording Studio on Santa Monica Boulevard wearing an extra-large white T-shirt and a nervous look in his eye. He marveled at the plaques on the walls—The Jackson 5's "ABC" had been recorded at Paramount, as had records by Frank Zappa, N.W.A, and Guns N' Roses—and held his head high as he passed into the muted warmth of the studio lights. After Darryl helped lay down the track, Mark stepped into the vocal booth and started singing. Unfortunately, the notes that came out lacked both passion and personality.

The stress started to leak out of Mark. This wasn't the same experience as cutting bedroom demos with his best friend; it was a claustrophobic shot at fame, gasping between hallowed walls. Painfully self-conscious, Mark asked everyone—the rest of the band, even Jeff—to leave the studio and loiter in the lobby while he recorded his vocals with Darryl. The day wore on. Everyone kept waiting.

Eventually, Darryl poked his head out of the recording booth and corralled Jeff outside the studio. "It's been a couple hours." The producer grimaced, relaying the bad news like a doctor delivering a fatal prognosis. "And I'm afraid he's not getting better."

———————

BUT DESPITE THE LESS-THAN-IDEAL RECORDING experience, Mark wasn't ousted from the band after the session. Xero played a handful of small local shows in the fall of 1998, including a Halloween gig at a frat house in Long Beach where Virgin Records A&R rep Danny Goodwin was among the crowd, and a November showcase for Reprise/Warner A&R rep Matt Aberle. The feedback was uniform: the vocalist was pitchy, the vocalist needs work, the band would be promising if the vocalist could just figure it out. There weren't a ton of eyeballs trained on Xero yet, but Mark was starting to feel the heat. "He would get like crazy ulcers and stuff from the stress of doing band stuff," Mike recalled. "Having to get onstage made him physically nauseous."

Everything building up inside Mark came to a head on December 10, 1998. The band members had booked an open label showcase at Whisky a Go Go—a self-appointed full-circle moment, after their first show the year before. In doing so, the band was going against the warnings of Jeff and Danny Hayes, who had been trying to finalize a label deal with Geffen Records, no showcase necessary, and knew Xero's live show needed too much work to invoke a bidding war.

Nevertheless, the band believed they had created enough industry buzz at that point to warrant a showcase for all the major labels. And they were right: thirteen months after playing the Whisky to a sparse, disinterested crowd, Xero returned to the same venue on that December night with iconic executives like Arista's Clive Davis, Sony Music's Tommy Mottola, Epic Records' Polly Anthony, and Maverick Records' Guy Oseary in their audience. These were the people who had discovered Whitney Houston and Mariah Carey, who were working with Michael Jackson and

Madonna, and now, they were waiting to see Xero to figure out what the fuss was about.

It's worth pausing to ask: Why? As in, why had the most powerful members of the music industry shown up to watch an unsigned band?

Xero had been hacking around the LA area over the prior year, gradually building interest with smaller showcases, and Jeff had possessed the A&R connections to put them on the radar of multiple labels. But everybody knows that the CEOs only show up when an artist has gold record potential.

Yet by that December night, the rap-rock market was the music industry's gold rush.

A few months earlier, in August 1998, Korn had released its third album, *Follow the Leader*. The project marked a significant turning point for the band: singles like "Got the Life" and "Freak on a Leash" flaunted a catchier form of their rapping-to-screaming aggression that casual listeners could plug into seamlessly. And beneath the surface were weird, fascinating sonic tics—frontman Jonathan Davis's scatted bridges amplifying his alienation, the horrorcore guitar work from James "Munky" Shaffer yielding a spooky sheen, the often out-of-nowhere beat breakdowns waving to hip-hop fans across the aisle.

Like Xero had been doing with their early music, Korn sank deep into their influences to bridge the gap between genres. "We were listening to tons of rap, but we also liked bands like Pantera and Sepultura, and as we evolved, I think we learned to mix those two styles better," Korn frontman Jonathan Davis later said about *Follow the Leader*. "Plus, I grew up on New Wave and I always wanted to make music that had lots of melody." The result was an album with immediate singles, deafening guitars, guest features by Ice Cube and The Pharcyde's Slimkid3, and, after years of subdued hits by alternative bands, a ravenous fan base ready to anoint Korn the future of rock.

"Got the Life" was the album's most exhilarating distillation of Korn's rabid yet playful sonic impulses, and its music video became a fixture on MTV's popular daytime countdown show *Total Request Live* in the fall of 1998—Davis's stringy blue hair, pierced eyebrow, and barked rap-singing played right alongside videos by Britney Spears and *NSYNC. Korn now sharing space with the teenyboppers was especially improbable, considering that they were pretty much ignored by rock radio: "Got the Life" missed the top 10 of both the Modern Rock Tracks and Mainstream Rock Tracks charts because radio programmers kept spinning alternative tracks even as teens voted for something different over on MTV. But there were plenty of Korn fans out there when *Follow the Leader* was released, debuting at No. 1 on the *Billboard* 200 with over a quarter million copies sold in its first week. The industry just needed a bit of time to catch up to them.

A few weeks after *Follow the Leader* was released, the Family Values Tour debuted as a traveling festival featuring rising hard-rock bands Limp Bizkit, Rammstein, Orgy, and Incubus; Ice Cube, for a bit of hip-hop cred; and Korn, in victory-lap mode, headlining every show. It's no coincidence that Family Values launched the same year that Lollapalooza failed to find a headlining act and was canceled for the first time, its chokehold on alternative music having loosened in 1998 as that scene turned bland and failed to produce any compelling new stars. Speaking ahead of the tour launch, Limp Bizkit guitarist Wes Borland said that Family Values "kind of brings back what Lollapalooza was originally shooting for, 'cause it turned out to be a corporate deal later."

The torch had been passed: Family Values proved an enormous success, hitting twenty-nine US arenas in fall 1998 and becoming the highest-grossing traveling festival of that year. Korn was doing big business as the marquee act of a new sound, and their peers were starting to bubble up as well.

Limp Bizkit embraced the posturing of popular rap and dialed up the macho anger; by late 1998, their hyper-aggro cover of George Michael's "Faith" was starting to get some MTV burn, too. Orgy were also earning *TRL* play with a rip-roaring metal cover of a beloved eighties pop single, New Order's "Blue Monday," and had worked with Korn's Davis on their perfectly titled 1998 debut, *Candyass*. Several other bands drawing swollen crowds weren't on that inaugural Family Values bill, from Static-X to Adema to Powerman 5000 to Staind, and a headbang-rap solo artist named Kid Rock who was starting to make waves out of Detroit with his album *Devil Without a Cause*. Papa Roach, a fiery group from Sacramento, were actually in talks with Jeff Blue for a development deal in September 1998, but Jeff thought they sounded too similar to Xero.

These artists were catnip for young, male, angry-at-the-world listeners; as longtime *Village Voice* editor Robert Christgau put it in his review of the Family Values Tour, Korn's music addressed "an alienated suburban proletariat-in-the-making." Some of their fans hadn't been old enough to experience the grunge boom of the early nineties, but all of them had grown up with hip-hop as a major force in popular culture. While bands like Korn and Limp Bizkit incorporated rapped vocals in their music, others just gestured toward rap music via their percussion, turntable scratches, collaborations, or fashion choices. Because *rap-rock* didn't quite corral every band in the scene, the term *nu metal* was created, encapsulating a style more than a sound, the word *metal* denoting how *serious* and *cool* this budding movement would be. And after a breakthrough 1998, 1999 would end up becoming the pivotal year of this budding genre.

Proof of concept works fast in the music industry: the same execs who didn't see the massive debut of Korn's *Follow the Leader* coming in August were starving for any band that resembled music's hottest new scene by December. And so it was that Xero beckoned every power player to Whisky a Go Go that night.

The room was so packed that the execs could barely move; nevertheless, Xero kept them waiting. Fifteen minutes passed from the planned start time, and the band still hadn't touched the stage—which was odd for an industry showcase. Finally, they strolled out looking a little shaky and started playing . . . but stopped playing after a few seconds. Then they began tuning their instruments.

Impatient mutters wafted from the crowd during the false start, a few executives peeling off to find something better to do in town. A few minutes later, Xero kicked back up, but Mark's vocals were completely out of key. He sounded irrefutably *off* and remained so for the whole set; the audience cringed, recognizing a band that wasn't ready, and quickly backed away from the stage. Maybe the nerves had gotten to Mark, making him jittery enough to delay the band's set time, or maybe his lack of inherent talent exposed itself at the worst possible moment. Maybe it was both.

The house lights came up to a mostly empty venue—the mass exodus had happened long before the final song. Scott Harrington, a legal partner at Danny Hayes's firm who would be instrumental in creating what would become Linkin Park, walked up to Jeff and Danny, looks of horror on both of their faces.

"You both have to go underground for six months after this show," Scott told them. "Seriously, don't show your faces."

MARK COULDN'T HAVE EXPECTED AN ambush when he arrived at dinner with Jeff, Danny, and the rest of the band in the waning days of 1998. The guys were a few weeks removed from the Whisky fiasco, and as he sat down at a large round table in the back of the five-star Westwood restaurant Gardens on Glendon, Mark figured that the expensive dinner represented a toast to a productive year—or, at least, a holiday gathering of friends.

After twenty minutes of pre-dinner small talk, however, Jeff brought up the unavoidable: the Whisky show had resulted in zero label offers. The main issue with the performance, Jeff said, was the vocals. He told Mark, point-blank, that his vocals had been weak, and Mark agreed with him.

Mark promised that he was going to work harder, to get better, but by that point, it was already too late. The Whisky show had been too conspicuous of a catastrophe for the band, in its current form, to recover from. "We all discussed it," Jeff told Mark, "and I honestly think it's best if we look at other singers."

They had *all* discussed it. At that moment, looking around that round table and realizing what was happening, Mark must have felt like Sonny Corleone pulling up to a tollbooth.

The truth was, Jeff and Danny knew that drastic measures needed to be taken after the second Whisky show had turned Xero into a laughingstock. They could have easily cut bait and shrugged off the band as a whole, but Jeff remembered the promise of their sound that had attracted him as a bystander at their first show—and, undoubtedly, realized their even greater commercial potential a year later, as rap-rock continued growing bigger by the month. Plus, Jeff's former intern, Brad, had become a close friend; there was a protective instinct at play that made him want to see this project through, even if it meant, as Danny's colleague Scott had suggested, going underground for a while so the group could make some much-needed changes.

When it came to figuring out exactly *what* Xero needed to change, all signs pointed to Mark—from the pitchy vocals of their first show at the Whisky to the off-key vocals of their second, with every underwhelming performance and uneven studio take in between. The week before the Gardens on Glendon dinner, Jeff and Danny had met with the rest of the band, sans Mark, in Jeff's office at Zomba and not-so-gently suggested that Xero find a new lead singer.

And though the band didn't initially want to fire their friend and frontman, they realized it was the best decision if they wanted to move forward.

At the dinner, when the rest of the band reluctantly admitted that they, too, wanted a new lead singer, Mark shot up from the table and stormed out of the restaurant. After Jeff caught up with him outside, however, Mark eventually stopped fuming, sunk his head low, and confessed that everyone else was probably right. He had been thinking of leaving Xero, actually. It stung to be summarily kicked out of a band, but it didn't look like that band was going to make any noise, anyway.

Mark wasn't a singer. But in his bones, he *knew* hard-rock music. And when his time as Xero's frontman ended that night in Westwood, Mark set off on a wildly successful post-singing career in the business. He joined Velvet Hammer, a music management group founded in 1997 by David "Beno" Benveniste, which remains one of the authoritative rock management companies today. Velvet Hammer took off as their client System of a

Down—the band that Xero opened for at that first Whisky show—became international stars in the early 2000s; Mark was credited for the idea of the iconic cover art for the band's mega-selling 2001 album, *Toxicity*.

As the VP of Velvet Hammer, having now spent decades as Beno's right-hand man, Mark has been instrumental in managing some of the most high-profile hard-rock acts of the past thirty years, including Deftones, Alice in Chains, Avenged Sevenfold, and, as of recently, Korn. He and Mike, many years after swapping cassettes and dreaming up their first songs together, have remained friends.

"Deftones was one of his favorite bands when we were in high school," Mike said of Mark. "Talk about a dream job—just working with bands that you love."

As Mark moved on, Xero endured three months of singerless purgatory in the early days of 1999, auditioning new frontmen while letting the stink of that Whisky show dissipate. For the remaining members, the fear that Xero was never going to break out must have grown more agonizing with each passing day. In fact, bassist Dave Farrell bowed out of the group in early 1999 to tour with his high school pop-punk band, Tasty Snax. Kyle Christner, a local bass player who was recommended by a colleague of Jeff, replaced Dave after being asked to learn songs that no one knew who would sing.

Jeff headed down to Austin for South by Southwest 1999, and on March 20, he met up with Scott and a few others for an afternoon drink at the Four Seasons in between sets by baby bands. The dreadful Xero showcase came up in conversation, and Jeff winced. But Scott had a suggestion: he knew a kid in Arizona who had recently left his band, and this guy could *really* sing.

Back when Grey Daze was hopscotching across Phoenix, the band had drawn the attention of an indie label called Real Records, and when they had been offered a contract, they'd reached out to Scott in LA to review the terms. Real Records eventually ran out of money, and the label deal never happened, but Scott developed a rapport with Grey Daze's frontman, Chester Bennington, and would even pass him demos every so often.

Right after drinks at the Four Seasons, Jeff convinced Scott to get his promising young singer from Arizona on the phone. Scott dialed, Samantha Bennington picked up, and everyone in Austin could hear the party music blaring all the way from Phoenix. It was Chester's birthday and the couple had people over. But Samantha still handed the phone to her husband, and Scott handed his to Jeff.

"Chester, hey, man," Jeff said into the receiver, "I have a band in LA that's going to be huge, and we're looking for a singer." He promised the singer he just met ten seconds ago a birthday present: Xero's demo tape, as well as another tape without vocals, that he would have sent out that day. Jeff wanted to hear Chester's interpretation of how the songs could become more popular, more urgent—*better*. And even though it was Saturday and Chester's birthday, he wanted to have Chester's demo sent to him by that Monday.

"I immediately was asking all sorts of questions, like, 'How old are they? How long have they been doing this?' because I didn't want to waste my fucking time," Chester recalled. He could have told Jeff to screw himself, gone back to his birthday party, moved on with his day job, and forgotten that this suit from LA was trying to force him back into the disarray of rock-band life. Instead, he accepted the demo and gave it a listen.

He heard the band that he needed to join. "Immediately," Chester said, "I was like, 'This is it. These are the ones.'"

CHAPTER 5

A REINVENTION WAS IN order: in the spring of 1999, the name Xero changed to Hybrid Theory. Joe had suggested the new moniker as representative of what their sound would be—a blend of rap and rock. ("We wanted something that had a close relationship with the style of music we're playing," Chester explained later.)

Here's the thing, though: the band wasn't actually *playing* any music when they settled on Hybrid Theory. No new songs had been finalized, no label deal was imminent, and the band was contemplating how they could stand out in an exploding nu metal scene just a few months after falling flat on their faces. The band members still had their development deal, but their specific style of rap-rock hadn't come into existence yet—Hybrid Theory was more of an idea than a fact.

The band needed to decide on the image they wanted to form, and to some extent, they found an early identity based less on what they stood for and more on what they rejected. For starters? That aforementioned exploding scene that the industry had lumped the band into even though they didn't want to belong.

"I never wanted to be part of nu metal," said Mike before acknowledging in the next breath that the genre had shown some promise before curdling in 1999. "There was a moment when that term, and what it meant, was actually pretty cool," he conceded. "It's almost impossible to imagine!"

If Korn's ascension in 1998 represented the fly-frozen-in-amber moment in which nu metal was still an exciting new prospect, Limp Bizkit's rise in 1999 served as a counterpunch to the gut for many of those

45

cautiously optimistic listeners. After opening for Korn, playing the Family Values Tour, and earning some early MTV buzz with their unhinged cover of "Faith," the Jacksonville band became inescapable when "Nookie"—an ex-treated-me-like-crap rap-rock sledgehammer that was knowingly vapid and undeniably catchy—was released as the lead single to the band's sophomore album, *Significant Other*, in June 1999.

The soft–loud dynamic of "Nookie," with Fred Durst rapping about his romantic regrets in the verses before yelling them plainly in the chorus ("I did it all for the nookie / So you can take that cookie / And stick it up your YEAH!"), functioned like an infantilized version of Nirvana's "Smells Like Teen Spirit," but MTV ate it up with similar fervor. Suddenly, Durst's soul patch and backward red baseball cap transformed into rock-star iconography. But unlike Kurt Cobain, who never wanted to be a leader to the masses, Durst was more than ready for the limelight. "Dude, I want to be massive," he told *Spin* in 1999. "And I think I can do it. I've got crazy vision."

Korn's breakthrough with *Follow the Leader* had turned them into the face of a new market, but Limp Bizkit's *Significant Other* was literally twice as big when it was released nine months later, launching at No. 1 with an astonishing 673,000 copies sold in its first week. The two bands were friends, collaborators, and former tour mates, but those paying attention to the nu metal scene could feel the dissonance of their warring approaches, particularly how Limp Bizkit's popularity commanded a gravitational pull toward their style.

If Korn was angry and insular, with pained vocals about trauma and loneliness, Limp Bizkit was showier and more commercial, with a jokester frontman who deployed choppy rhymes about being wronged by society and, in Fred Durst's words, "following these fat ass beats until I die." Limp Bizkit's rap-rock represented finely crafted dumb fun, and more bands like this followed in its lineage. Kid Rock, who had been grinding in the music industry for nearly a decade, caught fire in 1999 with pissed-off rap-rock credos "Bawitdaba" and "Cowboy," while bands like P.O.D. and Crazy Town released successful albums that year with similar rhyme cadences.

Rather quickly, the center of nu metal had morphed into a sleek, polished product for every frustrated suburban white boy with no real problems: angry-at-the-world rapping, speed-headbang hooks, frustrated grunts, gestures toward homophobia and misogyny. Limp Bizkit weren't actually that regressive, lyrically speaking, but they were tied to a lowest-common-denominator movement; all the universality had been squeezed out, replaced by mainstream-ready spectacle.

And in July of that year, nu metal got its big showcase: Woodstock '99.

Thirty years after the original Woodstock Music and Art Fair in Bethel, New York, represented a flash point in which songs could spread compassion across the counterculture generation in 1969, Woodstock '99 was imagined as the must-attend Gen X music experience. It was held at a retired Air Force base in Rome, New York, during a particularly sweltering weekend in July, the blacktop reflecting the intense heat and the four-dollar water bottles making the thousands in attendance even more sweaty and irritated.

And though the lineup included a smattering of late-nineties stars, from Dave Matthews to Jewel to DMX, the hard-rock acts—Korn, Limp Bizkit, Rage Against the Machine, Metallica, Kid Rock—made the predominant fan demographic "a lot of white boys wearing backwards baseball caps," as attendee Liz Polay-Wettengel put it in the documentary *Woodstock 99: Peace, Love, and Rage.*

With inebriated young men running rampant and security at a minimum, Woodstock '99 turned physically and morally gross—and very quickly. Pay-per-view cameras lingered on exposed breasts and drunk, horny guys groping and abusing women. Collapsed moshers were pulled out of pits due to heat exhaustion and dehydration. Porta-potties were upended; people rolled around in straight-up shit. By the time Limp Bizkit played on Saturday night, with Durst telling any lingering hippies to "take your Birkenstocks and stick 'em up your fucking ass" as he took the stage, drunk idiots were crowd-surfing on pieces of plywood during their destroy-everything anthem "Break Stuff." Any lingering thread of the original Woodstock's intent had been totally lost.

The eventual conclusion—multiple fires in the back of Red Hot Chili Peppers' crowd, shirtless rioters howling as the state troopers rushed to the scenes, trash piling up everywhere and broadcast around the world—was all too foreseeable and instantly burned into the brain of all music fans. No, nu metal music wasn't responsible for the chaos of Woodstock '99, but the sound had been inextricably linked with the fury. The perception was that a strand of rap-rock that had once held artistic promise got huge, turned commercial, and was now being consumed by assholes.

That view was flawed, of course. Nu metal contained nuance beyond "Break Stuff"—"Re-Arranged," another song that Limp Bizkit performed at Woodstock '99, is a contemplative midtempo jam—and a wider array of fans than was being presented on MTV. But the Woodstock footage was damaging enough that popular opinion and affinity for the emerging genre quickly crumbled. The fires raging for no reason became the perfect symbol of nu metal: the music of pointlessly aggrieved white youth.

———————

Xero became Hybrid Theory only a few months before Woodstock '99, and the group was still more than a year away from making its debut. They wouldn't have been ready to perform on that stage anyway, but as they watched the chaos unfold from afar, they were fully aware that they didn't belong to that scene.

Growing up in the eighties, Mike had plenty of practice rejecting the type of music that catered to an overwhelmingly white crowd. "I listened to 90 percent rap music, then I'd look at a lot of rock bands and I'd be like, 'There's something too white,'" he recalled. "That was one of the things that turned me off, especially hair metal. Hair metal felt like very white music and I was growing up in a very diverse city, so I didn't gravitate to it."

Mike's paternal grandfather had moved from Japan to the United States and planted roots for the rest of his family. In 1939, Mike's father, Muto, was born, the second youngest of thirteen children. The Shinodas built up multiple businesses in Orosi, California, including a grocery store and barbershop, but when Muto was three years old, he and the rest of his family were rounded up and forced to leave their home with only twenty-four hours' notice. In the months following the attack on Pearl Harbor, President Roosevelt issued Executive Order 9066, sending Japanese American families like the Shinodas to internment camps in 1942 out of a racist fear of mainland espionage during World War II.

Suddenly, Mike's father, who was born a US citizen in California, was waking up on a cot covered in dirt in the Poston War Relocation Center in Arizona. For Muto, internment meant years of sleeping in barracks, using communal bathrooms, coping with dust covering everything, and playing games with other kids to distract themselves from their grim reality. Some of Mike's relatives returned to Orosi after the camps closed in 1946, but by then, their once-thriving businesses had been vandalized, and they struggled to find new work. Even though the war itself was over, rampant discrimination carried on.

Decades later, as he was growing up in the eighties, Mike would ask a lot of questions about that time period, because he would occasionally overhear his father and relatives mention people they knew from camp, fragments of memories from those years. Yet they were always reticent to discuss details; the trauma mostly stayed buried in the 1940s. His family "made it sound relatively benign and they played a lot of things down," Mike recalled, "but if you dug into any kind of detail with them, you could tell it was really an awful experience."

Despite the fact that he was shielded from a great deal of this intergenerational trauma, Mike frequently grappled with his own racial identity as a kid. His mother, Donna, a white woman who was born and raised in Agoura Hills, was intentional in teaching Mike and his younger brother Jason about their Japanese heritage, as she learned customs from her husband and recipes from her in-laws. Although he didn't experience racism with the same vast hideousness as his father, Mike was still othered by the kids around him—made to feel that being Japanese American meant being classified as intrinsically different, if he was even classified at all.

"Mixed kids always have a very unique experience with the race subject because we are many times not obvious members of any group," Mike later explained. "For example, when I was younger, I would hear people make jokes about Asians around me because they wouldn't know that I was half Asian, so they assumed that I was maybe Hispanic or maybe Middle Eastern and they'd make a joke about Asians and I was the spy. I was the undercover receiver of this joke."

When Mike got to high school and studied World War II, he noticed two paragraphs in his history book: one dedicated to Pearl Harbor, and another waving away the 120,000 Japanese American lives upended by unlawful incarceration. He felt like his family's anguished journey deserved more space; he was frustrated that his ancestors' stories and persecution had been so redacted.

Throughout these experiences, however, Mike felt seen through rap music, appreciating explicit messages about systemic racism and the whitewashing of history. He would play Public Enemy and absorb the samples of Malcolm X, Rev. Jesse Jackson, and Thomas N. Todd that launched into the group's biggest hits ("I got a right to be hostile, man, my people are being persecuted!" Richard Pryor's voice declares to kick off "Prophets of Rage"), then swap an N.W.A CD into his boom box and listen to rhymes about bigotry and police brutality. These artists' points of view weren't being overtly represented in history books; as Mike later put it, "I felt I learned something about racism and discrimination by listening."

At Pasadena's ArtCenter College of Design, Mike bonded with Joe Hahn, a second-generation Korean American who also loved hip-hop and had learned his way around a turntable in high school. Joe's mother and father, a nurse and a miner, had relocated from Korea to West Germany in the seventies, then moved to the States; Joe was born in Dallas, and after his family moved to Glendale when he was eight, he struggled to fit in.

"It was very difficult to grow up as an Asian in America," Joe said. Fortunately, by the time he got to college, he found a kindred spirit in Mike, and his knack for mashing up melodic hip-hop and heavier rock came in handy when Mike was putting Xero together.

Their perspectives as Asian Americans didn't exist in popular US rock music during that time—or any time, really. Mike was initially turned off by hair metal for being "too white," but the truth was, *every* popular iteration of rock throughout his upbringing, from grunge to alternative to rap-rock and nu metal, had been incredibly homogeneous as well.

There were marginalized contributors to hard rock in the late nineties—artists like System of a Down, Deftones frontman Chino Moreno, Rage Against the Machine's Zack de la Rocha and Tom Morello, and Korn bassist "Fieldy" Arvizu, to name a few—and those contributions were meaningful, from Rage challenging capitalist nihilism to Deftones concocting a more inclusive form of post-hardcore. Yet their voices were often drowned out on MTV by big personalities like Durst and Kid Rock, white artists who had committed to giving angry listeners an unproductive form of release. As a result, the injustices being described in mega-selling nu metal in 1999 weren't about racial discrimination, social inequality, or domestic alienation—they were about having a crappy day and wanting to destroy things because of it.

Millions of fans—many of *them* white—connected to that message. Mike, however, could not. "That didn't resonate with me," he said. "And it wasn't just about race. I don't mean the color of skin. I just mean the culture of it."

At the time, Mike was a twenty-two-year-old Japanese American in a scene where barely any visible artists shared his heritage and where the loudest chants often left him bewildered. So even when he was uncertain of what type of rap-rock band Hybrid Theory would become, Mike was damn sure that they wouldn't function like any other group out there.

———

CHESTER, ON THE OTHER HAND, repudiated another feature of the Woodstock '99 set: the inherent recklessness. When he received that fateful call on March 20, 1999, he had just spent five years trudging across Arizona in Grey Daze while also physically and mentally recovering from an adolescence full of pain and hard drugs. Chester had chosen to give up the turbulence of the music grind for a nine-to-five life—and if he *was* going to rejoin that world, he wasn't looking for any of the party-hard hedonism that was increasingly defining nu metal. What he craved was professionalism.

The other members of the band he was potentially joining weren't exactly straight-edge—but for a group of early-twenties guys in a rock band kicking around Hollywood, they dismissed the party lifestyle with an almost shocking solemnity. When Xero played showcases for A&R reps in 1998, for instance, they raised eyebrows by avoiding the table of beers placed onstage for them. Even when they played clubs and frat parties, zero "rock-star hijinks" would ensue.

Rob Bourdon had also dealt with substance abuse as a teenager, around the time his band Relative Degree with Brad and Mark was disintegrating. "I went through a rough period in my life and was struggling with drugs and alcohol," the drummer recalled. "Although I never gave up playing the drums during this time, my mindset kept me from improving. Towards the end of high school, I got my life back on track." As luck would have it, Mike called him soon after about joining a band called Xero.

For the other members, partying simply didn't fit in with their plans of making it as a band. Who had time to get sloshed when there was more work to be done? "We'd rather go to somebody's house and write a song than go to a party," Mike said. "At parties, you knew what was going to happen. You knew who was going to get drunk. But when we got together to write songs, we never knew what was going to happen. It was much more exciting."

That approach perfectly aligned with Chester's mentality at the time; after all, he literally ditched his own birthday party to make music for the band that he knew had a shot to become huge. By March 21, the day after getting the call from Los Angeles, Chester had received Xero's demo tape in the mail and had already cut his vocals over the instrumental tracks. He offered to send it back via FedEx or hand deliver the tape; if he hopped on a flight from Phoenix to LA, Chester pointed out, he could out-hustle the shipping. And after spending years in a band that ultimately went nowhere, Chester didn't want to waste any more time.

Two days later, he was in Los Angeles, having quit his job and received his wife Samantha's blessing to make the trek. "Gut instincts are always so hit and miss," Chester said. "But with this particular situation, there was no doubt in my mind. The creativity of the music, and the different sounds that were coming out of it . . . When I listened to the instrumental tracks, all these melodies just started popping out of my head."

Chester showed up to the Zomba office on the Sunset Strip sporting glasses, dyed-black spiky hair, and a too-big glittery T-shirt on his slender frame, the design capturing reflected light below his huge grin. He certainly didn't *look* like a rock star; he looked a lot more like the geek that the rock star shoves into a locker in a high school music video. But Chester had the rock-star voice—that much was evident from his demo tape. And perhaps just as, if not more, crucially, he had the work ethic.

Every member of the band intrinsically understood how to bust their ass for an opportunity. At art school, Mike would endure twelve-hour days of college courses, squeeze in a few hours of band practice, knock out some paintings for class at home, then go to bed, wake up, and do it all again. Joe, who left ArtCenter College of Design after one year because it was too expensive, was hustling as a freelance illustrator in Hollywood, scoring storyboarding and character design work for *The X-Files* and *Species*. While interning with Jeff, Brad had helped send out Macy Gray demos while trying to get his own music off the ground, and Rob had scooped up shifts at a local bowling alley while studying accounting in Santa Monica.

The band's new lead singer needed to be a driven person to work within this industrious collective, and Chester, recognizing the chance of something real after years of living a rock-star mirage, poured himself into filling that role. While the rest of Xero held further auditions for Mark's replacement, Chester lingered in Los Angeles, jobless and driving back and forth to see Samantha in Arizona multiple times a week. He slept on the couches of family friends in California as Samantha put in her notice at work and tried to sell their house a state away.

Weeks passed, then a full month, and Chester still didn't know if he was in the band or not. The members of Xero understood that Chester possessed the raw skill, but did he match their style and personality? Some nights, as auditions continued, Chester even had to sleep in his car, which was so beat-up it couldn't go over thirty-five miles per hour. "Two lights were burned out," Chester recalled. "I had no money to replace them."

Chester had essentially pushed all his chips into the middle of the table with this band. Imagine the enormous sense of relief he felt, then, when the auditions finally ended, and the rest of the band told him that he, Chester Bennington, would be their new singer.

After weeks of preparing for this moment and a lifetime of dreaming up what it could mean for him, Chester was ready to work—passionately, furiously, with every fiber of his being and a full awareness of what this platform could signify. And to mark the dawn of a new era, the band name officially changed from Xero to Hybrid Theory.

Although they weren't initially sure exactly what they would produce, all the band members recognized the power of the raw materials at their disposal. Chester was an authentic lead singer, with pain in his past and a scream that could express it. Mike was a hip-hop disciple and sound tactician, ready to fight for the soul of a quickly decaying genre. Brad, Rob, and Joe possessed the talent and drive to efficiently supply a sonic environment. The band's approach was businesslike, and its hunger was real.

As the band's "hybrid theory" snapped into place, a singular, enduring identity was forged. The prelude was over; a new chapter had begun. Now, it was time to make a record.

PART II

THE SOUND

CHAPTER 6

"WHERE SHOULD I start? / Disjointed heart."

That's how Chester opens "And One," a song on a project that's mostly been buried down deep in the sands of time. Chester himself was feeling disjointed when he sang those words: still new to Los Angeles and the bandmates surrounding him, away from his native city and the broken home he grew up in.

The rest of "And One" plays out like a hyperactive grunge track, with a mucky chorus surrounded by Brad's rapid-fire guitar chug and Mike's canned-heat rapping on the bridge and outro. But the first verse is basically just Chester, alone with the alienation coursing through his veins. His voice is fuzzed out, thudding ever closer toward collapse.

"I've got no commitment to my own flesh and blood," he sneers in a lurching cadence. "Left all alone, far from my home / No one to hear me, to heal my ill heart."

"And One," much like the rest of the *Hybrid Theory* EP, is the sound of a band clearing its throat. Finished in June 1999, shortly after Chester had joined the band and moved to California, the six-song project marks the first batch of recorded music featuring both Chester's and Mike's vocals—momentous stuff, considering what that combination would go on to accomplish shortly after. You can hear the growing pains in every aspect of the newly named Hybrid Theory and its newly formed lineup, including the interplay between the two frontmen.

The self-titled EP was destined to be fodder for completist fans instead of the group's breakthrough material, but all these years later, it remains crucial to understanding how the group was able to gel in its early days. These tracks were like the rigorous practices leading up to a big game. Just because the stadium crowds don't see the warm-ups doesn't make them any less important.

Although some of the Xero demos would be revisited and repurposed later, by the time Chester joined the band, everyone wanted to focus on making new material. The main Xero songs had been kicked around for a couple of years by then, and that disastrous Whisky a Go Go show had contaminated them to some degree. Plus, they were bonding with Chester—learning the curves of his singular voice, interpreting the ferocity housed within that skinny frame—and wanted to invite his perspective into the creative process. "The idea," Mike said, "was to move forward."

For his part, Mike was growing as a leader and stylistic engine. He coproduced the *Hybrid Theory* EP with Andrew "Mudrock" Murdock, who had helmed Godsmack's breakout self-titled 1998 album and who would go on to work with hard-rock acts like Avenged Sevenfold and Powerman 5000. The process was simple and effective: Mike would first connect with Brad to tinker with the musical layout of each track, then bring the arrangements to Chester to discuss lyrical approaches. He was, by design, the central hub of Hybrid Theory.

Meanwhile, Chester struggled to adapt to his circumstances. Even though he was fully detached from Arizona, Chester still didn't have a permanent home—he had arrived, jobless, in LA barely two months beforehand, and his wife Samantha remained in the process of selling their Phoenix home and working on her move out to Hollywood—so he was bumming around in his busted car and catching z's on his new bandmates' couches and later in rehearsal studios.

As much as the rest of the band had welcomed him, the established group dynamics disoriented Chester. He had stepped into a collection of musicians that had already existed as longtime friends and collaborators: they had unlocked songs together, weathered shitty news together, spent multiple years learning each other's strengths and weaknesses. By contrast, Chester had auditioned for a spot to join them and was now expected to not just assimilate but also to become their voice. He was the new kid at the lunch table, a couple years older than everyone else, and from out of town, being forced to adjust to the group's in-jokes and impulses—and also help lead them.

"They're all best friends, and I was so focused on not going insane," Chester recalled. "When I would lose my mind, I couldn't lose it with them—why would they want to put up with my ass? I didn't want them to think I had lead singer's disease—always unsatisfied with everything."

Chester's first conversations with Mike—the band's two voices getting to know each other creatively and personally—helped, but they were far from easy. In addition to swapping musical influences and potential song ideas, Chester told Mike about his difficult childhood, history of abuse and drug addiction, and years of performing around Phoenix that hadn't led to anything substantial.

The hurt within those memories hadn't subsided. Yet Chester refused to paper over them, particularly when considering what he wanted to sing about with his new band. So what if his catch-ups with Mike, whose upbringing had been comparatively normal, were awkward as hell? Better to have those conversations early—get everything out in the open—and harness that suffering in the name of artistic growth.

For Chester, the ceiling of this new band was too high to risk being emotionally reserved. Hybrid Theory was never designed to work out their kinks in an underground scene; it was major-label-sanctioned mass appeal or bust, and time was of the essence. "I was fucking miserable," Chester said of that period. "The only thing that was keeping me going was knowing we had something special going on. I knew this was the one."

Mike already understood that Chester could make for a great frontman on the basis of the simple fact that his voice could level a city block. But the more time they spent together, and the more that the contrasts in their backstories became starkly evident, Mike realized that the phrase "Hybrid Theory" did not just represent the band's ability to rap and sing. Hybrid Theory extended to the many differences between the voices leading the group—differences that made "not only our friendship really strong," Mike said later, "but it played into the music. It was peanut butter and jelly."

Mike's and Chester's lives were nothing alike, but their experiences filled each other's respective gaps, and their personalities found a steady middle ground. And those early conversations—painful, yet productive—yielded their first songs.

EVEN THOUGH CHESTER HAD ALREADY fronted another band, recorded multiple albums, and performed on countless stages, he hadn't exactly figured out his voice just yet.

Yes, he possessed technical skills, but what exactly was his distinctive style? In his previous role, Chester had played a post-grunge journeyman and hadn't been pushed to fine-tune his vocal approach because he and the rest of Grey Daze were too busy focusing on the next gig. So, without realizing it, Chester would often slip into imitation, sounding like a mix of his biggest influences, from Depeche Mode's Dave Gahan to Alice in Chains' Layne Staley, and Mike would playfully call him out on it, laughing at the way Chester would turn an *r* sound into a yowling *arrrrr*.

Chester's voice sounds downright alien on "Part of Me," the final proper track on the *Hybrid Theory* EP. The way he gargles every syllable on the chorus and spits them out in a clenched holler ("I feel it *errrrvery dayyy* / I feel I *maaade my waaaaay*") produces a growl that's somewhere between Scott Stapp of Creed (a band that was blowing up at the time) and Wes Scantlin of Puddle of Mudd (a band that was about to). The affectation is jarring—especially on a song about being tortured by one's own flaws. Chester was clearly trying on some different skins while figuring out how to be comfortable within his own.

"Part of Me" actually started with a car alarm: a siren kept going off in the parking garage beneath Brad's apartment at the time, waking him up with exasperating regularity. Brad got back at the noise by recording it, then bringing the audio to Mike, who sampled and looped the alarm in a way that let Brad write a corresponding guitar line. It was a nifty flip that demonstrated how forward-thinking Mike, who coproduced the track with Mudrock, was already becoming in the studio. But he also needed to polish his flow: Mike raps confidently on "Part of Me," but he's still a little off-beat, barreling into the production instead of locating and sitting in the groove.

"Just do somethin' to tell you who I am, you know?" Mike opens "High Voltage," a rap showcase on the EP, this time with some choice record-scratching from Joe and a robo-voice hook that's very much indebted to Beastie Boys' "Intergalactic." "High Voltage" contains some lyrical references that pinpoint the song to that exact moment of the band's history: Mike calls himself "Akira," a moniker from the beloved anime that he was trying out at the time, and there's also a few shout-outs to Mix Media, the label that Hybrid Theory hastily created themselves to release the EP.

But even decades later, Mike's wordplay on "High Voltage" doesn't sound dated at all. Rhyming over a beat that would have worked for underground rap groups like Jurassic 5 and Blackalicious at the time, Mike snugly sinks into his metaphors: "Invented the mic so I could start blessin' it / And chin-checkin' kids to make my point like an impressionist / Many men have tried to shake us, but I twist mic chords to double-helixes / And show them what I'm made of." Mike definitely brought the bars on "High Voltage." Unfortunately, the band had no idea how to involve Chester on the track: he mostly accentuates Mike's loudest lines and otherwise lingers in the background.

So many of the Hybrid Theory demos play out like this: thickets of future sonic ideas, the moments when the band could see what the big block of marble in front of them could ultimately resemble but were still chipping away at it. At one end was the hip-hop braggadocio and turntable culture that Joe and Mike had grown up loving, manifested in songs like "High Voltage," "Step Up," the thirty-nine-second instrumental "Technique (Short)," and the untitled hidden track at the end of "Part of Me." Mike's lyrics even turn meta about the nu metal boom on "Step Up": "Rappin' over rock doesn't make you a pioneer / Rock and hip-hop have collaborated for years / But now they're randomly mixed and matched up / All after a fast buck, and all the tracks suck," he spits over ethereal production.

The kid who had watched Anthrax team up with Public Enemy had now grown up and was ready to drop knowledge on rap-rock authenticity. But he was also feeling his way around his own rap-rock formula, unable to clarify what separated these tracks from straight-up hip-hop songs. As such, the songs foreshadowed Mike's more rap-focused work with The X-Ecutioners and as Fort Minor in the coming years rather than what Hybrid Theory would become.

On the opposite side of that, however, were the flawed rock-leaning tracks that more closely hinted at the band's eventual sound, especially now that the lineup of the band had solidified (well, almost—Dave Farrell was still touring with his old band Tasty Snax, so Kyle Christner handled bass for the EP). "Part of Me" is overstuffed, with too many interludes precluding a radio-ready structure, but a few moments contain whiffs of the same musical chemistry that the band would use on "Papercut," with Brad's glistening guitar work crashing down like a tidal wave as Mike's urgent rhyming segues into Chester's rock hook.

Although "Carousel," an early demo revived when Chester joined the band, is saddled with a flimsy hook and directionless production, if you squint at its composition, you'll see the bones of "In the End," with Mike rapping about unmovable personal problems on the verses and Chester succinctly capturing those issues on the chorus. And even though Chester may have envisioned "And One" as a meaty grunge number, the song turns exhilarating during the bridge, when Chester's barked words go back and forth with Mike's jittered rapping and Rob's drums slam down with quickening regularity—real interplay between the frontmen at work for the first time.

The true diamond in the rough of these early sessions, however, didn't appear on the final cut of the *Hybrid Theory* EP. In May, just a few weeks after Chester joined, Mike and Brad strolled into Jeff Blue's office at Zomba and tossed him a CD carrying a few new songs and black Sharpie scribbles (including Mike's pager number—extremely 1999!). One of those songs was titled "Blue," and Jeff laughed at the unexpected homage.

"Blue" doesn't work on multiple levels: Kyle's bass line pops during the intro and Mike fires off some solid internal rhymes in the first verse, but the minor-key chorus jams Chester's and Mike's voices together with a mucked-up guitar riff from Brad. While the lyrics circle around universal angst, they end up too vague to be relatable. But with a minute left in the song, the percussion suddenly falls away and the guitar scoops up a kicky breakdown lick. A different beat sneaks in to join the guitar, and a few seconds later, the track erupts: Chester unleashes a melodic scream, Mike crashes in alongside him with some quick lines, drums are bashed, the record-scratching goes berserk, and the guitars are dialed all the way up. Then, without much warning, everything falls away into silence.

That minute may have been an outro of a song that wasn't even strong enough to make Hybrid Theory's self-released debut EP, but that minute blew Jeff away and reminded him how much potential this band had. Much later on, that minute would transform into the chorus of "Crawling." But for the time being, the band had a lot more work to do.

———————

ON JUNE 1, 1999, JUST as Hybrid Theory were recording their first songs together in LA, all the way over on the other side of the country at Northeastern University Shawn Fanning launched a beta version of a program called Napster.

The music industry, for decades dependent on jewel-cased physical products and big-box retail strategies, was about to experience a total digital transformation. For Hybrid Theory and countless other musical artists like them, the internet represented boundless possibility at the time. Even in this primitive stage, the idea of sharing files of songs before they were released on tapes and compact discs and then chatting with fans about those songs seemed revolutionary.

Before Hybrid Theory could find a record label and debut a fully formed sound, they were recruiting listeners online in the earliest iteration of the band's still-active online fan community. Message boards were becoming fertile, different subcultures cohabitating, songs (and reactions to those songs) being shared in real time across different parts of the world. The band's plan of action then was as much a relic of the time period as Mike's pager: they would upload MP3s of their demos and go into Korn chat rooms or the message boards of other bands and tell like-minded fans to check them out. "I would assign everyone in the band to go on the internet," Rob recalled, "and recruit five or six people a day."

Meanwhile, Rob's apartment became the unofficial headquarters of the band's self-run street team—mostly because Rob's place was located next door to a post office. "Priority Mail boxes are free," he explained, "so I would take all of their boxes and run out of there." When kids in chat rooms clicked on their MP3s and emailed the band asking for more music, the band would send them T-shirts, stickers, and self-made cassette demos, with instructions to spread the word far and wide.

"We would package the stuff in my apartment," Rob added. "My living room became a total mailroom." The band members spent hours preparing for bulky mail runs, while Mike designed the graphics of the band's very first website, trappings of engineering an early-internet grassroots campaign.

Although a fan base was starting to coalesce thanks in part to the *Hybrid Theory* EP, the band was still in need of a label home. As 1999 wore on, Hybrid Theory played label showcase after label showcase, garnering some intrigue but zero offers; the band performed between forty and fifty sets for interested record companies during that period, with major and indie labels uniformly responding with rejections. It was downright Sisyphean: the band needed only one label to believe in them enough, out of the dozens that they auditioned for, to score a deal and move into the next phase of their professional lives. But that boulder was too hard to push to the top of the hill, so they kept tumbling back down.

Part of the problem was that the band was still finding chemistry onstage, just as they were in the studio. Chester's lead vocals denoted a clear upgrade over Mark's, but Chester was figuring out how to coexist alongside Mike as well as how to appeal to label scouts in high-pressure situations. In one showcase for an executive at MCA Records, for instance, Chester got so close to the guy's face that some drops of scream-sing spittle flew into the exec's eye. At least *that* label rejection was an easier one to explain.

Another issue for Hybrid Theory: thanks to the rise of bands such as Korn and Limp Bizkit, the rap-rock bubble was perceived as either about to burst after a rapid expansion or at least oversaturated. Suddenly, the sound that had brought out so many execs to Xero's showcase was everywhere, and after Woodstock '99, its mainstream future was on shaky ground. "We were almost, like, 'We've been beaten to the punch,'" explained Brad.

Yet those concerns would have all been waved away by a label if Hybrid Theory had demonstrated one thing during those showcases: a clear hit single. Which they still didn't have.

The demos that constituted the *Hybrid Theory* EP contained flashes of the anthems that the band might someday produce, but glimmers of promise don't translate into radio play. So every label shrugged them off, Hybrid Theory got trapped in the music industry's no-man's-land, and the members had no choice but to keep grinding—more mailers, rehearsals, sleepless nights, and prayers that the next showcase would be the break-through. "We put in a good three years' worth of work in that nine or ten months," Chester recalled.

After banging their heads against a wall for so long, the group started to feel their doubts growing louder. Brad's parents were still pushing for law school as a possibility. Rob was practicing drum breakdowns for hours every day and starting to wonder if he was wasting his time. Chester was fully committed to his new band and believed with every fiber of his being that all the labels were wrong; at the same time, he was also broke, far away from his longtime home, and often separated from his wife. Even if Chester "knew this was the one," being rejected more than forty times takes a psychological toll. Was it *actually* the one? And what would he do if it wasn't?

At long last, the breakthrough happened—although not in the way the band ever expected.

Jeff, who had signed Xero to a publishing deal with Zomba, got a new job in the fall of 1999: VP of A&R at Warner Records. He had been dreaming of scoring an A&R gig at a major label for years, and when the opportunity finally came, he finagled a stipulation: he would join Warner *only if* they also signed his development project, Hybrid Theory, to a label deal. As part of his agreement, Jeff would bring the band onto the Warner roster and executive produce their debut album.

Jeff always wanted to discover and guide artists, even after they found their label home, and his first project at Warner would be—fittingly—the group he had been championing for years. Before the end of the year, the band brought in Rob McDermott—a New York metalhead who had started as an intern for Pantera and White Zombie and had been managing fellow Warner hard-rock group Static-X after moving to LA—to act as their manager, and he remained a long-term piece of their infrastructure.

The band toasted to their new major-label support before quickly hunkering down to record a hit single. After all, they didn't want the rock world to provide the same type of lukewarm response to their songs as those forty-plus label showcases. The tracks of the *Hybrid Theory* EP and the rest of their earliest demos with Chester were quickly retired as they started writing new music; as Mike would put it years later, "We played those songs a ton when the band name was 'Hybrid Theory,' and once we had a whole album to play, those kinda just went away."

For diehard fans, however, those demos will never go away, especially after multiple rereleases and special-edition reissues. Instead, these early songs represent the greatness that was still to come, and without those first attempts, who knows what would ever have been achieved. Slowly but surely, they were solidifying their sound. And before long, they were going to have to fight for their vision, too.

INTERLUDE

"I Felt Like I Knew Him My Whole Life"

Ryan Shuck was a member of Family Values mainstay Orgy when he first met Chester, and he would later form the band Dead by Sunrise with him and work with him in his band Julien-K. Here, he shares his first encounters with Chester, who would become one of his closest friends.

We were in NRG Studios—recording our second album, *Vapor Transmission*—and I heard some screaming in the hallway.

It wasn't blood-curdling. It wasn't bad screaming. It was something I hadn't heard before—loud, powerful. And it was ongoing. It just did not stop. I was like, "Dude, whoever's doing that is gonna lose their voice."

I was the social butterfly of Orgy. If something cool was happening, I would walk over there and start making friends with everyone, or if something weird was happening, even better, I was all over it. So I went next door, right to Studio B from Studio A, and I ran into this skinny little guy named Chester.

And I go, "Hey, is that you?" And he started laughing and goes, "Yeah." I was like, "How do you do that?" He's all, "Oh, yeah, I don't know! That's how I get warmed up!" I was fascinated, and he was also really cool, and we just walked out front and started talking. That conversation ended up being probably an hour and a half out there—just like old friends, and I had just met the guy. I believe at the time he was sleeping in a car, because he lived in Arizona, and he was out [in LA] to do this album. By the end of the conversation, I invited him to come live with me. "If you ever need a place to stay," you know, "come stay with me."

Chester and I continued our friendship. Honestly, it was as if we had known each other forever. It's the weirdest thing: I felt like I knew him my whole life, and I rarely felt that with anyone in my entire life—like a soulmate. He turned out to be one of my closest brothers of my life and one of my biggest advocates, teachers, students, all the above. It ended up that every single day they were recording *Hybrid Theory*, we were recording *Vapor Transmission*, and we were hanging out after that. Maybe the fact that I had opened my home to him broke down some more walls. And for me, just his sweetness, and the fact that the guy would sleep in the back of his car to record this album—that's the kind of stuff that I really respect, that I gravitate toward. He was also silly and goofy and fun, and we just connected on that level.

Through all that, I obviously was introduced to the guys before they were Linkin Park, when they were Hybrid Theory. I saw that a couple of them were really good artists and illustrators. I was just like, "What the hell? These guys are all so talented. What is going on with this band?" They invited me in to listen to some of the music, and that's when I really woke up—I heard some of the songs, and I was going, "Oh wow, this is something special." And the guy walking up and down the hall screaming? I heard it in the context [of the music], and it was interesting—to hear him scream in the hallway, it was weird and pleasing, but when I heard it on a song, I was like, "This belongs on the radio." At that point we were two times platinum, a pretty famous rock act, but we were talking about playing shows together someday, and I said, "Honestly, it's not gonna be long before we're opening for you." They all laughed—maybe they didn't believe me.

I remember that we sensed a huge market opening for something different. Every single person that was involved in any sort of heavy music was trying to look like Korn. Everyone was experimenting with dreadlocks, everyone had Dickies on, everyone had Adidas shoes on. And that speaks to the power of Korn, because they're the godfathers, they opened this door for everybody, and I love them. Anyone in a new band really had elements of Korn, and it was very powerful, but a guy like me always thinks, "What can I do to stand out from that, to do something unique?"

That type of thinking led to Orgy—we were into Duran Duran and Depeche Mode, and simultaneously into Stone Temple Pilots, Metallica, Pearl Jam. Korn not only kicked the door open, but they brought up other bands around them and helped create this genre. It was like Korn created the universe, and then other bands like Limp Bizkit, all these different sounds, started emerging in their wake. We decided we were gonna come out with a new guitar sound and do full-on electro—and Korn backed us and helped us launch. The rap-rock thing was certainly extremely pervasive, but you'd also have these weird outliers like Marilyn Manson and Orgy.

In some ways, I think Linkin Park is sort of the supergroup of our era. I always thought that Chester could be the biggest pop singer in the world—but then, he could turn on his demon as well. So he could do these verses where he literally sings, and this is not derogatory, better than a singer in the Backstreet Boys or *NSYNC. Chester can inhabit literally the most insane, impossible vocal tone—and then in the same breath, go to something that rivaled these incredible pop singers. And then you have Mike, who's bringing this legit hip-hop feel and everything. It was like a super formula, and I think the timing was really perfect, where the right kind of groundwork was laid. They came out and just hit a nerve in a way that I just can't even describe.

No one can make the tone that Chester makes, and I definitely noted it when we were in the studio together. When we were recording, we didn't have him in a vocal booth, he was just standing or sitting right next to me. And that is an interesting way to hear a singer like that sing: Chester had this harmonic that his vocal cords did, where it was like another voice, within his voice. And you can only hear it when you're not listening to it amplified or through a mic—you can hear it in the room. And I had to sit there and listen to that for a thousand hours, and I've never heard anything like that. To be next to someone like Chester, recording and making stuff, just makes the hair on your arm stand up, because there's just nothing like that.

And I'm grateful, as an artist, because it taught me a lot. But could I ever be what he is? No. He's the voice of a generation. He just eclipsed everyone. And there are other voices of other generations, for sure. But he's the voice of ours.

CHAPTER 7

THERE WAS SIMPLY no way that the tension wasn't going to spill over into the music. The years of forming, reconfiguring, swapping singers, changing names, garnering intense doubt from the industry, and now sowing seeds of uncertainty inside the studio, on the precipice of something spectacular or maybe nothing at all—it built and built and demanded release.

The band that would become Linkin Park knew this. They could hear their own walls rattling when the coarse, chunky riff of the opening ten seconds of "One Step Closer" exploded into the rest of the song. They could feel hours of frustrated calls and not-quite-right pulling-your-hair-out studio tedium melt away when Chester's voice rips into the bridge. It's all there, in every word and scream and drumbeat.

"One Step Closer" is a miracle, a timeless piece of intense beauty and pummeling anger. It's the type of perfect debut single that any band would love to have but would hate to have to earn.

Hundreds of points of exasperation, the ones that made the band members wince and sigh and shake their heads in the years leading up to their first album, could be felt in the "I'm about to BREAK!" immediacy of "One Step Closer." But in late April 2000 at NRG Recording Studios in North Hollywood, Chester and Mike were *actually* about to break.

Not with each other, of course—they had formed a symbiotic relationship within the band at that point, and the rest of the group recognized the power of their bond. But producer Don Gilmore, brought in to helm their debut album following the Warner Records label deal, did not. He kept prodding the band to tweak a song that was originally titled "Plaster." It was good, but it wasn't quite right.

Incomplete sections needed to be filled out, according to Don. Lyrics needed to be changed, then changed again. As he kept pushing for rewrites, attitudes started to blister to a worrisome point. Chester became so furious with his producer that he started writing lyrics about how furious he actually was—seeing red, then scribbling down every pissed-off word he could squeeze out of his pen.

Chester wanted his ideas to be heard. But more than that, he wanted the person seemingly trying to drown them out to shut the absolute hell up.

———————

EVEN IF EVERYTHING IN THE studio had been copacetic, this would have still been a pressure-packed moment for the group, just as it would have been for any band trying to cut through a crowded scene. The demos from the *Hybrid Theory* EP and its castoffs hadn't made a dent in scores of label showcases, and the band was still tinkering with ways to combine rap and rock music that felt new yet urgent. The song that would become "One Step Closer"—which Mike and Brad had first pitched as a demo, then the band rerecorded at NRG within the four weeks of creating their first album—had the potential to be their opening statement, a lead single and introduction to something bigger than themselves.

If the band and their producer weren't seeing eye to eye on how that statement should function, that would have been a simple enough problem to solve: compromise, find common ground, or try another producer on for size. Yet this conflict took place as multiple voices surrounding the band believed that they should change not only a few things about their sound but also the very fabric of their being, as if what made them unique was actually a wrinkle to be ironed out. And from the band's point of view, the one allowing that chorus of naysayers to creep into the studio—who wasn't telling anyone floating ideas from the periphery to kick rocks—was their producer.

The band had initially struggled to find a producer for their debut album after signing to Warner Bros. but finally landed on Don Gilmore, a studio veteran in the alternative-rock world. Don had been an engineer on Pearl Jam's blockbuster-selling *Ten* album and then produced late-nineties crossover rock hits for bands like Eve 6 and Lit. To put it simply, he was an adult in the room, a technical pro leading a band that was still figuring out studio nuance.

But Don also had a self-admitted blind spot: he had never been involved in making anything that even *resembled* hip-hop music. And when he signed on to helm the band's debut album, Don essentially shrugged at half of Hybrid Theory's sound.

"In choosing Don Gilmore as a producer, we were really hesitant," Mike explained. "Don had more of these radio-alternative songs, and we knew that he would get that part of our sound right, but he knew nothing about hip-hop. Not a thing! And he said that to us when he met with us. He was like, 'Here's the deal, the part of your sound that I can't contribute to is the hip-hop part. I know that's a big part of your thing. But I like how you do it, so I will try to just get out of the way in terms of the beats and raps and stuff, I will leave that to you.'"

The band didn't need a producer telling them to "do their thing" at that point—they needed a champion and defender, someone who recognized the potential of their sound and swatted away creeping doubt about its details. But the executives and A&R reps at Warner Bros. felt similarly to Don: they saw promise in the band, but not in the parts of the band's identity that skewed toward hip-hop or electronic music. According to these longtime industry men, the rapping in the demos had to be toned down, and the DJ scratching needed to be muted. Ultimately, the band had been signed as a stipulation of Jeff's employment but still hadn't proven a damn thing yet, so their identity was considered fungible. And because Don couldn't explain why those features were essential to the rest of the product, the band realized that he couldn't quell the anxieties of the suit-wearing cynics.

"In making that record, we weren't completely understood by the record label, mainly because there was a categorization of what bucket you fit in," Joe said. "Being a rock band, but trying to have a firm foundation with our hip-hop and electronic influence that we bring to the music. The formats were alternative rock and active rock at the time. I remember the label at one point asked us to have less rapping and less scratching."

Once, the band even caught wind of the label's plan to have Mike stick strictly to the background of the band—or even be replaced by an outside rapper. The argument was that the band had replaced Mark with Chester, so why not swap out another perceived weak link for a better MC?

Naturally, those suggestions were met with outrage from the whole band, including Chester. After years of professional instability, he remained loyal to his new band of brothers and waved off attempts to position himself as the sole leader of a traditional hard-rock group.

The truth was, it would have been easy for the band to buckle under the pressure, to feel the weight of the major-label suggestions to streamline their sound into something more digestible, and to cater to a veteran producer who had helped score multiple rock hits. But they never really wanted to be a "traditional hard-rock group" in the first place. Even after Chester joined the lineup and gave them a radio-ready singer, their influences were still a pastiche of hip-hop, industrial, pop, post-punk, electronic, and alternative—everything from Timbaland to Nine Inch Nails to Aphex Twin to Red Hot Chili Peppers—and they were intentionally refracting those sounds through a metal prism. Telling the band to just play straight-ahead hard rock was like telling a running back to never move left or right on the football field; there was never going to be a clear path forward.

Unfortunately, timing was no longer on their side. The group had to work through their debut album in the first half of 2000, a moment when any major label would have viewed rap-rock as a sound that was starting to feel played out on a commercial level. Artists like Korn, Limp Bizkit, Kid Rock, and Staind were still huge, but most of these groups were already experimenting with different sounds and distancing themselves from the nu metal delineation post–Woodstock '99. The music industry is forever looking ahead for the next big trend, and a rap-rock act named Hybrid Theory undoubtedly felt like a backward glance by the time "One Step Closer" was in the works.

Considering all these circumstances, it makes sense that the band wrote a potential breakthrough song about being at the end of their rope. After so much arduous work and so many iterations, the industry had apparently turned them into an afterthought—that is, unless they were willing to completely change who they were. They were losing the power struggle over maintaining their essence to opinionated A&R reps. And now Don, the producer who couldn't fully support their vision, was questioning everything about the song still titled "Plaster," dissecting and disassembling lines to the point of exhaustion.

"We were losing our minds," Mike recalled. "At that point in the process, it was just like, 'Why don't you trust us? This is *our* album.' Our A&R guy doesn't have to have his fucking name on the front of the CD and play this music onstage every day. We knew, if we put anything on this record that we don't like or that we're not feeling, we're gonna have to live with it. Like, this is our career!"

So Chester and Mike balled up that frustration—at Don, at the label, at everything and everyone, but mostly at Don—and hoisted it into what would become "One Step Closer." The seething, spit-through-the-teeth opening—"I cannot take this anymore / I'm saying everything I've said before"—is literally directed at the producer who demanded more rewrites. The chorus cry of "Everything you say to me / Takes me one step closer to the edge" captures their escalating rage. And when it came time to write lyrics for the combustible bridge, Chester needed something pithy and powerful that could silence his biggest critic.

———————

THERE'S A REASON THE BAND considered the song that would turn into "One Step Closer" a potential lead single even before it was completed. Within their early demos and then within the jam-packed hard-rock scene and now within Linkin Park's whole discography, "One Step Closer" stands out. Every second either boosts the tension or dissipates it in a whooshing release, allowing the listener to translate their own problems onto its baked-in catharsis. Before any vocals are introduced, the instrumentation—quicksilver guitar riff, DJ scratches to suspend it in air, then full-band assault with blistering percussion—moves with kinetic energy and a menace that feels purposeful.

"'One Step Closer' is a good representation of the group," Chester said in 2000, prior to the single taking off, "as far as the riff and the power of the song. The aggression of it."

As it so happened, the opening guitar riff was a total accident. The band was doing a photo shoot in the underground parking garage of Joe's apartment building—not a real shoot with a professional photographer, mind you, but a shoot with someone they knew who could capably handle a camera and was up for taking some early band snapshots. Brad was sitting in a car with its door open, bored out of his mind, but fortunately, he had brought his guitar along. He fiddled around with a few licks, then messed with the guitar's tuning, tweaking the bottom string to a D and working through a few riff ideas.

Brad played a combo in drop D that sounded particularly springy, then played it again, his hands guiding the gleaming bounce across the strings. Mike heard the riff and stopped the faux photo shoot: "I was like, 'Dude, record that. . . . Don't lose that riff!'"

The "One Step Closer" riff musically separated the song from the rest of the band's demos for their debut album, which were heavy but not necessarily combative. Whereas a song like "Crawling" felt spacious and contemplative in their synthesis of rap-informed hard rock, "One Step Closer" was downright spiky—the sound of a band shoving the general public into the dirt to get its attention.

That sense of confrontation begins with Brad's sledgehammer of an opening riff but continues coursing throughout the rest of the song. The band wrote "One Step Closer" in Mike's apartment after the guitar line—played throughout the entire track—was finalized, and the structure came together quickly. Brad's riff drives the song, but instead of bogging down the arrangement through repetition, the rest of the instrumentation slides into place around it: the sleek cymbal rides on the chorus, the chattering beats expand the arrangement, the scattered DJ scratches dial up the chaos on the bridge. And for everything that sounded modern within the song, the band was smart enough to understand that the age-old quiet-to-loud contrast remained an effective tool: the percussion dropping away before the chorus, then crashing back into view provided a sense of movement, as if Chester and Mike were in cruise control before slamming down the gas pedal.

When the band was recording their debut album, Jeff told Chester that he thought "Crawling" was their surefire smash, a perfect distillation of their softer and harder edges. But Chester wasn't so sure. He told Jeff that, for one, "Crawling" was more difficult to sing, and two, Mike wasn't featured on the vocals that much—at least, not as much as he was on a song like "One Step Closer," which still had the working title "Plaster."

Chester was singing lead on both tracks, but "Crawling" featured a few quick rhymes from Mike on the pre-chorus, whereas the song that would become "One Step Closer" braided their vocals together on the hook—Chester's furious howl overlapped by Mike's quick-jab rapping. The two cadences balanced each other out sonically, volleying the song's intensity back and forth. Lyrically, they finish each other's thoughts: Chester sings, "Everything you say to me . . . ," then Mike swoops in with "takes me one step closer to the edge, and I'm about to BREAK!" And as an opening statement, what better way to introduce your band to the world—and push back against the label execs dissuading your hip-hop influences—than to hoist up the song exemplifying the dual sides of Hybrid Theory?

The fiery lyrics that Chester conjured in the studio after Don kept crumpling up his words and telling him to find more ultimately helped turn the song into an anthem. Because Chester was so livid with his producer and just wanted to hit upon something that worked, each line that made the cut is purposefully straightforward—no frills, just raw emotion.

As such, the lyrics possess a sort of blunt-force universality that can be adopted for any at-wit's-end scenario. The second verse goes, "I find the answers aren't so clear / Wish I could find a way to disappear / All these thoughts they make no sense, I find bliss in ignorance / Nothing seems to go away, over and over again." The song is ostensibly about Chester being fed up in the studio, but most people listening to the song don't know its backstory, so to them, the words represent the general experience of banging your head against the wall while nothing around you changes. Turns out, that's a feeling millions of listeners could relate to. In any scenario, the lyrics worked.

But the song still needed a bridge, and nothing Chester or Mike came up with met Don's standards. Mike imagined a part like the breakdown of Rage Against the Machine's "Killing in the Name"—that "Fuck you, I won't do what you tell me!" refrain—fitting into one of the band's songs and thought something like that might work for the bridge here. The problem was that he just couldn't find the right words, and their producer kept telling him and Chester to keep trying.

Chester was fuming at Don, to an almost inconsolable point. He jotted down the words "shut up" just to privately vent. Mike loved it. What if *that* was the bridge? It was simpler than anything he and Chester had come up with so far, but simple might be what the passage required. Chester thought about it for a moment, then agreed.

Chester and Mike entered the studio and told Don to pull up the track—they were ready to record the bridge. "Don was like 'Well, tell me what it is,'" Mike recalled later with a laugh. "And we go, 'No, no, no, it's better if we just record it. Listen to it in its full concept.'"

So Chester entered the vocal booth, and Don cued up the track without knowing what his singer was about to sing. Weeks of tension, months of hard work, years of willing this into reality had all built up to the moment in which Don pressed play—and Chester proceeded to breathe fire.

SHUT UP WHEN I'M TALKING TO YOU!
Shut up! Shut up! SHUT UP!
SHUUUUUT UUUUUPPPP!!!

In the wrong hands, "One Step Closer" could have sounded like a temper tantrum, an ill-conceived expression of angst that landed flat on its face. The song also could have been perceived as a lesser version of similar hard-rock tracks. After all, Limp Bizkit had sung about wanting to "Break Stuff" a year before Linkin Park's "I'm about to BREAK!" hook. And a few weeks before "One Step Closer" was recorded, Papa Roach had released "Last Resort," a similarly intense rap-metal opus that served as that band's mainstream breakthrough.

Betting on "One Step Closer" as the band's de facto introduction hinged on the belief that the song possessed the gravity to be taken seriously and enough personality to distinguish the band in a packed field. Once that bridge was recorded, though, any lingering uncertainty was laid to rest, and the decision to go with "One Step Closer" was a no-brainer. The song wasn't like anything else out at the time, because it was *better* than everything else out at the time.

"Everyone agreed that was the first single," Mike said. "When you got to the 'shut up' part in the bridge, we all felt like, 'People are going to remember this band when they hear the song.'"

"One Step Closer" not only contained the force to shake radio listeners and CD buyers awake but also appealed to ticket buyers. After the song was fully recorded—it's the only song on the band's debut album that features bassist Scott Koziol, who was brought in after *Hybrid Theory* EP bassist Kyle Christner departed the group after a months-long run—and mixed by Andy Wallace in New York, the band started thinking about their first proper tour in support of their debut album. They knew that "One Step Closer" was the type of song they wanted their audience to know by heart, its hooks shouted back at the stage as their fans' eyes bulged in delight. Anyone who's ever been to a Linkin Park show where "One Step Closer" serves as the boisterous finale or has selected the song to scream-sing in a karaoke bar knows that it's fun as hell to sing. Before it was even released, the band knew that, too.

"We didn't know anything about picking singles," admitted Rob, "but it was important for us to start off with a heavier and more aggressive song, because it represented the energy of our live show in the most accurate way. Bringing a ton of energy to our live show has always been top priority."

Before the band could start blasting through the song at their shows, their label told them they needed to yet again change their name and ditch Hybrid Theory. A UK dance group called Hybrid was part of the extended Warner Bros. ecosystem, and the label group couldn't support both Hybrid *and* Hybrid Theory.

The guys decided to keep *Hybrid Theory* as their debut album title, and after a few more naming mishaps—they were almost called Plear and also considered Platinum Lotus Foundation—they settled on Lincoln Park, an homage to a community space in nearby Santa Monica. They wanted to be a little easier to find online, though, so they tweaked the spelling, and with that, Linkin Park was born.

A few weeks later, Brian "Big Bass" Gardner, who mastered *Hybrid Theory* in early July 2000, recommended an obvious title change to the song still being called "Plaster." The phrase "One Step Closer" was used in the chorus, and it was way catchier for both fans and programmers.

Soon, the radio brass at Warner previewed a few songs by the band newly named Linkin Park, including the newly titled "One Step Closer," for rock programmers. The response was ecstatic, and KROQ, the enormously influential rock station in Los Angeles, started playing the song.

The fuse was lit.

Naturally, success relieved much of the tension that had mounted as the band carved out the sound of their debut album. Those label concerns about Mike Shinoda's rapping and the electronic elements in their songs? They dissipated once "One Step Closer" raced up the rock airplay charts. And Don was no longer the villain for failing to silence those concerns or for challenging the band to perfect their lyrics—after producing all of *Hybrid Theory*, he would continue working with the guys on their next album, which would have been impossible to imagine at many infuriated points.

Over the course of their career, Linkin Park would score bigger hits than "One Step Closer." The song wouldn't even be their biggest hit on *Hybrid Theory*. But as the warning shot that set the tone for the band's sound and its many permutations, "One Step Closer" was indispensable, an artistic affirmation that made all the struggle and hard work that preceded it feel like prologue. Most successful bands take a few swings of the bat before connecting with a commercial breakthrough, but "One Step Closer" made Linkin Park a hit immediately—crashing through the Hot 100 chart, streaking into the top 10 on alternative radio, scoring listenership across three continents, setting up the release of *Hybrid Theory*.

None of this was by mistake, however. "One Step Closer" took off precisely because the band fought so hard to maintain their identity and preserve the disparate elements that made their sound so singular, even when no one else around them could see the vision. They may have recorded "Plaster" as Hybrid Theory, then released "One Step Closer" as Linkin Park, but they knew who they were—and anyone who was trying to tell them otherwise needed to "shut up."

CHAPTER 8

A GROUP OF HIP-LOOKING teenagers is hanging out in a dark alley at night, as Cool Teens do. While chatting with a dude sporting impossible sideburns and an eyebrow ring, a girl wearing a sporty one-shoulder crop top and baggy pants looks to her right. At the other end of the alleyway: a figure in a black hooded robe. An apparition? A ghost? A wizard?

The girl points out the mysterious man and decides to follow him, leading Sideburns Guy by the hand through a busted door in the alley and into an underground tunnel. Waiting for the teens down that rabbit hole: multiple masked men—who begin to hover in midair! Linkin Park is there, too, surprisingly unbothered by the mystical figures floating among their instruments, and they're ready to rip.

As a de facto introduction to the band's visual aesthetic, the "One Step Closer" music video now looks like high-octane, turn-of-the-century silliness. And the guys look like they're savoring every moment in that tunnel. "Somebody just told me that they heard that most bands don't have a good time shooting their video or they don't like their first video," Mike said soon after filming the clip. "I think we had a blast."

A cheap blast. Linkin Park was still an unknown band on a major-label roster, and though they had carte blanche to make whatever kind of video they wanted, they were operating on a shoestring budget. Fortunately, Joe knew how to stretch a production dollar from the time he spent hustling in the film industry after art school, and he linked up with Gregory Dark, a former softcore porn director (sample film title: *Sins of the Night*) who had jumped to helming music videos in the late nineties and had worked with everyone from Britney Spears to Ice Cube.

Gregory and Joe devised the treatment together, strategizing how to pull off the gravity-defying special effects, including the big stunt during the breakdown of the song, where Chester is physically inverted and screams "Shut up when I'm talking to you!" from the ceiling. They decided to shoot in an abandoned tunnel that used to be part of the Los Angeles subway line, adjacent to a deserted Veterans Affairs hospital and sixty-three feet underground.

"The air was very thick and filled with minerals and dust and dirt," Mike noted. "It's very hard to breathe down there." Yet the band (including stand-in bassist Scott Koziol, making his only Linkin Park music-video appearance) was thrilled to be finally shooting its first visual, air quality be damned. They set up their instruments, lit some torches, and even hung some pieces from art-school friends on the walls of the tunnel for an extra pop of personality.

At a moment in time when regular rotation on music-video channels remained a crucial pathway to a band's mainstream success, the utility of the "One Step Closer" video was pretty clear: Linkin Park needed to introduce themselves to MTV viewers as their debut single was taking off on the radio and earning them a sliver of buzz. The video functionally accomplishes this mission. When it debuted, viewers unfamiliar with Linkin Park—that is to say, the overwhelming majority of viewers—could easily discern that the band had a singing frontman, a rapping frontman, a guitarist who wore headphones, a DJ who did not.

Viewers also used the video's tone and color palette to scan Linkin Park as a hard-rock group that was still accessible to non-hard-rock fans. Even in an underground tunnel, the video is never explicitly *dark*; instead of leaning into the murky disorientation that bands like Deftones and Korn had adopted, Linkin Park exists in a green glow, and the guys are never obscured by the shadows. Chester and Mike are positioned front and center like they're leads in a play, and their wild-eyed stares are captured in medium close-up—mad, but not menacing.

Unfortunately, the visual details around them suggest that the band is much goofier than its music. The smoke machines, tiki torches, and turn-of-the-century onlookers are straight out of a *Goosebumps* episode and immediately remove any sense of grit. Then there's the *hair*: Chester has a shock of blond spikes above his piercings and goatee tufts; Mike's hair is improbably dyed the color of cherry licorice. When the duo knocks forward in rhythm prior to the opening verse—Chester in a black sleeveless tank top, Mike in a white tee and baggy bomber jacket—their red and yellow heads bob up and down. They look like they're offering a choice of condiments: Ketchup or mustard?

What's more, it's hard to take them too seriously when they're inexplicably flanked by hooded fighter guys. Those "floating monks," as Mike would call them, have black-and-white face paint and a selection of martial-arts poses; some of them brandish ancient-looking swords and daggers, while others perform little flips when they're not hovering midair. You could watch the "One Step Closer" video twenty times in a row and still have no idea what their deal is. Are they a secret society? Are they time travelers? Are they aware that a band is playing their debut single in their underground lair? If so, why does Chester get to join them in midair during the bridge?

The answer to every question is: don't worry about it. "'One Step Closer' was just for fun," Mike said in a 2000 online fan Q&A when a listener from Sweden asked what those floating monks were supposed to symbolize. "It was an escapist action movie video."

Timing is everything: in 1999, *The Matrix* had become a box-office smash thanks in part to gravity-defying action set pieces and wire-work martial-arts choreography, and big-budget studio projects would mainline its influence for years to come. Action films like *Romeo Must Die*, *Mission: Impossible 2*, and *Charlie's Angels* cribbed some of its moves the following year, and a few weeks after the "One Step Closer" video was released, Ang Lee's *Crouching Tiger, Hidden Dragon*—a martial-arts epic full of flying warriors and fantastical stunt work—was released in theaters, eventually earning over $200 million internationally and four Oscars.

In a video interview filmed from the "One Step Closer" set, Brad sits on a couch in a trailer—Chester scrunched next to him, arm slung lovingly across his back—and declares, "The vibe is pretty much, like, *Blade Runner* meets *The Matrix*." Brad says it proudly, pausing to smile and slowly nod, and after a beat, Chester chimes in with a twinge of nervous energy: "Hopefully, we can pull that off!"

A few other music videos from 2001, such as Missy Elliott's "Get Ur Freak On" and U2's "Elevation," harnessed the *Matrix* influence, but for the most part, rising rock-group music videos still followed a simple formula of showing a band performing in a tight space while surrounded by rabid fans—think Papa Roach's "Last Resort," System of a Down's "Chop Suey!," Alien Ant Farm's "Smooth Criminal." The idea was to capture the exhilaration that the band's music provides their up-close fans and suggest to the average MTV viewer that they could—and should—join that crowd, too.

That concept was apparently the original game plan for the "One Step Closer" video. It definitely would have been safer, and probably more effective, than the high-flying approach. But the Linkin Park guys were still in their early twenties, consuming the same multiplex fare and borrowing the same DVDs as everyone else. They wanted their visuals to be ambitious.

They wanted floating monks.

———————

WHEN HE WAS IN ART school with Joe, Mike would work on a painting every week, putting in anywhere from six to twelve hours on one piece, then hang it on the classroom wall. After that, "twenty-nine other people tell you why it's horrible," he recalled. The criticism could be brutal, especially after such concentrated effort. But the idea was not only to improve as an artist but also to develop a thicker skin—to understand "how to leave the ego at the door," Mike said, "and walk in and do what's best for the art."

Joe focused his drawing skills on character design for film and TV storyboarding during his one year at the ArtCenter College of Design, and Mike graduated with a bachelor's degree in illustration in 1998, the year before the band landed a record deal. In the years between forming Xero and breaking through with Linkin Park, illustration and graphic design were always Plan B in case the band went haywire. Rock groups don't offer the steadiest career paths, so between the nights and weekends of band practice, Mike worked overtime to earn his backup-option degree. Either way, he figured, he was going to be an artist.

Mike grew up loving anime, connecting to the Japanese animation flourishes and inhaling the genre's classic films: *Akira*, *Ghost in the Shell*, *Ninja Scroll*. He also became a fan of the *Astro Boy* manga and TV series and played through classic video games like *Metroid* and *Mega Man*. His illustrations in art school drew from that same sensibility; later, anime would become integral to the Linkin Park fan community, with home-made mash-ups of their songs and animated visuals. But back when it was time to think about the artwork for the band's debut album, Mike and Joe, the self-appointed visual captains of Linkin Park, wanted something that captured the band's rap-rock duality, so they looked elsewhere for ideas.

Frank Maddocks, an LA-based artist who had just designed the cover to Deftones' 2000 classic *White Pony*, said that Mike and Joe showed up to their first meeting together wielding books and magazines as reference points for the *Hybrid Theory* cover. Frank was impressed by their intent—young bands typically didn't have such professional focus—and started cycling through ideas with the pair.

"We came up with this kind of a militant vibe," he recalled. "We were all really interested in Banksy at the time and stenciling and this kind of propaganda." During the nineties, the anonymous England-based street artist Banksy developed his signature style as a freehand graffiti artist in the Bristol underground scene and established a stenciled aesthetic, often with an anti-capitalist and anti-war bent, by the end of the decade. A street-art feel—a little like the graffiti the band's friends had added to the tunnel walls in "One Step Closer" but with a more striking subject—felt like the right move.

The guys settled on the image of a soldier, but searched for some sort of juxtaposition—the cover couldn't just feature a soldier without it being softened to some degree. Frank started taking notes and sketching out ideas, at one point suggesting they put butterfly wings on the soldier. They landed on dragonfly wings and thought about "making it look like someone had painted them on the street," Frank explained, "like you had the soldier initially, but then someone came along and added to that piece. That was the desired effect, this push and pull of images."

Mike and Joe handled the primary artwork themselves—they're credited in the *Hybrid Theory* liner notes for "line art sketches + drawings"— and Frank solidified the design, rendering the main image as a graffiti spray atop a cloud-colored background. Stray lyrics from the album are tucked into the artwork, and the band name is presented in a blocky grunge font, the *N*s in *Linkin* twisted backward to provide the effect of a custom street-art logo (and, undoubtedly, function as a tip of the cap to Nine Inch Nails for their influence on the band).

Mike drew the soldier as a stencil, generalized but easily identifiable, similar in visual scope to Banksy's Flower Thrower masked man, which was first presented in 2000 and became an iconic mural in 2003. The soldier charges forward carrying a thin flag, the helmet tilted down in duty and the face a formless shadow. Behind them: dragonfly wings, dripping down like still-wet paint, delicate and beautifully detailed. The contrast was intentional. "The idea of bringing heavy elements and some softer elements of music together was represented through the visual art of this album," Chester said in 2003.

Creating a memorable image that subtly hints at a new band's sonic approach is a daunting task—which is why most groups opt for a band photo on their introductory album cover. Yet the *Hybrid Theory* cover fit the ascendant band to a tee. The dragonfly wings tempering the imposing facelessness of the soldier inject a vulnerability into an otherwise hard exterior, just as the band's melodic intent and lyrical approach functioned within the hard-rock scene. And the mix of stencil art and graffiti-spray design—as if the soldier was created on a wall with a spray-paint can, and the wings were added by someone else with a differing voice swinging by that same wall—communicated a DIY mashing of styles, which was ultimately the band's goal.

Simple, striking, effective: the *Hybrid Theory* cover didn't necessitate a long gestation period, and the guys nailed it on the first try. Years later, the soldier with dragonfly wings has become iconic—an idea dreamed up by a band still honing their visual approach transmitted to the world—and countless fans have adorned their bodies with the image.

"Obviously, I know it's because the music is so special to them and I'm happy to just lend a hand to that," Frank said, "but I got to think somewhere, if the art was really lame, it probably wouldn't be tattooed."

———

As THE BAND HAMMERED OUT its visual aesthetic early in the *Hybrid Theory* album cycle, the hand-drawn artwork was, understandably, easier to nail down than their three-dimensional identity. How exactly did Linkin Park want to present themselves to the world? Coming up with a striking cover image was one thing; conveying their status as a rap-rock band (but not like all the *other* rap-rock bands), heavy but not pitch-black, a bundle of influences and distinct personalities, was something much trickier—especially when that presentation was condensed into a three-minute video or a twenty-five-minute opening-act set, as was often the case.

After Chester joined the band, the majority of their shows in 1999 were label showcases, followed by a few gigs around West Hollywood and in Tempe, Arizona, during the first half of 2000. The rest of the year was jam-packed with spots on other bands' club and music-hall tours: The Union Underground in July and August, Kottonmouth Kings in September and October, P.O.D. in November, Papa Roach in December. Linkin Park would shuffle onstage and rip through a few songs in front of a crowd that was there to see another band, as Xero had done way back at that first Whisky show, although depending on the month, a lot of those unfamiliar fans had at least heard "One Step Closer" on their local rock station.

Immediately before and after releasing their first album, the members of Linkin Park were also fleshing out their stage personas in short bursts—and the key was always getting fans to understand the frictional force between Chester and Mike. The tactics weren't too subtle when they started, as demonstrated by the "different hair colors for the singer and the rapper" approach in the "One Step Closer" video. But the more shows they logged together, even as a rushed-out opener, the more the band's two frontmen developed a rhythm side by side, feeling out each other's movements while first presenting the songs they cocreated.

"What's up, New York! We're Linkin Park," Chester exclaimed while pacing the stage at Manhattan's Roseland Ballroom on September 20, 2000, during a radio show that also featured Disturbed and Fuel. The performance was the band's first of two stops at Roseland that fall—the P.O.D. tour brought them back to the venue on November 20—with *Hybrid Theory* scheduled to come out nearly smack in the middle of them, on October 24.

At the September show (which exists in astonishingly good quality on YouTube, as do a handful of their early gigs—Linkin Park fans are master archivists), Mike fidgets with his in-ear monitor and Chester gets a bit tangled in his mic cord, kids still learning how to physically exist onstage. More noticeable is the way they crowd each other onstage, fumbling some of their ad-libs and midsong banter. They have to restart the set-capping "One Step Closer" midway through the opening riff, causing Chester to turn to the crowd and let out an "Oh, shit!"

The energy is high, and the talent is evident—especially whenever Chester unfurls his vocal power in front of the unsuspecting crowd. "A wonderful instrument" is how Mike described Chester's voice, "and he spent so much time learning it and getting in tune with it and unlocking it." But back then, there was still a clunkiness to their interplay, like two point guards needing time to figure out how to share the ball.

Fast-forward to the November show at Roseland, however, and every aspect of the band has been tightened and finessed: the setlist, Rob's tumbling drums, Brad's razor-slick guitar lines, and most importantly, the dynamic between the two stars at the front of the stage.

What a difference two months can make: by that second show, the vocalists showcased a natural reciprocity, from their complementary stage movements to Chester's playfulness with the crowd (at one point dropping a "What's up, ladies?") and Mike's impeccable timing. He knew exactly when his counterpart was going to punctuate a lyric (on "Papercut": "A face that awakes when I close my EYES!! / A face that watches every time I LIE!!!") and how to turn Chester's scream into a springboard for himself. And both Mike and Chester loved to simultaneously double over in full-body quakes when a riff really landed, emphasizing to the crowd that, yes—it's time to lose your mind.

In their earliest performances as Linkin Park, the band understood the sincere giddiness of rock-show release. What they learned over the course of those first few months of touring, however, was how to translate what made them so special to *listen to* into something that also made them special to *see*.

The crackling tension between the soft and hard in their sound had been effectively visualized in the *Hybrid Theory* album cover, less so in the "One Step Closer" video. But watching Mike and Chester onstage in the back half of 2000, gradually becoming stronger performers and co-leads as they worked toward headliner status, crystallized the image that Linkin Park envisioned for themselves, the one that set them apart from every other band like them. Nobody else had *those* guys.

As time wore on, the shows got bigger and better, as did the music-video concepts. "Joe started to get more confident about asserting himself in the process," Mike said about following up "One Step Closer" with a visual for "Crawling," a song the band wasn't even playing in all their sets but that would soon become crucial in their story. "He really got in there and probably learned a lot and asked a ton of questions," Mike added. Joe eventually moved from dreaming up treatments to directing the videos himself, and by Linkin Park's third video, he was incorporating references to Miyazaki's *Princess Mononoke*, one of the band's favorite anime films.

In a different era of the music business, every single detail of Linkin Park's visual style wouldn't have been so important to unlocking their sound to the general public. Nowadays, as we forge deeper into the streaming era, rock groups are putting less emphasis on music videos (MTV, which was so crucial to the industry at the time, has essentially stopped playing videos), and without record stores for fans to browse, album covers aren't catching the eye of unfamiliar consumers in retail stores.

But in 2000, Linkin Park *had* to nail those details. The videos, the photos, the artwork, the show setups—they *all* needed to exist as parts of a whole to convince music fans that this was a band worth investing in long term. It's the difference between "One Step Closer" being a one-hit wonder and the start of something bigger, the start of a legacy. It's the difference between a nominally successful debut album and one that sells ten million copies.

INTERLUDE

"Once We Heard It, We Knew"

Sonny Sandoval, the leader of rap-rock veterans P.O.D., reflects on first meeting Linkin Park in 2000 and sniffing out the band's potential while hitting the road on one of the band's first tours.

We had been doing it already, since '92, independently and underground, and built our own little following and had our first major release, [1999 album] *The Fundamental Elements of Southtown*. When Linkin Park came out, we were headlining a tour with (hed)p.e. and Project 86, and we had heard their single on rock radio. We got a call to take out Linkin Park, as a way of doing Warner Bros. a favor—but once we heard that song, and we knew that they were supported by Warner Bros., we were like, "Aw, dude, these guys are gonna blow up!" I mean, they were new, they hadn't been around—they just came out of nowhere. But once we heard it, we knew.

And so we took them on tour. They opened up, the first of the four [bands] on the tour, and I think they played for, like, fifteen minutes. And you could just tell. All the bands knew—(hed)p.e., all of us, were like, "Yep, they're blowing up."

They were obviously young and ambitious and just ready to go. And we loved them right from the start. I mean, they were always simple guys, quiet. Chester was always the most fun and had the most experience with playing in bands. The bass player [Dave] was in a Christian band, and we'd known about that band—I think [our bassist] Traa even had a sticker of his band, just because we were familiar with the scene—so when he jumped in with them after they recorded the album and he started playing with them live, we were stoked for him. But like I said, they were just ready. I think that was the first time they had actually toured, but they had the single, they had the record, they had all the support in the world, and they just hit it running.

I remember listening to one of their interviews, a live interview on a rock station—I knew we were taking them out, so I wanted to get familiar with the guys. They were on the radio, and Mike and Chester were talking, and Mike kept saying, "I'm the rapper, and he's the singer." At the time, there were so many bands trying to do that. But they were definitely a lot more ear-friendly to me—obviously, I liked Chester's voice, and also Mike's rapping in between, and that [combination] is what drew me in. It was done in a tasteful, catchy, hooky, radio-friendly way.

When P.O.D. had come up, we'd come up from the underground, but [our song] "Rock the Party" got a lot of press and on MTV. There were still the Korns and the Limp Bizkits, but they were viewed a little differently— "Rock the Party" was a little bit more friendly, a little bit poppier. It wasn't as in-your-face, mad-at-the-world, angsty hardcore rock. We were on the *TRL* chart, so I think in that pop world, they were a little bit more, "Okay, cool, I can get down with this stuff." And then when Linkin Park came in, they checked all the boxes for that pop-rock world. They were friendly, and they weren't mean. And then obviously, when you listen to a lot of their lyrics, it gets a lot deeper than that. But I do think their timing was perfect.

With Linkin Park, I had heard that a lot of the early crowds, the metal crowds, were hesitant—like, "We're metal, and we don't wanna accept any- thing else!" And they had to get through that to prove them wrong. I think a lot of it had to do with the rap stuff, too. Us and Linkin Park were some of the more well-known bands that were doing it, and that crowd didn't want to like rap. Korn never did that, Deftones never really did that—they never really rapped. And Limp Bizkit was doing it, but I don't think people ever really took Fred as, like, a hip-hop head, even though he can rap. When Linkin Park came out, it was very distinct—Chester was the singer of the group, and Mike is the hip-hop guy, and it was clear he could rhyme. So even if a lot of the metal heads weren't ready to mix the two just yet, they were still paying attention, and a lot of them eventually accepted rap-rock.

Watching Linkin Park [on the early tours], we really just felt like the older uncles—watching these guys go out there with excitement, ready to get their feet wet. They were excited about the opportunity to be doing this. For me, Chester would always be the standout, because he was on a different level than everybody else. Sometimes, everybody else could have been a little bit serious, or maybe even intimidated, still being very green in the game. And Chester was living it up! He wouldn't be afraid to walk in everybody's dressing room and be like, *"WHAT'S UUUUP!"* He was always familiar with your band and always a fan of your music. There was never any ego on any of the members, but Chester was the one who would make you feel the most welcome.

We would have talks, going back to the hotel or whatever, and they would always just listen to our horror stories about breaking down in the middle of nowhere and sleeping in parking lots and not having enough money to make it to the next venue and stuff like that. And they were always amazed at our big-brother stories. Chester had put in some time in other bands, and he knew what we were talking about, but the rest of the guys didn't have that experience. So when they were coming up so quickly, Chester understood what a privilege it was. I think Chester realized, "I'm not taking this for granted."

We've been on those tours with bands where, like, you don't even talk to the lead singer of the band until the last day of a two-month tour, and you go, "This is stupid, dude. Who do these people think they are?" Not Chester. Never.

CHAPTER 9

O VER THE MONTHS that Linkin Park put the finishing touches on its debut album, the following songs were enormous on MTV and Top 40 radio: *NSYNC's "Bye Bye Bye," Britney Spears's "Oops! . . . I Did It Again," Backstreet Boys' "Larger Than Life," Mandy Moore's "Candy," 98 Degrees' "Give Me Just One Night (Una Noche)," Jessica Simpson's "I Think I'm in Love with You." The year 2000 represented the commercial peak of teen-pop, with harmonizing, choreo-loving boy bands and beautiful, melisma-slinging young women selling millions of albums and seemingly producing even more shrieks outside of the Times Square studios of *Total Request Live*.

The hysteria was era-defining: turn-of-the-century bubblegum had been on the rise since the mid-nineties as a new generation of perfect-looking young stars took over MTV, but 2000 saw a total pop-culture takeover as the biggest artists scored their biggest album debuts. This was the year that *NSYNC's *No Strings Attached* sold a mind-blowing 2.4 million copies in its first week of release—a record number that would stand undefeated for the next fifteen years—while Britney Spears and BSB each scored seven-figure album bows.

These teen-pop songs were full of sugary hooks that were often produced by a cabal of studio polymaths in Scandinavia and sung by young people who had either appeared on *The Mickey Mouse Club* or been cobbled together via record-label auditions, or both. As such, the teenybopper movement faced understandable criticism for being inauthentic: plastic music manufactured in a lab and transmitted by former child stars who now looked like models. Non-pop artists started taking shots.

"I'm sick of you little girl and boy groups / All you do is annoy me, so I have been sent here to destroy you," Eminem rapped on "The Real Slim Shady," mere seconds after making an oral sex joke about Christina Aguilera. At Woodstock '99, multiple bands took a less pithy approach: during Limp Bizkit's set, Durst asked the crowd how many of them "really like *NSYNC" and was met with a chorus of boos. Meanwhile, The Offspring propped up cardboard cutouts of the five Backstreet Boys onstage at Woodstock, then destroyed them with baseball bats.

Being deemed a "manufactured" act equated to grounds for dismissal of any artistry—as if they were AI music decades before that was actually a thing. If every piece of their musical presentation had been constructed *for* them, why should their music be taken seriously? So, when Linkin Park debuted in 2000, found a little bit of success, and were almost immediately accused of being a label-created group, the band members took that personally. How could they not?

"There was a rumor going around that we were a manufactured boy band," Mike recalled. "Like Backstreet Boys or *NSYNC or New Kids on the Block or whatever. And no knock on those guys, but that was an industry-created phenomenon and group. Those guys didn't, like, grow up at junior high school together making music . . . and we were!"

The gossip got so bad that when the band started doing their first interviews, Chester would candidly discuss his personal history of drug problems and sexual abuse, lest anyone think his more serious lyrics were ringing hollow. This was a different, less sensitive time with regard to prodding musical artists about personal trauma, and Chester felt forced to publicly process his issues to prove his authenticity. "It was like, 'There's a lot of songs about depression, fear, and paranoia. Are you just making it up?'" Chester explained. "And I said no."

So, why did the band face these charges of "just making it up"—being a toothless rap-rock industry plant—in the first place? Linkin Park were far from major-label marionettes. If anything, their relationship with Warner Bros. Records had been frayed by the executives' attempts to shove Mike into the background and potentially bring a new rapper into the lineup. The label hadn't manufactured their image; on the contrary, the label had wanted to rearrange it entirely! But MTV viewers and radio listeners weren't aware of those behind-the-scenes tensions, so they assumed Linkin Park had signed off on how they were being presented to the masses as opposed to conceptualizing it themselves.

Although Linkin Park was lumped into the omnipresent rap-rock movement, the band never existed in any sort of music scene prior to their major-label debut—never gigged around the underground or spent time grinding out dive-bar shows to scoop up a few new fans, as Chester had done in Phoenix with Grey Daze years earlier. Xero scored their publishing deal after one show; Chester met the other members through industry connections. Plus, they were acutely professional—in a way that was inauthentic, per the rumors. "We did get a reputation for being a business rather than a band," Mike later admitted. "But that was because we were so focused on getting our stuff done."

In this instance, the members' work ethic worked against them: if they were a *real* rock band, they'd be getting loaded and causing chaos instead of honing songs and hitting deadlines, right? The band had spent years refining their ingredients, but with mainstream ambitions, no home base, and a distinct lack of drama, the perception was plain: they must have been conjured out of thin air to take over the world.

Plus, there was the band's decision not to use any curse words on their first batch of songs—not a moral objection but a conscious choice to rid their songwriting of four-letter crutches. "When Mike and I sat down and wrote the lyrics," Chester explained, "we wanted to be as honest and open as we could. We wanted something people could connect with, not just vulgarity and violence. We didn't want to make a big point of not cussing, but we don't have to hide behind anything to show how tough we can be." The result was that Linkin Park's debut didn't include a Parental

Advisory sticker, a move that undoubtedly broadened their fan base. At the same time, hard-rock fans were openly skeptical about this suspiciously family-friendly new group.

Let's be real, though: all that was background noise and snarky nit-picks. Here's the actual reason why Linkin Park faced bogus claims of being manufactured: they were too good too fast.

The band's peers, from rap-rock predecessors like Rage Against the Machine and Red Hot Chili Peppers to concurrent superstars like Korn and Limp Bizkit to genre-straddling peers like Deftones and Papa Roach, all followed a similar trajectory: start off raw, tinker with an aesthetic, use a second album (or a third album or, in the case of the Chili Peppers, a fifth album) to capture mainstream imaginations. Take a band like Korn: their self-titled 1994 debut was gnarled and unrelentingly bleak, but by 1998, their third album *Follow the Leader* included MTV-ready singles. They had started out with okay sales, but over multiple years, they were able to cultivate a real fan base and rely on that same base when they later sharpened their sound and put out a blockbuster hit.

For most bands, that path would bring in thousands of new supporters, whom the day-one fans would squabble with online and at shows. Ultimately, these listeners were all part of the same gigantic crowd that record labels craved—arenas full of people who had latched on to an artist at different moments of their streamlining process. Refinement was often needed to produce a hit song or album, and it was widely understood that this process would take place over multiple years and projects.

However, that was decidedly not the case when Linkin Park emerged with their debut album. *Hybrid Theory* effervesces in synthetic beauty, its soundscapes purified to the point where every band member corresponds with each other cleanly, and even the most aggressive outburst is pristinely aligned with the elements surrounding it. Don demanded perfection of the band, who in turn demanded it of themselves—rewrites, endless song mixes, a refusal to waste time "jamming" when they could be recording. And the result was almost *too* perfect.

The most cynical rock fans took on the role of smarmy teachers suspicious of a cheating student. When it arrived, *Hybrid Theory* was so good, in fact, that the only explanation a faction of listeners could accept was that the band didn't make it themselves.

———————

IN REALITY, LINKIN PARK *DID* experience that same refinement process— it just happened before they were called "Linkin Park." The band was distilling their aesthetic after years of discarded band names and a different singer. The upside of this process was that some of the band's earliest demos from their Xero days with Mark had never been heard by the general public, so they could be scavenged, improved upon, and considered for the debut album.

Resurrecting old Xero songs for Linkin Park's first album carried an inherent risk: after all, these demos had been rejected by the music industry at large when the guys were trying to score a label deal. But with Chester in the fold, Mike feeling more confident with studio software, and Don on hand to help fine-tune every track, the band approached their demos like a chop shop—stripping down demos to their most essential parts, then building them back up with better raw materials.

"Runaway," for instance, came from the Xero demo "Stick N Move," which worked well at their early shows and felt like a puzzle that the band should solve. "We completely disassembled the song and rewrote it," Mike said. "We kept the chords and some of the drum grooves but added a bunch of new stuff to it and rewrote all the lyrics, and it became 'Runaway.'" A similar remodeling happened to the guitar line on the song "Points of Authority": "Brad wrote this riff, then went home. Mike decided to cut it up into different pieces and rearranged them on the computer," Rob recalled. Eventually, the guitar became a phantom of its former self, and "Brad had to learn his own part from the computer." Brad didn't mind—that sawtooth riff *roars*.

Anchored by Rob's funked-up drum fills, the production of "Runaway" and the setup of the chorus are discernible from the "Stick N Move" demo, but the rap verses have been overhauled as an emo-leaning sing-ing showcase for Chester, who oscillates from agitated metaphors ("Paper bags and angry voices, under a sky of dust") to one of the album's best snarls on the chorus ("I wanna know the answers / no more lies!"). Ches-ter hated "Runaway"—the song eventually fell out of favor in the band's setlists—but it remains one of his most complex early vocal performances. Listening to the demo and the finished product side by side feels like flip-ping through a book of cartoon sketches, then watching those cartoons spring to life as 3D animation. The band's sturdier sonic approach, Ches-ter's technical skill, and Don's studio polish turned the rough ideas into compressed, virtuosic intensity.

"Runaway" was one of the band's very first tracks, dreamed up by Mike and Mark when just the two of them were writing songs together. Mark also received a writing credit on fan favorite "A Place for My Head," which was originally called "Esaul" (the first name of a friend of the band) and which eventually became one of Linkin Park's most frequent set clos-ers, along with "One Step Closer." The members of Xero always liked the energy of "Esaul," and the track was the first demo that Chester recorded for the band; the muted intro and whispering bridge set off the rest of the song like a firecracker and served as a strong template to start mosh pits. "I think that was our goal," Joe said, "to somehow lyrically and musically convey this feeling of frustration and tension, almost like you're stuffing a bottle full of those emotions and then you're shaking it up until it explodes. I think that song does that very well."

Across several versions of the song, from rough draft to finished product, the spindly rap-hardcore structure of "Esaul" remains mostly intact on "A Place for My Head," from Brad's fingerpicked intro with the piezo pickup to the head-slamming second half of the bridge. The pro-duction adds some heft, but the pit euphoria was always preserved. The main change, however, is the lyrics, which are nearly unrecognizable from "Esaul." Mike's verses were fully rewritten, Chester tweaked Mark's chorus lines, and the refrain of that crucial bridge has changed from the internal-rhyme word salad "Soon, the Aztec moon will heat my room, heal my wounds" to the more arena-ready "You try to take the best of me, go away!"

Some of that refurbishing surely came from Don giving studio notes, but "A Place for My Head," a song that was always about feeling detached from family, also improved because the band members were becoming more thoughtful writers. "We're attacking these universal themes of depression, of anger, or of frustration. I mean, we approached those things from the eyes of someone who's twenty years old," Mike pointed out when discussing "A Place for My Head." Years had elapsed between when the song was started and when it was finished, and the band could "attack those thoughts with a little bit more confidence," Mike explained, "and also talk about some things that go beyond those things."

By the time they started recording *Hybrid Theory*, all the members of Linkin Park had reached their early twenties, but you can still hear the teenage angst across the record, remnants of bygone frustrations that were carried over and projected on the widest screen imaginable. There are inner demons pointing out mistakes, petty betrayals in relationships, desires to shut the world away, wounds that will not heal.

On "By Myself," another resurrected demo that used to be called "Sad," Mike raps in a teen-drama daze, sputtering out rhetorical questions: "Do I trust some and get fooled by phoniness? Or do I trust nobody and live in loneliness?" "Forgotten" is all nightmares and bad memories, the sound of young artists identifying painful realities versus illusions; the song formerly known as "Rhinestone" had been around since Xero's first demo tape, and some of the high school lit-club metaphors ended up making the final cut.

Still, Mike and Chester understood how to take that pre-adulthood vulnerability and make it universal. The lyrical sadness and resentment on *Hybrid Theory* are the products of two frontmen talking through their experiences, and even though they may be rooted in their youth, their words spoke directly to every demographic of listener who was feeling misunderstood and searching for a release.

One of the hallmarks of *Hybrid Theory* is the lack of lyrical specificity: songs are often a battle between "I" and "you," and gendered pronouns and proper nouns basically don't exist. That's all by design. The band members' own pain was authentic and personal, and Chester's words drew from the more traumatic details of his past. But Linkin Park wanted to make an album onto which *anyone* could graft their feelings—to become the "I," to rage against the "you," to find connection with their voices, in whatever situation they were facing.

"There are all these different things that can trigger the same emotions—getting kicked out of school, having your parents get divorced, or losing a boyfriend," Chester explained. "All of those things can trigger anger, depression, aggression, self-doubt. When I'm writing, I'm constantly thinking about myself, because it's the only experience I have to draw on. And I don't see an exact reflection of myself in every face in the audience, but I know that my songs have validity to them, and that's why the fans are there."

———————

BEFORE THERE WERE THRONGS OF fans, there were Chester and Mike screaming in a tiny room as faceless listeners slammed on the walls around them.

"By Myself" was one of the songs that the two frontmen figured out together in Mike's modest apartment in Glendale—a lot closer to Hollywood than where most of the band had grown up in Agoura Hills, although still not quite there. Mike's neighbors hated him, especially during the "By Myself" nights. It was tireless noise, rerecorded over and over—but the leviathan cries had to be captured just right for the song to work.

"The walls were paper-thin, Chester's screaming the chorus, and they must have thought we were murdering somebody in the room," said Mike, the memory cracking him up. "We were both just shouting, and I'm going, 'No, LOUDER!'" The neighbors would typically thump on Mike's wall at 10:00 p.m. on recording nights—*enough, lights out*—but sometimes

Chester and Mike were feeding off each other's energy and had their head-phones strapped on, so they couldn't hear the rattling. "They're literally punching the wall," Mike recalled with another laugh, "trying to get our attention and tell us to shut the fuck up."

"By Myself" underwent several iterations and studio tweaks, from the initial "Sad" to an early 2000 cut called "SuperXero" to a near-finished version with a slightly different vocal take on a Warner Bros. Records hard-rock sampler CD called *Raw Power* in May 2000. Throughout that evolution, however, the blunt force created in that banged-upon apart-ment remained. The production of "By Myself" became more intricate as that seed sprouted across studio sessions—Brad's guitar stops on a dime with an effect that sounds like a shriek, and the atmospheric produc-tion and Joe's subtle scratches ground Mike's longing in the verses—but, really, the song works because Mike says the word "myself," then Chester goes "MYSELLLF!," and it makes the listener want to sprint through a brick wall.

"That's what was kind of magical about Mike and Chester as front-men, partners, and covocalists—to have that sort of Jekyll-and-Hyde type moment," Joe noted. "Two vocalists that could pull that off together really made us stand out from everyone else."

Mike said that the guys wanted the soft–loud contrast on "By Myself" to reference Nine Inch Nails and Ministry more than their hard-rock peers. Those kinds of left-turn influences—conscious attempts to produce a more sophisticated sound than the average nu metal group—are every-where on *Hybrid Theory*. "Cure for the Itch," an instrumental spotlight for Joe full of wobbly beats and programmed strings, was inspired by Joe's and Mike's shared love of nineties electronic pioneers like Aphex Twin and DJ Shadow. "My December," a fan-favorite ballad recorded for KROQ's *Almost Acoustic Christmas* show in 2000 and released as a *Hybrid Theory* B-side, possessed a velvety soft-rock texture that hinted at how Ches-ter's voice would be deployed on future releases. And the intro to "Points of Authority," where Mike dices up his own flow into a sort of scat-rap opening, can trace its influences back to The Roots—Mike heard Black

Thought doing something similar on their 1996 album *Illadelph Halflife* and thought it sounded cool.

With its sleek rap-metal gallop and hyper-processed beats, "Points of Authority" was one of two songs that Don liked from the band during preproduction. The other was "With You," which had been created with and cowritten by a duo known as the Dust Brothers. Over the previous decade, Michael Simpson and John King had earned a reputation as pastiche geniuses, helming found-sound masterpieces like Beastie Boys' *Paul's Boutique* and Beck's *Odelay*. Jeff Blue had been roommates with Simpson's stepfather and tried to link the band with Simpson and King back in the Xero days, to no avail. Once Chester joined the band, however, the Dust Brothers agreed to try a song with them, sending over drum loops and Moog sounds for the group to explore. "They basically gave us a bunch of stems from an unused remix that they had, so we constructed that into the song," Joe explained. "Some of the sounds at the beginning, like that '*Dun-dun. DUN*,' some of the loops and drum breaks in there are from them."

Mike described "With You" as more "of the time"—that is, a song that fit in with music being released by their rap-rock contemporaries—the product of the band reassembling stray pieces of Dust Brothers material into a nu metal song about struggling to move forward in a relationship. For all its moving parts, however, "With You" doesn't have an ounce of fat on it. The scratches, kick drums, synth loops, guitar pops, and rap verses shuffled into a guttural hook, then back out again—everything is lean, disparate pieces stitched together (over, not surprisingly, several versions of the song), and sewn up into a quick, seamless whole.

The tiny details of "With You" amount to a type of mathematically sanctified catharsis: lab-tested fury, designed to make a listener's neck hairs stand up. And it's exactly those types of details that help Linkin Park's debut album stand the test of time.

Of course, they didn't have a ton of time to coalesce: primary sessions for the album took place over just four weeks at NRG Recording, so a lot of that tinkering had to be completed across endless days and sleepless nights.

After the album was completed, the revolving door of bassists—Scott Koziol played on "One Step Closer," Ian Hornbeck played on three songs, Brad essentially took on the rest—finally closed when Dave Farrell left The Snax to rejoin the band, at long last solidifying the lineup.

Andy Wallace, who most famously mixed Nirvana's *Nevermind* but also coproduced such albums as Jeff Buckley's *Grace* and Bad Religion's *Stranger Than Fiction*, mixed *Hybrid Theory* at Soundtrack in New York City in June 2000, sharpening the edges as Mike nodded in approval behind the console. "One Step Closer" started picking up radio traction in August, and the interest in the single caused the label to push up the album release from Q1 2001 to Q4 2000; the thought was, "Hey, maybe this new band's debut CD would make for a tidy stocking stuffer that holiday season."

The night before *Hybrid Theory* was released on October 24, 2000, the band was between tour stops outside of Seattle, parked outside of a record store and waiting for the clock to strike midnight so that Linkin Park could buy the first Linkin Park album. While they waited, the band started guessing how many copies *Hybrid Theory* would sell in its first week. "I thought it would be awesome if it sold three thousand copies," Dave said. Chester thought it would be higher: eight thousand copies. Dave heard that number and became worried: "My gut reaction to that was panic. You've got to set your expectations high, but you don't want to be stupid."

The final first-week number: nearly fifty thousand copies. *Hybrid Theory* debuted at No. 16 on the *Billboard* 200 chart—a sign of how many listeners were soaking up "One Step Closer" at the time. No. 16 was not a boy-band-worthy ranking at that time, but after years of grinding toward a first album, it was a damn good start. By the end of 2000, Linkin Park had successfully brought the first iteration of their sound to thousands of music fans. In 2001, they would deliver it to many, many more.

W HAT IS LINKIN Park without "In the End"? Where would the band's journey have led and what would their legacy have become had they not summoned those quintessential three minutes and thirty-six seconds for their debut album?

Hybrid Theory could have feasibly been released without "In the End," and based on the success of the album's first few singles, Linkin Park would have been a rock-radio mainstay without it—at least for a little while. Had this been the case, they might have just fit in with their peers instead of eclipsing them all.

The history of popular music is full of colossal near-misses; from "(I Can't Get No) Satisfaction" to "Billie Jean" to "Smells Like Teen Spirit" to "Somebody That I Used to Know," iconic songs have a tendency of nearly imploding mid-formation and barely scraping toward release before shifting pop culture forever. And not only did Linkin Park's most earth-shaking hit struggle to reach the finish line, but this timeless song also almost never existed in the first place.

It starts with one night in the spring of 1999 when Mike sauntered over to the band's rehearsal studio on Hollywood and Vine by himself. That part of Los Angeles now exists as a cabal of juice bars, Walk of Fame stars, and upscale burger joints, but back then, that area "was, like, drug addicts and prostitutes everywhere," Mike said, "so you wouldn't just want to go in and out of there." Mike's plan, then, was not to go out once he got in. He flicked on the lights in the empty studio at around seven that night, looked around the windowless room full of the band's gear, and locked the door behind him, knowing full well that he wouldn't step back outside until morning.

Chester had recently joined the band, and the newly formed group had already created a handful of tracks that they thought might work for their debut, in addition to a backlog of demos. Things were moving, but there was still something missing. The song sketches—including tracks that would eventually become songs like "A Place for My Head," "Runaway," and "Forgotten"—punched hard, but not enough of the demos were hummable, the refrains often too aggressive to stick in anyone's head long term. It was a problem not only as a matter of the album's balance but also for a band attempting to reach an audience wider than the mosh pit.

"We knew that we needed more melody," Joe noted. "We knew we needed to round out what we were doing. People don't want to be screamed at for a full record—well, some people do."

Mike took it upon himself to come up with something actively catchy: "I was having this moment of, I knew it was on me, I had to find it," he said. So Mike locked himself in the rehearsal studio and started writing. The room didn't have a table or chairs, so he sat on the floor, huddled in front of the world's bulkiest desktop, and worked with both Pro Tools and an MPC2000 sampler that was positioned by his hip. Because there were no windows in the room, Mike didn't know what time of the night it was, and he started to feel woozy, disoriented—but he kept writing, jotting down notes and lyrics on looseleaf, creating a potpourri of ideas in a quiet room.

When Rob showed up to the studio the next morning to check on his fervent pal, Mike finally exhaled and played him the bones of "In the End." He was exhausted, but he watched his drummer's face light up at the eerie piano melody, the immediacy of the hook lyrics, the chorus that suggested something towering to come. The song was nowhere close to finished, but Rob said that it sounded damn near plucked from his own fantasies of what the band could accomplish.

"I was dreaming," Rob said, according to Mike, "imagining that we needed a melodic song that took us to the next level, where the chorus was just the undeniable thing. *This* is the song." Pretty good validation after pulling an all-nighter.

From there, the rest of the band built on Mike's foundation—the song was, rather improbably, set to be named "Untitled" back then. (The release of D'Angelo's R & B masterpiece "Untitled [How Does It Feel]" in January 2000 eventually made the band change course.) Joe added the stuttering DJ scratches to supplement the piano melody, and Rob replaced the original beat that Mike had come up with in the verses with a simple rhythm that could easily segue into the hook's enormity.

Brad came up with the guitar part in the verses as a series of harmonics: he wanted the chiming, high-pitched tone to upend expectations, as if the band was another instrument where a traditional riff would be. "With the right effects and the right performance harmonics on, a guitar can sound like a keyboard or strings," explained Brad, who also played bass on "In the End," "and more rooted in an approach that works well with the hip-hop and electronic influences in our songs."

Mike, Joe, Brad, and Rob had been trying to fine-tune their amalgamation of musical styles for years by then. "In the End" effectively solved the puzzle. The rap verses fed into the rock choruses seamlessly; the guitar and the bass pulled back, then crashed down, to account for the alternating sounds; and the mix of beats, sampling, and scratches solidified and pushed forward a viscous electro-rock underbelly that added without distraction.

Of course, the piano melody distinguishes "In the End": ecstatic in its sense of melancholy, that fluttering loop of hopeful A-sharp notes spiraling down to the D-sharp minor base notes served as the earworm woven throughout the song and its prologue and epilogue. Overall, the mix is titanic—the chorus crashes down with colossal weight and then the bridge somehow grows the song in scope and tension—but it also *runs*, refusing to linger on one interesting sonic detail or catchy hook for too long.

The lyrics needed to be finalized, and the vocals perfected. A demo version of "In the End" from early 2000 features totally different rap verses from Mike and a bit more wounded crooning in the mix. But the song possessed an undeniable spark, and when he finally left the rehearsal studio on Hollywood and Vine, Mike felt like he had accomplished something significant. "The moment I played that demo for the other guys," he said, "they knew that song was special."

ACTUALLY, CHESTER DID NOT. UPON first hearing it, he thought the song was . . . okay. But he didn't believe the melodic lightness of "In the End" fit the tone of the rest of the album. And in any regard, it was definitely not how he wanted the band represented in the mainstream.

"I don't really participate in picking singles," Chester said years later. "I learnt that after making *Hybrid Theory*. I was never a fan of 'In the End' and I didn't even want it to be on the record, honestly. How wrong could I have possibly been?"

Thus began the long-standing rumor that Chester hated "In the End," which his bandmates still have to clarify today. "No, no, no, no," Mike said in a 2023 interview when asked if Chester disliked the song. "That's actually a misconception. Some people think that he hated the song. He liked the song, he just loved really heavy stuff, and so when people were like, 'This should be a single,' he [shrugged and] was like, 'Ah, whatever!' It's not the one that he would have chosen."

For a while, nobody else chose "In the End," either: amazingly, it wasn't the first, second, or even third single from *Hybrid Theory*. The same A&R reps that had suggested that Mike's rapping needed to remain in the background—or even that he be entirely replaced as the band's rapper—balked at the idea of leading Linkin Park's debut album with a song so hip-hop-oriented when they weren't sure the right person was rhyming. Mike recalled "a lot of drama" around his verses on "In the End," where his original lines were picked apart by one A&R rep who was hell-bent on sowing seeds of doubt. The verses were eventually rewritten, and the band fought for the song formerly known as "Untitled" to make the track list—but "In the End" was pushed off as a single option until after more rock-focused songs had been served up to radio.

So "One Step Closer" was followed by "Crawling," the most straightforward vocal showcase for Chester on the album. Although Mike's rapping isn't as prominent—he rattles off a few quick lines during Chester's pauses in the pre-chorus—"Crawling" represented a left turn from the relentless aggression of "One Step Closer," with a soft–loud dynamic that the band had been utilizing since its Xero days.

"Crawling" alternates between Chester's delicately delivered confessions in the verses and his gut-wrenching screams in the chorus; the outro of the band's demo "Blue" had been excavated and repositioned as the hook. Before Chester bends his shrieks into an undeniable melody, he's presented with a ghostly keyboard riff that was directly influenced by Depeche Mode, a childhood favorite that he daydreamed in fourth grade would save him from his mundane life.

When "Crawling" was released as *Hybrid Theory*'s second single in the spring of 2001, "it represented a different side of what we do, intertwining something very intimate with an outpouring of emotion in the chorus and bridge, and even with some screaming," Joe noted. "Funny thing, too, because ['One Step Closer'] was such a big deal at the time—and then we come out with 'Crawling,' which is more of a softer side of what we do. I think if you got the album, you really understood it, but people that didn't were like, 'How does this song have anything to do with that other song?'"

The connective tissue between the first two singles was the vocal force and simmering emotion of Chester, who was increasingly sounding like an authentic rock star. Most of the singing parts on *Hybrid Theory* were written together by Mike and Chester, with Mike passing his co-frontman lines and phrases to consider and make his own—but for "Crawling," Chester wrote the majority of the lyrics, putting his vulnerability on full display.

"Crawling" is "probably the most literal song lyrically I'd ever written for Linkin Park, and that's about feeling like I had no control over myself in terms of drugs and alcohol," Chester admitted in 2009. He sings about the psychological and physical effects of addiction: paranoia, depression, endless discomfort, the feeling of crawling in your own skin. Many of the lyrics—"Against my will, I stand before my own reflection / It's haunting, how I can't seem / To find myself again"—are heartbreaking. But Chester viewed "Crawling" as personally enlightening.

"That song is about taking responsibility for your actions," he stated in an earlier interview. "I don't say 'you' at any point. It's about how I'm the reason that I feel this way. There's something inside me that pulls me down."

That message resonated with both radio listeners—"Crawling" reached the top 10 of both the Mainstream Rock and Alternative charts—as well as MTV viewers, who were given a darker, more visceral video for "Crawling" compared to the clip for "One Step Closer." As the band (which now included Dave on bass, in his first video as part of the group) performs within the shards of a cracked mirror via green screen, model/actress Katelyn Rosaasen stars in starkly lit, slow-motion sequences depicting abuse and the way music can help alleviate pain.

Joe worked closely with directors the Brothers Strause on the "Crawling" treatment in February 2001, and compared to its predecessor, everything about the visual—from the narrative concept to the outfits to the interplay between Chester and Mike—appears more professional, as if the floating monks of "One Step Closer" were already a distant memory. With MTV starting to take notice of Linkin Park after "One Step Closer" had made noise in the rock world, the "Crawling" video "was really an important part in introducing people to the band," said Mike.

While "Crawling" was still growing as a rock hit in the first half of 2001, another *Hybrid Theory* track, "Papercut"—a band favorite that was intentionally positioned as the album opener—was serviced to Europe as the third single. "The whole ethos of the album was to smash genres," Brad said, and with that in mind, "Papercut" is perhaps the most complete testament to the band's myriad musical influences on *Hybrid Theory*.

With its electroshocked guitar bounce, double-time rapping, slamming chorus that yields a soaring bridge, and whooshing beat that Mike said was inspired by Timbaland, the song is in-your-face and unclassifiable, in exactly the way the band members wanted to be at the time. Maybe it wasn't the catchiest song on the album, but the way that "Papercut" grabbed the well-worn nu metal formula, then refracted it through their own prism of sonic ideas, made the members particularly proud.

"To me, the two songs [on *Hybrid Theory*] that were the most important were 'Papercut' and 'In the End,'" said Mike, pointing out the tiny details on "Papercut"—the ending that blended the bridge and final chorus together, the way the beat is introduced, the fact that Chester is faintly rapping alongside him in the verses—that made the song so effective. "'Papercut' was all of the identity of the band packed into one song," he added.

As the first song on the first Linkin Park album and a Swiss Army knife of the band's sonic DNA, "Papercut" was always destined to be a fan favorite and live-show staple. But it wasn't a hit with the general public. Although the song peaked higher on the UK's Official Charts than either "One Step Closer" or "Crawling," "Papercut" never made the Hot 100 in the United States and stalled at No. 32 on the Alternative chart. Yet the whole idea of offering up "Papercut" as a single overseas was in part to synchronize the promotional push for what would follow.

"'Crawling' was still going strong at radio in the States," Mike explained, "but the European radio market moves faster, so they'd already burned through two singles and they needed a third one." Thus, "Papercut" fed the international demographic during the summer of 2001 as "Crawling" kept chugging along in the States, with both campaigns wrapping up in the early fall.

"And then," Mike said, "we could go worldwide with 'In the End.'"

———

LINKIN PARK'S BIGGEST HIT IS all about failure. A sadness pervades all of *Hybrid Theory*, but whereas the band rages against inner demons and unrequited longing elsewhere on the album, "In the End" is pure defeat, crushing in its simplicity: "I tried so hard, and got so far, but in the end, it doesn't even matter."

Mike said that those lyrics "just popped out" when he was originally putting the song together and that he had been thinking about the band's journey together up until that point. That checks out: by the time Mike had started the "In the End" demo in 1999, the band had spent years trying to break through, and the roadblocks had far outnumbered the success markers. They were still multiple months and dozens of showcases away from landing a label home, and nothing was promised after they found one. The band members weren't getting any younger ("Time is a valuable thing, watch it fly by as the pendulum swings," Mike raps in his reworked verses), and everything felt like a battle that they might not win and that no one would ever see ("I kept everything inside / And even though I tried, it all fell apart").

Of course, "In the End" doesn't work as a literal rant against music-industry disillusionment; the banging-your-head-against-a-wall frustration that the band was experiencing had to be turned universal, in the same way that any listener could understand the boiled-over anger of "One Step Closer." So Linkin Park rendered "In the End" as an epic monument to futility. They drew from their own personal and professional losses but ultimately used the song as a shrine to all our respective despairs.

"We like to talk about things that we can relate to," Chester said. "When we write music, there has to be honesty in it. We're not trying to say, 'I've gone through this, you have to feel sorry for me.' We're saying, 'I've gone through this, and we know other people are, too.'"

That sentiment holds true even with "In the End"—after all, there are two voices on the track, overlapping with and confiding in one another. Out of any song in Linkin Park's discography, "In the End" features the strongest seesaw between Chester's and Mike's vocal performances. Chester oscillates between controlled and guttural, and Mike's rapping possesses a crisp, concentrated intensity, but crucially, their tones complement each other to the point when it's impossible to imagine "In the End" with one of those voices swapped out or removed. Chester and Mike function as a sort of conscious and subconscious on "In the End"—rap and rock as alternating foreground and background, their thoughts crashing into each other across different planes of reality.

The bridge of "In the End" features Chester repeating the same four-line collapsed declaration twice, first solemnly and then as a howl. When Linkin Park performed the song live, their crowds picked up on the second half themselves, shouting along louder and louder, until Chester's wail is slowly drowned out.

"Naturally, at some point, we just stopped playing at that moment. Chester and Mike would just hold out the microphones and turn the lights on," Brad recalled. "The incredible outpouring of personal emotion; it's a crowd singing together, but each individual person is in love with the song, because they're investing their own life story into it." It was the type of deeper connection that the band had been trying to make with their sound for years. It also hinted that "In the End" was going to get very, very popular.

"One Step Closer" and "Crawling" established Linkin Park as a successful core rock-radio band, but then "In the End" raised the ceiling of their commercial prospects an *incalculable* amount. Those first two singles had peaked at No. 75 and No. 79 on the Hot 100, respectively; "In the End" climbed all the way to No. 2 in March 2002 and logged an impressive thirty-eight total weeks on the chart.

MTV was on board, playing the "In the End" music video—a big-budget epic full of CGI whales, thorny bushes, rain machines, and a tower growing in the desert, which listed Joe as a codirector for the first time—on repeat, both in its rock video blocks and on *TRL*. Alternative and pop radio also embraced the single, which became the rare song to top both the Alternative Airplay and Mainstream Top 40 charts.

Before "In the End," Linkin Park had yet to fully transcend the nu metal tag, a band that sang and rapped during the rap-rock boom. But Korn and Limp Bizkit never had a song come anywhere close to the runner-up spot on the Hot 100. And *Hybrid Theory*, which never topped the *Billboard* 200 albums chart but kept briskly moving copies following its October 2000 release, ended 2001 as the biggest-selling album of the whole year.

Linkin Park had effectively surpassed their peers and proved an industry full of naysayers wildly wrong. But, for the band, revenge was never the point. By the end of 2001, Brad, Rob, Dave, and Joe could stop playing during the bridge of "In the End," and Chester and Mike could at last extend their mics to the masses. They could hear their words of admitted failure sung back to them by thousands of fans, all of whom felt seen by their message.

For so long, Linkin Park had worked together to hone their sound. Now, they could simply hold out their mics and feel its echo resonate around the world.

PART III

THE FAME

CHAPTER 11

O N August 9, 2001, amid an avalanche of performances and exhaustion, Linkin Park went bowling with a superfan.

MTV's Canadian counterpart, MuchMusic, had arranged the group activity for the series *Gonna Meet a Rockstar*, in which a lucky listener would spend an afternoon with their favorite band before watching the band's show from backstage that night. So, before Linkin Park performed at Jones Beach Theater in Wantagh, New York, their bus bumped along to a bowling alley on Long Island with Jamie, an excitable twenty-something with a puka shell necklace and eyebrow ring, and Jamie's quietly supportive girlfriend, Glendine.

Under the washed-out fluorescent light of the alley, in between chowing down greasy snacks, Chester yelling at bowling pins to fall in his favor—"You're MINE, sucker!" he taunts a completed spare—and Dave nonchalantly doing the suck-it sign after avoiding a gutter ball, Jamie sparks up conversations with individual band members. Chester chats freely about his tattoos, telling Jamie that once you've gotten two done, you're going to want to get twenty done. Joe shrugs off a question about how he helps conceptualize the band's music videos. Brad gives a diplomatic nonresponse to a question about the band fighting on the road (*"Uhhhhm* . . . physically? Or do we argue a lot?"). But the highlight is when Mike, in a backward cap and baby-blue tee, scores a straight-on strike, high-fives Jamie a little too hard, plops down on a stiff plastic chair, and tells him about the band's too-packed Des Moines show in October 2000, the time right around the release of *Hybrid Theory*.

"It was 95 to 105 degrees outside, real humid," Mike explains to Jamie, who audibly oohs and aahs offscreen. "The people in the club were all drunk. And with the humidity and the show, and them just getting out of control, people were passing out. When we were done playing, Brad almost passed out. And I threw up all over the place." Mike leans back and wraps his hands around his elbows, hugging himself. The smile that crept across his face breaks into a toothy grin; he's delirious, downright giddy. "It was a *crazy* show."

This was a season of release for Linkin Park: following years of behind-the-scenes preparation, they were finally let loose in the real world, like a wind-up toy streaking forward after countless turns of the spring. After spending much of the back half of 2000 on the road around the release of *Hybrid Theory*, the band toured the globe in 2001—165 shows, four continents, zero months of the calendar year without a gig. There were headlining tours, support dates, hard-rock package runs, radio one-offs—at long last, concrete amphitheaters were full of flailing limbs and slammed heads, after too many nights expended perfecting songs in small rooms. The tour was promotion and catharsis tied together, the six members of Linkin Park meeting the listeners they had conceptualized for so long, now converted into reality. There were road-life difficulties—both the endless-travel-doldrum kind and the pass-out-throw-up kind. But in the right light, even *those* could be viewed as invigorating evidence of the band's success.

Plus, Linkin Park gained commercial momentum the entire time they were on the road; after "One Step Closer" impacted radio and MTV in 2000, "Crawling" became a hit in the spring and summer of 2001, and then "In the End" turned into a smash in the fall of 2001 before peaking on the Hot 100 in early 2002. All the while, *Hybrid Theory* copies kept scanning across the country. By the time Linkin Park finally returned home to Southern California in March 2002, they were dramatically bigger than they had been when they set out twenty months earlier.

"If you've never seen anything about our band, and all of a sudden you're hearing three songs on your local radio station, I'm sorry," Brad says to the camera, sporting a sheepish smile, in the band's first tour documentary. "You might think that this is an extremely new phenomenon, and in one sense, yeah, it's been very fast, because everything we've done has been becoming more intense exponentially, in terms of our schedule, in terms of all the things that we're trying to do relating to the band. However, we started out as a band over five years ago!"

Released in November 2001, *Frat Party at the Pankake Festival* is now a sort of skeleton key for that nonstop year, full of intense stage footage of Chester screaming into tangled knots of arms, as well as sleepy clips of the band waiting around for bus arrivals or fast-food orders. Brad gripes about spending his per diem too quickly, desperate for a real meal; Dave grips a PlayStation controller on the tour bus while Rob narrates to the camera, explaining which members like to sleep in (Brad and himself), which one requires the most footwear options (Chester, with ten to twenty at a time on the road), and why tour manager Bob Dallas is indispensable for keeping things orderly. The mini-fridge on the tour bus is filled with peanut butter, soda, and a soggy bag of Arby's leftovers—a trifecta of early-twenties nutrition. Rob opens the bathroom, points to the toilet, and tells the world that no one is allowed to shit in it.

And the tour doc doesn't just focus on Linkin Park. Members of Slipknot, Disturbed, and Crazy Town all make cameos, and bad room-service food gets hurled out of a hotel window. There's an elaborate joke about swapping Deftones' onstage water bottles with vodka, which doesn't actually happen. The hijinks are low-stakes and decidedly PG-rated, a band of decent young dudes clowning on each other and finding their place within the contemporary hard-rock ecosystem. "We were just stupid kids, man," Mike said, "so immature and doing dumb stuff. . . . We didn't know how to behave on a bus or anything, so it was just, like, trying to find ways to entertain ourselves and keep ourselves sane."

After spending the fall of 2000 as a support act in the United States, the band headed to Europe for select dates in January 2001, then returned to the States on their first headlining run, the Street Soldiers tour, through February. After that, they crossed back over to Europe to support Deftones in March and spent the rest of the spring scooping up dates in far-flung markets—Australia, Japan, Germany—they hadn't yet hit. These consecutive treks were dubbed the "endless winter" tour by the band, who found themselves chasing cold weather around the world and constantly passing each other sicknesses in the too-tiny quarters of the tour bus. When Linkin Park finally returned from Europe in the first week of June, they were worn out—but *Hybrid Theory* was still in the top 20 of the *Billboard* 200. Linkin Park had four days off, and then they were off to Ozzfest—the annual metal road show thrown by Ozzy Osbourne and his wife, Sharon—for the entirety of the summer.

"I'm doing more work now—working harder, with longer hours—than I've ever worked in my life," Chester said in July 2001. Fortunately, the band members were still young enough to endure the nomadic pressures, and what's more, they'd failed for long enough to appreciate the wins, regardless of the form and function. Fatigue and bad food were bearable when a line of fans were waiting, clutching jewel cases and band tees for you to sign at all hours of the day.

"You don't even have the sleep out of your eyes, you're barely conscious, and you're in a bad mood because you're not a morning person," Chester continued. "But you've gotta get beyond yourself and say, 'Look, this kid's bought an album, he's probably got four or five of his friends to buy the album, he buys the T-shirts at the show.' You can't deny the people who've put you where you are."

———————

IN A DELETED SCENE ON the *Pankake Festival* DVD, Chester shows off his tattoos for the camera—the flames on his forearms, the Pisces fish near his shoulder, the black loop around his ring finger, that last one a relic of a time when he was too poor to buy wedding bands for Samantha and himself. He's immortalized the band in tattoo form as well; the soldier with dragonfly wings from the *Hybrid Theory* cover runs across his left calf, and the words LINKIN PARK adorn his lower back. "I made a bet with my tattoo artist," Chester smirks, showing off the name of his band, "that when we went platinum, he'd have to do this for me for free."

Chester proudly wore his band on his body. He had always possessed the vocal skill of a rock superhero, and now that he'd found the right group, he could take it one step further to physically embody the intensity of his own voice. As his bandmates were gelling onstage and Mike was rattling off rap verses with cool precision, Chester was thrashing the hardest, deflating his lungs and jumping off risers, his skinny frame ready to fly.

As naturally as playing the rock star onstage came to Chester, however, navigating the idiosyncrasies of that transient life proved more difficult during 2001. He had started three straight years in a completely different space: in Phoenix, resigned to leaving music behind on New Year's Day 1999; in Los Angeles, with a new band of brothers and demos to work through in 2000; in Paris, for the first of dozens of overseas shows in January 2001. Even someone preparing for the moment needed to develop sea legs.

Plus, rock fans were still trying to pinpoint a collective perception of Linkin Park, especially as the first wave of nu metal bands began to crash or wholly change course by summer 2001. Limp Bizkit's ludicrously titled third album, *Chocolate Starfish and the Hot Dog Flavored Water*, came out just one week before *Hybrid Theory* and sold over a million copies in its opening week, but it was lambasted by critics and hard-rock purists, and the band (especially Durst) had fully become a pop-culture punchline. Korn was between albums and off the road, and Kid Rock was shifting toward country-rock balladry. The scene that Linkin Park never wanted to belong to in the first place was starting to evaporate, leaving a void and lots of bubbling questions in its wake. Who was this rap-rock band that was suddenly all over MTV, and how did *they* fit into this evolving hard-rock landscape?

As part of the 2001 lineup for Ozzfest, Linkin Park particularly struggled to fit in on a bill that included Black Sabbath, Marilyn Manson, Slipknot, Papa Roach, and Disturbed, among others. Chester chafed under the stricter corporate policies of the tour—no stage-diving, no hand-slapping, stay in the area of your designated stage.

Meanwhile, some Ozzfest attendees weren't thrilled to watch a band that not only didn't curse but also was getting played on pop radio and showing up on *TRL*. "There were a lot of our fans there, but they were so far back on the lawn, whereas the hardcore Ozzy fans were front and center," Rob said. "So, we were playing to these guys that had been up drinking since ten in the morning, and they just, you know, didn't want to hear it."

Chester would sometimes squint into a formless crowd that wasn't jumping around at all and conclude, *Oh, they think we're lame*. "We're not trying to force ourselves on anybody," he explained in the middle of the tour. "We were invited to do this show, and we were paid a lot of money to do it. Ozzy and Sharon asked us to come out on this show, and we're friends with everybody on this bill. We all respect each other, but the fans don't get that."

Contributing to Chester's Ozzfest grievances: an enormous spider bite on his ass.

Some sort of black widow sank its teeth into the singer while he was asleep on Linkin Park's tour bus, causing an enormous welt on his butt cheek—pretty amusing, until his neck started swelling up and his brain became cloudy. Instead of it being a Marvel Comics origin story for Chester, the bite made him delusional, caused onstage stumbles, and ultimately required an emergency prescription of the antibiotic ciprofloxacin. "I thought I had cancer," Chester later admitted about the incident.

Against doctor's orders, he finished the tour in September, and the ordeal made for a bitter pill on an imperfect festival run—but there was no time to sulk, because the band was quickly off to make their MTV Video Music Awards debut with a performance of "One Step Closer," then head to Stockholm three days later for another two-week European run.

Around this period, as the overseas dates led straight into a prominent slot on the Family Values Tour in October, Chester started drinking heavily. During the Ozzfest run, Chester had found a kindred spirit in Jacoby

Shaddix of Papa Roach, whose "Last Resort" started getting played on MTV a few months before "One Step Closer" was released. "He's a punk kid like me, from a fucked-up small town," said Shaddix, a native of Mariposa, California, whose family was homeless for part of his childhood. "I'd have to sneak him away to go party—the other guys in [Linkin Park] would be like, 'Keep it straight,' but I'd pull him away."

Blowing off steam with a fellow singer during a hectic period was one thing; drinking to the point where the rest of the group avoided Chester and he had to travel to cities on a different bus than his bandmates was another—and it was no one's fault but his own. Nobody else in Linkin Park was getting high, but back then, "I never performed a show completely sober, I was always smoking weed right up until the moment we went onstage," Chester admitted. "Immediately after we finished the show, I'd go and get hammered."

Being on the road for months on end, driving all night to make it to the next market, constantly catching colds, summoning energy onstage to play the same songs for the hundred thousandth time—it was all difficult for young men to shoulder when they were so fully locked in. Plus, the band was overseas traveling across a different continent when the terrorist attacks of September 11, 2001, took place. They canceled their scheduled show in Hamburg that night.

"And so in the midst of all of that," Mike recalled later, "having a guy who would sneak out—he'd just go missing and come back obliterated. You couldn't even talk to him, he's just so wasted. . . . There was an element of Chester, he was very fun sometimes when he was that way! And then usually the next day, it'd be, like, so dark. He's super hungover, he's angry at everybody, yelling at everybody, and you're kind of just like, 'Let's get through the day.'"

The addiction that had marred so much of Chester's early life returned at a critical moment in the band's trajectory. As "In the End" was becoming a smash and sending *Hybrid Theory* sales into the stratosphere, Linkin Park's singer felt disconnected from his bandmates, once more a stranger in a group of longtime friends, as old habits returned.

Chester and Samantha were also arguing constantly—sadly, Sam had suffered a miscarriage earlier in 2001—and the strain of so few days at home together that year made a difficult period unbearable. Chester felt "like I was doomed to be this lonely person," he confessed, even as his wildest dreams were being realized.

Fortunately, a year of endless touring had to end at some point. After a few more US arena dates and radio-show gigs in early December, the band enjoyed a fifty-day break around the beginning of 2002. Chester detached from the road and sprinted home—where a pregnant Samantha was waiting for him, their first son together already on the way, due in April.

On January 2, 2002, Chester officially gave up drinking. If 2001 was the most successful year that he and his bandmates had ever experienced, the next year had to be better.

———————

THE FINAL SALES NUMBERS FOR *Hybrid Theory* during its first full calendar year of release staggered the band, who had spent the year incessantly promoting their debut and watching intangible measures of its connection without knowing the seven-figure details. Over the course of 2001, *Hybrid Theory* sold a total of 4.81 million copies—the first and (to date) only time a hard-rock album was the year's top-selling album since Luminate (formerly Nielsen Soundscan) began tracking music sales in 1991.

Hybrid Theory was the year's top-selling album, out of any genre? More than albums like *NSYNC's *Celebrity* (4.42 million) and Shaggy's *Hot Shot* (4.56 million)? The guys couldn't comprehend the statistic. "We were like, 'What does that even mean? That's ridiculous!'" Mike said. "Imagine getting that news and we're like, 'I don't understand. We're just kids from the suburbs of Los Angeles. I lived in my parents' house not too long ago!'"

As exciting as those numbers were, they also had consequences; even though "In the End" still had a few months to go before peaking on the charts at the start of 2002, Linkin Park was already feeling the pressure to focus on a new album. The band was craving new material after months of performing the same dozen songs—"I'm ready to explode," Chester replied when asked in a 2001 interview about that desperation—but as the *Hybrid Theory* numbers kept growing week after week, so did the expectations for its follow-up, even before primary work began. "No matter what we did, we knew it would probably be considered a disappointment," Dave admitted. "Clearly, there was no way we could repeat the insanity of *Hybrid Theory*."

They had started sorting through new ideas while they were out on tour in 2001, in a cramped digital-recording studio that they had squeezed into the back of their tour bus, with Mike shrugging off road-show misadventures to click-and-drag melodies across a monitor. In *Pankake Festival*, Mike gives a tour of his studio cubby—a keyboard, a pair of computers, a Pro Tools unit, all ancient-looking under a modern lens. Mike points to the speakers on the bus playing the instrumental of an in-the-works song that he, Chester, and Joe had been hashing out. Eventually, that snippet would turn into the intro of "Somewhere I Belong."

More crucial than any song chunk summoned on the road was the time Mike and Chester spent side by side, endless hours across dozens of cities as different tours spilled into each other. With *Hybrid Theory*, the dynamic between the band's two voices had to be worked out in compressed time and space—but now, their paths had been intertwined for over a year on the road, and even though it wasn't always perfect, the proximity helped them bridge the emotional gap.

"Back then, Chester could tell me a story about himself that I hadn't heard—and for me, that's hard to even imagine," Mike explained. "We were living and breathing every minute together, which is a lot. But it resulted in, when it came time to get in the studio and when we were writing the songs, we were definitely really synchronized."

Linkin Park would spend the majority of 2002 off the road and in the studio, but before that, they still had one more live run scheduled: Projekt Revolution, a twenty-two-date North American trek that marked the band's first proper arena headlining tour. They had already completed some new material by the January 29 kickoff in Colorado Springs, but the band declined to preview anything for the audience, opting instead to put a bow on the *Hybrid Theory* promotional cycle in their largest headlining rooms to date. Some of the same songs they had first tried out before a scattered, half-interested crowd at Whisky a Go Go would now be gobbled up at twenty-thousand-seat-capacity venues.

The band brought West Coast rap veterans Cypress Hill, rising post-grunge band Adema, and legendary mash-up DJ Z-Trip out with them on Projekt Revolution. They also hosted local DJ battles at each tour stop, with unsigned talent getting the chance to square off against each other and win the chance to open for the band at their final tour stop in Mexico City. Members of LP Underground, the official fan community the band had launched in November 2001, were encouraged to bring their membership cards to the shows and huddle with like-minded fans in the pits. After spending extended time on traveling festivals and as opening acts themselves, Linkin Park saw Projekt Revolution as their singular vision for an arena show: genre-splicing, actively engaging, with fans connecting and imprinting their identities onto the scene.

And when it came time for the headliners to hit the stage, Linkin Park declined extravagance—just some raised platforms for Rob to drum and Joe to scratch, the soldier with dragonfly wings billowing behind the stage. At that point, the band didn't need any bells and whistles to batter an arena: Linkin Park's live show was a well-oiled pulverizer, with Mike and Chester in total lockstep on each song, Brad blasting out riffs with hunched-over concentration, Dave slamming out bass notes in a power stance, and Rob and Joe playing off each other's percussion in the background.

The efficiency stands out in the footage of those shows, each member of the band understanding precisely how to deploy and pull back their force within each song so they could all shine. So do the crowds of thousands, all there to see Linkin Park and scream along to the band's quickly growing collection of hits.

Following its 2002 launch, Projekt Revolution evolved into an annual touring series, spanning multiple Linkin Park albums across the next decade and eventually grossing over $40 million, according to Boxscore. At the conclusion of its first iteration, however, the band wasn't thinking about how the brand would expand. They had just finished the most grueling tour schedule they would ever face, and they'd done so on their own terms. They had traveled the world and watched their audiences swell—an incredible, career-altering run, to be sure. Now, mercifully, it was done.

"The experience was simultaneously rewarding, but absolutely draining too," Dave said later, reflecting on that tour. "I'm glad I did it, but I never want to have to do it again."

CHAPTER 12

W HEN THEY WON the Grammy, everyone knew who should hold it.

On the night of February 27, 2002, Linkin Park attended their first Grammy Awards, right after wrapping up the US dates of their first arena headlining tour. The guys had been up for Best New Artist, the only band in that year's nominees, but lost to Alicia Keys; meanwhile, *Hybrid Theory* came up short against U2's *All That You Can't Leave Behind* in the Best Rock Album category. There's no shame in getting beat by a pair of Grammy darlings—and yes, even in her first year in the game, Keys was already a Grammy darling. But Linkin Park didn't go home empty-handed: "Crawling" prevailed in the Best Hard Rock Performance category, trumping songs by Alien Ant Farm, P.O.D., Rage Against the Machine, and Saliva.

The Rock and Alternative categories at the Grammys mutated over the years, as genres merged into each other: in 2002, there were nine Rock categories; in 2024, we have six; and Best Hard Rock Performance hasn't existed since 2011. "At the time, I didn't know the difference between 'hard rock song' and 'hard rock performance,' since they had Grammys for both," Mike explained. But because the song had won for its performance, Mike said, "eventually I was like, 'Oh, this is a Grammy for Chester's vocal.'"

The full band's studio recording had facilitated their first Grammys win, a watershed moment in their history—"but if we really want to be super honest," Mike continued, "the reason we got that Grammy was because Chester's performance on that song was bananas." So when the band went up to collect their award and posed triumphantly on the red carpet step-and-repeat, Chester was the one carrying the Grammy, facing forward in the center of the collective and cradling the tiny golden gramophone close to his chest. In one photo, Dave's right arm is extended in presentation of Chester and the trophy, as if to confirm, *Ta-da, he did this.*

In between the roughly three hundred shows that Linkin Park performed in the period around and following the release of *Hybrid Theory*, the band squeezed in stops at the various checkpoints of commercial success in the early 2000s, boxes ticked off to demonstrate proof of enormity. The Grammys win was significant, but so was the network television debut a year earlier: the band had flown straight from London to New York in January 2001 to perform "One Step Closer" on *Late Night with Conan O'Brien*, Chester flailing around Studio 6A and into millions of homes while wearing a cowl-neck sweater and chain wallet.

A few weeks after Ozzfest 2001 wrapped in August, Linkin Park was back in NYC at the MTV Video Music Awards, being introduced by NASCAR star Dale Earnhardt Jr. ("These guys might not run 190 mile an hour, but they sure bring the noise!" he stiffly read from the teleprompter) and performing an extended version of "One Step Closer" to rattle the opulent walls of the Metropolitan Opera House. Linkin Park returned to the VMAs the following year—but as part of the MTV elite instead of as the hot new rock band. Mike and Chester got to copresent a Moonman award to Jennifer Lopez, and when Linkin Park won Best Rock Video for "In the End," David Lee Roth and Sammy Hagar announced the band name from the stage, voices from a bygone music-video era theatrically anointing the current stars.

In 2001, one could still posit that Linkin Park's astronomical success—the sold-out shows, the millions of albums sold, the radio adoption of "One Step Closer" and "Crawling"—could be credited primarily to hard-rock fans. But by 2002, after "In the End" raced up the Hot 100, that argument fell apart. Linkin Park were now full-blown A-listers.

None of the band members had the brash personality of Fred Durst, mugging for the cameras and blowing up boats (an actual thing Fred Durst once did during MTV Spring Break). But the popularity of the music turned Linkin Park omnipresent, the smash singles plentiful enough to make the voices behind them into regular pop-culture fixtures.

By March 2002, Linkin Park was gracing the front of *Rolling Stone* ("Rap Metal Rulers" was the cover line) and getting shout-outs from Nelly Furtado and Willa Ford on MTV. They were the band mentioned breathlessly by pop stars discussing their affinity for rock's new big thing. Even the show's hosts weren't immune to the sounds of Linkin Park. "I'm a huge fan of your band," Carson Daly gushed to the guys during a stop at *TRL*, the teenage crowd in the studio audience and Times Square streets smiling and squealing. "The record is *so sick!*"

Because the band had existed in the public eye for some time by that point, the years preceding their debut album—followed by the extended *Hybrid Theory* promotional cycle and snowball effect of its biggest hits—prevented the members from feeling like an overnight success. "One Step Closer" had already been playing on rock radio and MTV for roughly eighteen months when the band finally left the road in early 2002, new to public opinion but accustomed to seeing their images and hearing their voices out in the wild. "It's eerie," Mike said of those first glimpses of themselves. "It felt natural, even though we knew it wasn't. Like an overwhelming of déjà vu."

Even with a somewhat gradual climb into the spotlight, however, the effect of leaping out of the touring circuit and parachuting into the world of Grammys and cover stories was jarring. As the shows became increasingly robust, so did the fan communication—the signed merch, the meet-and-greets, the adoring letters from listeners explaining how Linkin Park's songs had helped them through difficult periods or prevented them from running away from home. In a *Spin* cover story, Mike and Chester talk about a fan who needed to undergo a brain operation that required her to stay awake during an eight-hour surgery—so she asked the doctors to play *Hybrid Theory*, on loop, for all eight hours.

By early 2002, Linkin Park Underground, the band's official fan club, exceeded ten thousand members and received regular messages from the band. The LPU connected listeners around the world, offering a space to gather, discuss their favorite band moments, receive news and updates, and press play on LPU-exclusive music.

Every major musical fandom has forums for their most hardcore supporters, but Linkin Park Underground distinguished itself thanks in part to the band's official annual *LP Underground* releases—exclusive CDs containing song demos, live tracks, and unreleased ideas, which were often shipped to members around the holiday season as fan club stocking stuffers. The *LP Underground* albums became a yearly highlight for diehard listeners, beginning with the *Hybrid Theory* EP in 2001; the band hand-signed five hundred copies of their 1999 demo as a thank-you to the fans who helped make the *Hybrid Theory* full-length the best-selling album of that year.

By now, Linkin Park was getting more and more familiar with the idea of having superfans. They had just spent all 2001 accruing them, sweating for them, hearing them scream their lyrics. The band members had all been kids themselves, finding solace in their own favorite songs, not too long ago. Mainstream fame was something else entirely, though. Although they never belonged to a traditional scene coming up (and rejected the one, nu metal, that they were most associated with at the start), the band's extended time touring the world with bands like Deftones, Papa Roach, and Disturbed had indoctrinated them in scores of hard-rock ticket buyers . . . and yet, *here* they were, giving away VMAs to J. Lo.

Linkin Park was crossing over in a genre-rigid musical ecosystem in a way that could have been perceived as a betrayal of the hard-rock base they had just created—the same reason some Ozzfest attendees shrugged them off as poseurs and the accusations of label-manufactured inauthenticity lingered. Fortunately, appealing to listeners of different sounds had been the band's entire point.

"Sorry, man, if the 'wrong' kid buys your record, if your idea of the 'wrong kind of fan' buys your record, bummer for you!" Chester said.

"If somebody who has only been buying Britney Spears and the Back- street Boys buys our record, I feel like I've accomplished something. I've expanded this kid's horizons, you know what I mean? The same thing goes for the kid who's bought nothing but Pantera albums. Which kid is worse? Which one is the kid you don't want? I would never tell anybody they can't like our music."

Linkin Park's openness to other musical styles, and their correspond- ing fan bases, proved absolutely crucial in a prestreaming music industry, back when the question "What kind of music do you listen to?" often yielded a single genre in response. After *Hybrid Theory*, the band could have chased approval from the Ozzfest set and shrunken away from the spotlight, limiting their commercial prospects in favor of a heavy-rock core. Or they could have gone all-out pop and called up super-producer Max Martin to further streamline their sound, shirking off fans in the pit to ensure the *TRL* screams lasted a little longer.

They did neither. Instead, Linkin Park adjusted to fame by trust- ing their creativity to keep expanding. At a time when the logical move would've been to pore over a sophomore album that could appeal to the widest possible audience, the band pivoted, focusing on a side project that would prove to be an ambitious, unexpected, downright weird detour.

DURING THIS TIME, THE MEMBERS of Linkin Park had already been thinking about making music outside of their traditional band structure. In 2002, Chester recorded background vocals on "Karma Killer," a spin- dly post-grunge rocker from Cyclefly, chiming in on the track's chorus after he met the Irish band while kicking around the LA club-show scene pre–*Hybrid Theory*. A few weeks before "Karma Killer" was released, a song on the metal-heavy soundtrack to the vampire horror film *Queen of the Damned*, an Anne Rice adaptation starring Aaliyah in a posthumous per- formance, was credited to "Chester Bennington of Linkin Park."

The song "System" did not originate with Chester; Korn's Jonathan Davis had worked with film composer Richard Gibbs on the music for

Queen of the Damned, some of which would be performed by the vampire Lestat's band in the movie. But because Korn was signed to Sony BMG and the soundtrack was coming out on Warner, Jonathan was contractually denied from having his vocals appear on any of the songs. So he asked his pals in the Warner Music Group ecosystem—including Disturbed's David Draiman, Static-X's Wayne Static, Orgy's Jay Gordon, and Chester—to be his voice.

Chester performing a song cowritten and coproduced by Jonathan Davis constituted a full-circle moment: after watching Korn help kickstart the rap-rock revolution from afar, Linkin Park had become that sound's biggest name, had taken over the Family Values Tour, and now, Chester was actually working *with* Davis, singing what was ostensibly a Korn song. "System" gurgles, then seethes, Chester re-creating Jonathan's twitchy delivery and chorus roars. Evidently, he was nerding out on the opportunity to work with both the Korn leader *and* the source material. "I'm such a big fan, I have read all the books," he said of *Queen of the Damned*. "I think I can kind of relate to Lestat a little bit more than someone who doesn't know the film or the books."

Three weeks before the *Queen of the Damned* soundtrack arrived, Mike and Joe were featured on "It's Goin' Down," a single from the hip-hop DJ collective The X-Ecutioners. The group formed in New York City in the late eighties and had spent over a decade as underground turntable heroes when executives at Loud Records spotted a crossover opportunity; they were heralded as "the first DJ crew to sign with a major label," then plied by the label with various collaborators to perform over their concrete-hard beats. One Loud exec brought a copy of *Hybrid Theory* to the studio, and the group's Rob Swift reached out to Mike to potentially work together. Luckily for him, Mike and Joe were already hardcore fans.

"They are pioneers of deejaying," Joe gushed. "As turntabling developed, they were one of the original crews to come up." Joe directed the video for "It's Goin' Down" at the Park Plaza Hotel in Los Angeles during the break between Linkin Park's final 2001 shows and their arena shows in early 2002, and after the single was released that January, it became the only new track that Linkin Park performed on the Projekt Revolution tour. In the video, The X-Ecutioners invade a hard-rock rehearsal space (Rob and Dave are shown jamming with Wayne Static), start scratching themselves, then set off a rap-rock party. Chester, Brad, Xzibit, members of Adema, and (həd)ᵖ·ᵉ· all make blink-and-you'll-miss-it cameos, but Mike remains front and center, the star of the show.

"It's Goin' Down" represents a road not (yet) taken: although it's not a solo track from Mike, and in fact samples the Linkin Park demos "Step Up" and "Dedicated," the song sounds like the conjecture of a solo career. The guitar line and boom-bap beat ground the song in rap-rock, but "It's Goin' Down" is very much an East Coast hip-hop song, engineered by an MC who has long inhaled rap music and wants to honor his influences. "The combination of a vocal caress / With lungs that gasp for breath from emotional stress / With special effects and a distorted collage / Carefully lodged between beats of rhythmic barrage," Mike spits, his vocabulary providing a lacquer to the boasts. What "It's Goin' Down" lacks in emotional resonance it makes up for in rap-pastiche polish and calculated flow—it's not a transcendent song, but it's an effective head-knocker, which is all it needs to be.

It was a minor hit, too: unlike "System" or "Karma Killer," "It's Goin' Down" reached the Hot 100 at No. 85, earned regular MTV rotation, and The X-Ecutioners eventually scored a top 20 album. That success certainly helped give additional cover for what the band, and specifically Mike, wanted to do next: deconstruct *Hybrid Theory* and release a full-length, hip-hop-leaning remix project.

Reanimation didn't begin as an album. While the band was working through ideas for their second full-length record on the road in 2001, Mike would send stems of *Hybrid Theory* songs to other artists and ask them to rearrange their elements. "I thought I was just going to do a remix or two," Mike said, "and other people were going to do all the work." Instead, the project ballooned to include over a dozen artists and producers, alongside the band's multiple self-produced remixes—and Mike was tasked with "overseeing the whole thing and juggling over thirty artists' work and schedule."

That guest list predictably included several hard-rock brand names Linkin Park had crossed paths with on the road, like Jonathan Davis, Marilyn Manson (with a creepy last-minute remix of "By Myself," delivered in time to become a B-side), Staind's Aaron Lewis, and Orgy's Jay Gordon. Yet *Reanimation* also reaffirms the band's left-of-center hip-hop and DJing interests: Aceyalone, The Alchemist, Black Thought, Jurassic 5's Chali 2na, Pharoahe Monch, and Dilated Peoples' Evidence all crossed genre lines to contribute, too. Chester quipped that the project was "a chance for us to show what our music would sound like if we took all the guitars out." That was an overstatement—but not by much.

The band started referring to the project as a collection of "reinterpretations," not remixes: "It's about the songs and reinterpreting them in a way that's artistically exciting," Brad noted. Linkin Park wanted to get avant-pop maestros Björk and Aphex Twin in there, too, but unfortunately, they couldn't make it work in time—Mike was already sorting through dozens of demos. The release of *Reanimation* had to be pushed from May to July 2002, and what could have been a time of post-tour tranquility was overwhelmed by what quickly became a gargantuan undertaking.

Most remix albums are unsubtle cash grabs, a simple way of regifting a proven commodity in a shiny new package. In the Spotify age, they've become "deluxe editions," with leftover tracks glommed onto an original album to juice streaming totals. *Reanimation*, however, was the polar opposite: a passion project that actively delayed the recording of the highly anticipated proper follow-up to *Hybrid Theory*, full of underground voices after "In the End" made them crossover stars, and firmly outside of the hard-rock world after a year touring within it.

Reanimation was constructed explicitly for the hardcore fans, and it was almost brazenly anti-commercial—even the song titles are inscrutable for casuals, "In the End" remixed into "Enth E Nd." It was a Mike project, and even though Chester had just won the band a Grammy, he didn't mind the diversion: "In terms of what we did—a remix album of a highly successful album—I think it was a huge success."

WAS *REANIMATION* ACTUALLY A HUGE success? Although the album didn't produce any new hits—"Pts.OF.Athrty," the "Points of Authority" remix from Orgy's Jay Gordon, was released as its lone single and peaked at No. 29 on the Alternative chart—the full-length still sold in droves, released at a moment when anything Linkin Park touched turned platinum.

Reanimation debuted at No. 2 on the *Billboard* 200 (Linkin Park's first top 10 album!) and has sold over four million copies to date, a staggering number for any twenty-first-century album, much less a stopgap between official full-lengths. By nearly any standard, it's one of the most successful remix albums of all time, and in just two and a half years, Linkin Park would release another collaborative set that was smaller in size, but much bigger in impact.

Of course, the product is imperfect, but it was destined to be that way: at sixty minutes—nearly twice the length of *Hybrid Theory*—*Reanimation* is purposely overindulgent. The lean song structures have been diced up, dashed with DJ scratches, and plied with a mixed bag of guest vocals, naturally casting aside the cohesion of the original. The highlights move swiftly: "P5hng Me A*wy," featuring Taproot's Stephen Richards, expands the wounded world of the original, while "1Stp Klosr" with Davis shoves the "One Step Closer" chorus back behind multiple verses and gauzy production, an interesting case of delayed gratification. Yet even the coolest remix album from the biggest-selling band of the year cannot alter its remix-album DNA. *Reanimation* was always destined to become message-board debate fodder rather than radio fare.

The lasting power of *Reanimation* is neither artistic nor commercial, though. Arriving at a moment when the band was getting invited to more red carpets and feeling the weight of newfound fame, *Reanimation* functioned as a symbol of the band's artistic autonomy: after years of chasing labels and pleading for the industry to hear their voices, the *band members* were now in charge and wanted to flex their creative muscles during a Midas-touch commercial run.

The album could have been stuffed with superstars for more MTV resonance—if they'd really wanted to, they could've tried to get, say, Eminem and Usher to hop on remixes. "We could have gone out to more mainstream collaborators, and we chose to do the opposite. We chose to show people some of our influences," Mike explained.

Linkin Park's popularity gave them the power to make a deviation, one that certainly would not bring them back to the Grammys stage but that would show the world more of the band's soul and help them establish a bit more cred. "We've always had that instinct to balance things that will work [commercially]—the fans are gonna maybe expect this, and it's gonna check a box for them, something like having Jonathan from Korn on the record is something that could be so cool—with stuff that we know might not be on their radar," Mike continued. "And I think that's carried through our entire career, you know? Our entire career has been that balance of doing things that we think are smart to do and doing things that we don't care if anybody likes."

Their newfound artistic leverage extended to their label dealings as well. That same year, Linkin Park created Machine Shop Records as their own imprint (distributed through their Warner Bros. label home) that would sign and develop other artists, with Mike and Brad having a hand in the A&R process. Machine Shop became the label home of such artists as Canadian punk band No Warning ("The rock world needs something that's as heavy, melodic, and passionate as they are," Mike gushed about the band) and underground rap group Styles of Beyond, and it also became a hub for Linkin Park releases as well as the LP Underground releases, beginning with 2002's *LP Underground 2.0*.

Meanwhile, after a period of prolonged friction with Jeff Blue that dated back to the *Hybrid Theory* studio days, when there was talk of replacing Mike, Linkin Park decided to cut off their creative collaboration with the A&R exec prior to the *Reanimation* release. According to Jeff in *One Step Closer*, the tensions that extended into the single selection process for

Hybrid Theory during its promotional run—as the band kept pushing for "Points of Authority" to get its day, only to be rebuked—got too heated, and the relationship was too badly frayed to be repaired. One day, band manager Rob McDermott told a stunned Jeff that he'd only be involved on an administrative level moving forward.

A new regime was being installed at the top of Warner Bros. Records anyway; Tom Whalley—the Interscope president who had signed artists like Tupac Shakur, Nine Inch Nails, and The Wallflowers—was brought in as Warner's new chairman/CEO. Tom had known Rob McDermott for years and became the main label contact for Linkin Park, who were increasingly a flagship artist at Warner Bros. It's worth mentioning here that Tom gets thanked by the band in the *Reanimation* liner notes, whereas Jeff, who would soon move on to a new role at Interscope Records, does not.

As *Reanimation* sold tens of thousands of copies each week in the second half of the summer, the band shed the skin of the *Hybrid Theory* era, which had been successful enough to effectively last two years. Now back home in California and sorting through new song ideas, the guys' lives were totally different in many ways. Chester and Samantha had a new baby boy named Draven and enjoyed panoramic ocean views from their new mansion, while Mike was getting ready to marry Anna Hillinger, a writer Mark Wakefield had introduced him to back in the Xero days. Yet, despite their domestic developments, the two frontmen would still bunker down regularly, gab about life, and tinker with various snippets and songs, figuring out where their newly minted collective should go next.

The band had improbably entered the worlds of Ozzfest, the Grammys, *and* the hip-hop DJ circuit and had come home bigger than ever. But the members of Linkin Park were still working the same way they always did and were still trusting in their craft, which had been validated beyond their wildest dreams. The "balance" that Mike referenced—locating the midpoint between fan service and artistic expression—gave Linkin Park a singular feeling of freedom as their second album, *Meteora*, started to take shape.

"Our next record," Chester said in 2002, "could sound like anything."

INTERLUDE

"It Was One of Those Once-in-a-Lifetime Collaborations"

Rob Swift, an original member of hip-hop DJ collective The X-Ecutioners, discusses how an unlikely team-up with Mike and Joe for the rap hit "It's Goin' Down" changed his group's trajectory.

Around 2000, The X-Ecutioners inked a record contract with Loud Records, which was one of the most powerful hip-hop record labels at the time. They had groups like Wu-Tang and Mobb Deep, artists like Big Pun and Xzibit signed to them, and we were their first all-DJ crew. It was four DJs—myself; Roc Raida, who passed away in 2009; Total Eclipse; and Mista Sinista.

So we're working on this album called *Built from Scratch*, and we're in studio putting together one of the songs, and our A&R at the time—a guy named Sean C., who was, ironically, an original member of our DJ group, the X-Men, that we started out in the late 1980s—walked into one of our sessions. And I remember he turned to us while we're sitting down with our engineer putting together some ideas for a song, and he says, "There's this group called Linkin Park. They're really dope, man. It's two vocalists—one guy sings, another guy raps. And they got a DJ, this guy named Mr. Hahn, and he gets busy on the turntables!"

This is before they blew up—when they were just on the cusp of going global. So Sean's like, "Yo, I think you guys need to do a song with them, because A, they're dope, and B, they're about to fucking blow up." So he looks at me specifically, and he's like, "Rob, here's Mike's number. Call him now." So I grab my phone, call Mike, and he's like, "Yo, Rob Swift! What's up, man! Sean mentioned to me that you were gonna call me and, dude, I'd love to put together a song with you guys. I think this will be fun and super creative for us."

And his vibe over the phone was just so cool and warm and welcoming. And the way he talked to me, I could tell that he knew about the group. It wasn't like some guy that wanted to cash in on this new DJ craze—I could tell that he respected what we did as The X-Ecutioners. And so within days, we started putting together the song that became "It's Goin' Down."

Mike rhymed his ass off on that song—flow, lyrical content, energy. Honestly, he complemented us in a way that I think the average rapper at the time probably wouldn't understand how to complement us. He was never a guy who was exploiting rap—he is a hip-hop artist, you know what I mean? Hip-hop accretes by attaching itself to all genres, which is why it's such a global, impactful genre of music. It's not jazz or rock or R & B or soul or funk—it's all of that, combined into one. So when people ask me, "Well, how was that experience working with a rock group?" they're asking as if it was going to be hard. Hip-hop borrows and takes from all genres, and that's how it grows, how it gets its power. So for us, it was a no-brainer to work with Linkin Park. And the process was super easy, because we scratched rock songs as kids—like, I learned how to loop a drumbeat by taking duplicate copies of "Walk This Way" by Aerosmith and slapping them on the turntable and cutting them up. So it's just dope for me, the arc of all that, leading to this group of DJs collaborating with this rock group. We were these Black kids from the inner city of New York City working with these kids from the [California] suburbs, but the chemistry just blended so smoothly and effortlessly. It just made sense! And that's why the song was so fucking popular.

At the time of the song, the movie *Scratch* [a 2001 documentary about turntable culture] had been out for maybe about a year, and that helped bring this underground movement of DJs to the forefront, this movement that was taking place in the nineties that was super underground. But then when we did "It's Goin' Down," that song catapulted us to new galaxies. It's not like you had YouTube or Instagram or Facebook or TikTok around in the early 2000s, right? So you could be in New York and on top of the DJ world, and everyone knows you—you're walking around and people stop and ask you for your autograph—and then go to Nebraska and no one knows who the fuck you are. But people knew who Linkin Park was!

So we shot the video, directed by Mr. Hahn, and then we're getting played on MTV. And then the song is being played on stations like KROQ, then Linkin Park ended up bringing us on the road, and then they invited us to perform at the 2001 MTV Video Music Awards, as a way to introduce us to their fans. Those guys—specifically Mike and Mr. Hahn, but really, the whole band—they took us under their wing, and they didn't have to. And I think it was all because there was a true appreciation for what we did as DJs. I remember touring small spots in the Midwest that honestly weren't gonna book The X-Ecutioners, but they allowed us to piggyback their platform. And because of that, we blew the fuck up. Maybe we would have blown up anyway, but they definitely sped up the process. It exposed us to a different demographic of music lover, as Linkin Park fans became X-Ecutioners fans. They probably didn't even realize it, but in working with us, Linkin Park introduced DJing to a completely new audience. People that didn't know that scratching existed got turned on to DJing! So that whole experience was revolutionary to me. It was one of those once-in-a-lifetime collaborations.

If you listen to all their albums, there's distinct growth from one album to the next. Today, we live in an era in music where artists don't necessarily concern themselves about the art of what they do and are more focused on the glamour, attention, and buzz that comes with it. And so I feel like anyone that was around during the early 2000s and experienced Linkin Park's full run in music, you saw growth. I remember watching them perform on the first tour that we did with them and then seeing them perform again later on, after "It's Goin' Down," and that whole little time period ended, and they were on to other, bigger shit. They wanted to always get better and hone their craft. They wanted to make music that was timeless. When I think of them, that's the first thing that comes to mind.

CHAPTER 13

"Somewhere I Belong," "Faint," "Numb," "Breaking the Habit." *Meteora* is more than its biggest singles, but any serious conversation about Linkin Park's second album needs to begin with those four ground-rattling hits. They not only dwarf the other album tracks in terms of artistic achievement but also crystallize that period for the band when arranged alongside each other. They're interlocking pieces, and when taken together, they're also a time capsule.

The fabric of who Linkin Park was in that moment, and what the band was trying to do, is woven into those four songs. And each of their purposes couldn't have been more different.

The songs are, first and foremost, a product of pressure. The process of creating "Somewhere I Belong" was a direct result of the band's need to re-prove themselves following a massively successful first album. *Reanimation* had been a well-liked stopgap, but it merely bent the years-old *Hybrid Theory* songs into new shapes and styles. Linkin Park could still be viewed by critics as a one-trick pony, even after remixing that trick.

On the road, the band workshopped tunes for their second album, coming up with nearly eighty song concepts—notebooks and hard drives full of ideas, in varying degrees of completion—in a back-of-bus studio space so small the members couldn't even stand up in it. Still, they weren't sure if *any* idea was good enough to follow up one of the biggest debut albums ever. "It was basically an impossible task," Brad said. "Not to mention that we were on the road for years for *Hybrid Theory*. The joke is, you have your whole life to make your first album, and you have three weeks to make your second."

Brad credited Don Gilmore, the producer who had driven them batty with his endless notes in the *Hybrid Theory* sessions, for once again "helping us get there, encouraging us, challenging us." Back in June 2002, the band had considered tapping other producers for their sophomore album, but because Don had been the right voice to amplify the strongest hooks of an unknown band the last time, they ultimately decided to return to NRG Studios with him that August. They understood Don would once again be a drill sergeant in the studio—they anticipated that the dulcet tones of his calm, endless *this-doesn't-work*s would get in their heads. Above all else, it would be excruciating, but they knew it was exactly what they needed.

"For me as a producer, working with artists like Linkin Park that really want their music to be as good as it can be, we'll rip a song to shreds and then build it back up, and then rip it down again, if that's what it takes," Don says in the *Meteora* making-of documentary. The hook of "Somewhere I Belong" is Exhibit A: the band tried a mind-boggling thirty-nine different choruses for the track, lyrics swapped in and deconstructed. Each time, Don told them that what they had wasn't exceptional and pushed them to try again.

The band swallowed its frustration, fully aware of what they signed up for. They would write a "Somewhere I Belong" chorus, play it for someone in the studio, and then be told that it sounded "cool." Linkin Park didn't need "cool"—that wasn't going to sell millions of records or be worthy of *Hybrid Theory*'s follow-up. So they went back to the drawing board, hoping to turn "cool" into "mind-blowing."

However accepted it was, Don's perfectionism was still painful to live with for months on end. Rob said he was "spending probably eight to ten hours a day practicing, almost seven days a week"—he was even having dreams about drums, haunted by fills that he couldn't get quite right the previous day. Dave hadn't been a member during the *Hybrid Theory* recording sessions, and he received a crash course of his own in the grueling process; Don himself was a bass player, so his pinpoint maneuvering made Dave question his own skills on the four-string as he struggled to match him.

Even Mike and Chester, who tracked their vocals at the end of the process, started to bug out. In the *Meteora* doc, Chester is shown sitting in a dimly lit studio room with his hands on the sides of his face, fingers digging into his cheeks, fully spent after dozens of takes. In another clip, Mike staggers along a sidewalk and explains why he can't fall asleep until three in the morning. "I was thinking about the album," he says droopily, "and thinking about all the stuff, all the crap that we've gotta do and that we're worried about."

Disaster struck during the final week of recording: Chester became sick as work on the album was finishing, just before the "Somewhere I Belong" chorus was finalized. With Chester unable to sing at NRG Studios, the band was forced to finish the song from across the country in December 2002, while it was being mixed by Andy Wallace in New York because if Chester's voice sounded different in any way, they would have had to scrap the song—or push the album back multiple months to rerecord it.

But when "Somewhere I Belong" was released on February 24, 2003, the rest of the world couldn't perceive any of the frantic behind-the-scenes stitching. The fortieth chorus had been a perfect match. And *Meteora* possessed its radio-ready lead single.

Beyond some interesting production choices—the reversed riff is actually Chester on acoustic guitar, chopped up and flipped backward by Mike, and Joe's scratching nudges that riff throughout the intro—"Somewhere I Belong" operates as a sequel of sorts to "In the End." The structures are startlingly similar: slightly spooky introduction, Mike's rap verses with murmured interjections from Chester, a loudly sung guitar-rock chorus, an even louder bridge. The hopelessness of "In the End" has been replaced by a sense of yearning ("I wanna heal, I wanna feel / Like I'm close to something real / I wanna find something I've wanted all along / Somewhere I belong"), but Chester zeroes in on an identical level of intensity, breathing a replicable quantity of fire in each word.

The precision is what sets "Somewhere I Belong" apart from past iterations of its recipe. Even as every inch of the single is calibrated for maximum impact, and the vocals were recorded in different months on different coasts, Chester and Mike mesh together more naturally than before, the endless months of sharing small spaces during the *Hybrid Theory* tours subtly evident in the way their cadences ricochet off each other.

Their personalities shine through the song's highly manicured environment, its endless refinement juxtaposed with human connection. As *Meteora*'s lead single, "Somewhere I Belong" announced that Linkin Park and their market-tested formula were back for round two.

—————————

As Linkin Park returned with its second album, nu metal no longer existed at the forefront of popular rock, a style fossilized by the wreckage of Woodstock '99 as a cautionary tale. By 2003, Korn had scored the final No. 1 album of their careers, Rage Against the Machine were done making albums altogether, and Kid Rock was crooning adult-contemporary ballads with Sheryl Crow ("Picture"). Bands like Deftones and Slipknot would continue releasing successful hard-rock albums for decades, but they were divorced from the nu metal sound and name by that point. And Limp Bizkit, the once-mighty kings of the movement, had already seen guitarist Wes Borland depart the group and would release only one more album—2003's scattershot, pretty good *Results May Vary*—before packing it in as recording artists for many years.

Of course, second-wave nu metal bands like Evanescence, Seether, Three Days Grace, and Trapt *were* finding major success by drawing from post-grunge, hardcore, and . . . bands like Linkin Park, while still distancing themselves from any whiff of Woodstock mayhem. But in the same way that the sudden collapse of grunge had caused a fractured "alternative music" scene a decade earlier, the fall of nu metal's original wave was followed by a grab bag of popular rock styles in the early 2000s.

In addition to the post–nu metal class, the garage-rock revival intermingled with an indie-rock scene that relied on the proliferation of the early blogosphere; bands like The Strokes, Yeah Yeah Yeahs, and Interpol earned acclaim on the increasingly influential website *Pitchfork Media* while shambling around New York City. Meanwhile, pop-punk and emo bands with devoted followings were turning basement shows and Warped Tour slots into crossover hits and headlining tours. The week that *Meteora* was released in March 2003, the Alternative chart encapsulated just how splintered rock music had become, with The White Stripes' "Seven Nation Army," Good Charlotte's "The Anthem," The Used's "Buried Myself Alive," and Evanescence's "Bring Me to Life" all sharing space around the top 20.

So, where did Linkin Park fit in? They had returned to the stage as a triumphant rap-rock band at a time when rap-rock had shrunken from the mainstream. Some of the pressure the band felt involved not only following up *Hybrid Theory* in a way that would satisfy their millions of listeners but also innovating enough to push themselves forward in a new rock landscape and transcend a fading sound. "We went into the album realizing that it was our opportunity to break outside of those expectations—what people thought the type of music we made was," Mike said.

"Somewhere I Belong" demonstrated that their proven techniques were still intact, but they were going to need something more than that, something different from that, something *evolved*. Linkin Park needed a follow-up single like "Faint."

The song dates back to Ozzfest 2001, when Brad came up with the guitar part in the band's studio bus, then Mike sped up the riff so that the beats per minute were nearly doubled. "The guitar line in the chorus was originally the chord structure—it was power chords doing that, and it sounded very aggressive," Mike explained. "But we just had this feeling that the song was hitting a ceiling, in terms of being as good as it can be, and not as melodic as it could be."

Though there were loads of other songs to choose from, Mike circled back to "Faint" over and over, like it was a puzzle he needed to solve. One day, he was in the driveway of NRG Studios, "and I couldn't run from my car to the control room fast enough, because it hit me just as I pulled in!"

he recalled. "Let's change that thing to octaves, play them higher, and then put chords underneath it already. That's what sounds great with the vocal already there. [We] came in and knocked it out immediately. And it was like, 'Oh my God, this is, like, my favorite song on this record.'"

Meteora wasn't a sharp left turn in terms of sound or identity, but it did include slightly more instrumental experimentation than *Hybrid Theory*, from "Nobody's Listening" (which was built around a loop of a Japanese bamboo flute called a *shakuhachi*) to "Session" (which featured digitally enhanced DJ scratching that was nearly impossible to play live). But in the order of both the track list and the single releases, "Faint" was the loudest declaration of change—a new pigment coloring the band's recorded presence from the second the live strings open the track in piercing, theatrical swoops.

Arranged by Dave Campbell—who, fun fact, is Beck's father—the violins, violas, and cellos form the melody that Mike had searched so long for, positioned as a backbone of a body of breakbeats, battering guitars, and quicksilver drumming. The verse-chorus-bridge structure is static from songs like "In the End" and "Somewhere I Belong," but the whole affair *slams*, with Mike's "I! Am!" verse refrain electric in its energy, and Chester's "Hear! Me! Out! Now!" breakdown on the bridge causing spine shivers. "Faint" was breathless, throttling, unquestionably exciting rock music. Even to this day, it remains one of Linkin Park's most thrilling songs.

Following the somber music video for "Somewhere I Belong," in which Joe cast the band in dramatic lights and set a bed on fire, the "Faint" visual became a raucous palate cleanser, with director Mark Romanek staging a Linkin Park performance in front of a thousand members of the LP Underground in downtown Los Angeles. Romanek filmed the video from behind the band onstage, and they finally turn around to face the camera on the final lyric, "I won't be ignored." This move allowed him to focus on the frenzied crowd of fan club members—an ocean of arms bristling before the band's silhouettes, orange stage lights capturing the human wave.

A month before the release of *Meteora*, Linkin Park debuted the majority of the new album on the sixteen-date LP Underground tour, which was designed as a series of underplay shows where fan club members would get first dibs on tickets. The tour wound through Europe and major US markets before ending on back-to-back shows at the Wiltern in Los Angeles, the nights before and after the album release. After waiting for *Hybrid Theory* to come out while parked outside of a Tower Records on the outskirts of Seattle, Linkin Park now took over the Tower Records in LA as the clock struck midnight on March 25, 2003, and signed four thousand *Meteora* CDs for the fans spilling out of their sold-out gig.

The spirit of those LP Underground shows is alive in the "Faint" clip, a salute to Linkin Park's most dedicated supporters as the band's sonic universe was expanding. The music video was also a pretty great tour advertisement and a peek at what was still to come—more Projekt Revolution runs, arena headlining shows, and even the band's first stadium dates were not too far away.

———————

IN 2013, THE CULTURE WRITER (and my professional pal) Chris Molanphy coined the term "the AC/DC Rule" to describe the phenomenon of a band scoring their biggest chart debut not with what would stand as their classic album but with the album that *follows* their classic.

This makes a lot of practical sense: typically, a major album gradually multiplies an artist's fan base over months of tour dates and single promotion, so when that artist comes back with something new, a much bigger crowd is ready to support them. Molanphy called it the AC/DC Rule because the metal great's 1980 classic *Back in Black* only peaked at No. 4 on the *Billboard* 200 chart, despite eventually becoming one of the biggest-selling albums ever, but it was their forgettable 1981 follow-up, *For Those About to Rock We Salute You*, that gave the band their first No. 1 album. Adele's *25*, which earned the largest sales week of the modern era in 2015 simply because it was the Adele album after her gargantuan previous full-length *21*, is a perfect recent example of the AC/DC Rule in action.

In 2003, Linkin Park's *Meteora* was all but guaranteed to score a sizable launch because of how well *Hybrid Theory* had performed in the two and a half years since its release; when you sell nearly five million copies of your debut album in a calendar year, the lead single of your second album could be a recitation of the phone book, and that album is still going to hit No. 1. Indeed, *Meteora* soared to the top of the *Billboard 200* with an astonishing 810,000 copies sold in its first week—more than fifteen times the first-week sales of *Hybrid Theory*, and more than twice as big of a debut number as major 2003 albums from Madonna, Beyoncé, and DMX.

When the final numbers came in, the band, preparing to kick off Projekt Revolution 2003 in a matter of days, toasted the first No. 1 album of their careers. Next up: figuring out how to *stay* on top.

Linkin Park had developed a rock-solid touring base by the time of *Meteora*'s release, but their mainstream presence had never been assured to last beyond one album, especially if their new project didn't carry something close to an "In the End"–sized hit. "Somewhere I Belong" and "Faint" both received plenty of MTV play and topped Alternative Airplay, but neither became a crossover smash. On the Hot 100, they peaked at Nos. 32 and 48, respectively—a far cry from the momentous No. 2 peak of "In the End."

In the spring and summer of 2003, Linkin Park once again toured the world, first on the Projekt Revolution tour in the United States, next across Europe, and then as support to Metallica on their Summer Sanitarium stadium run. They played plenty of new material but lacked that surefire crossover hit from their latest record. Their setlists often ended with "Crawling," "In the End," "A Place for My Head," and "One Step Closer," not dissimilar to their setlists from tours two years earlier.

But just as "In the End" gradually changed the commercial trajectory of *Hybrid Theory* as its third single, "Numb" spent the fall of 2003 gathering steam, snowballing into the new album's biggest pop hit, and reaching noncore fans by the beginning of 2004. "Numb" is indispensable to *Meteora* for many reasons, one being that it helped the album become more than "the follow-up to the huge, hits-packed album," and was an enormous success on its own merit.

Whereas "Somewhere I Belong" is marked by the flipped-guitar sample and "Faint" by its rush of strings, the defining sound in "Numb" is that ghostly keyboard hook, each hollowed-out note guiding the song's melody among a relatively straightforward rock arrangement. Really, though, Chester's voice is the sun of the song's solar system, the gravitational force that every component must revolve around.

The range of Chester's delivery—from the exhausted admission "I'm tired of being what you want me to be," to the forceful declaration "I've become so *numb*, I can't feel you *there*," to the gentle pleading "Can't you see that you're smothering me?" to the raging shriek "And I *KNOW* I may end up *FAILING*, too!"—remains authoritative. He gives the type of performance that elevates a good song to greatness. And the words themselves, a meditation on conformity and the draining of personal passion, connected Linkin Park with more fans than ever before.

In early 2004, "Numb" finally reached No. 11 on the Hot 100, but its cultural impact extended far beyond the *Meteora* campaign—into video games and movies, as one-half of a later blockbuster mash-up, covered and played endlessly, grown into what now is arguably the band's signature hit. They never stopped performing it and never grew sick of it. In early 2023, Joe stopped by Mike's house to help accept a Spotify plaque: "Numb" had at last crossed one billion streams, two decades after its debut.

"It continues to go," Mike said of the song's lasting relevance. "It continues to show up in things and be relevant. The band and the song will trend for seemingly no reason at all. We couldn't be more grateful for that."

───────────

THOUGH THE ALBUM IS TYPICALLY remembered for its hits, *Meteora* is full of impactful moments that never got single consideration but that still held their own: the scratch-heavy bounce of "Don't Stay," the sinister guitar crunch of "Hit the Floor," the mountainous vocal takes of "Easier to Run," and the creeping rhyme cadences of "Lying from You" all have their champions, and deservedly so. "From the Inside," a chiming hard-rock track with a 6/8 time signature (courtesy of Dave, who had desperately wanted to play a song in 6/8) and Chester's most prolonged screaming on the album, is a clear highlight—and was actually serviced as the album's fourth single. "From the Inside" received some international play as Linkin Park made their touring debut in parts of Asia, Australia, and Europe, but the song never took off in the States, failing to crack the Hot 100. No matter: "Numb" continued racking up radio plays, *Meteora* easily went platinum, and really, the fourth single from an album is just gravy anyway.

Yet the campaign wasn't finished. Although Linkin Park had re-proven themselves commercially with their second album, the band felt a need to prove themselves sonically, too. They were already thinking ahead to future projects: they hadn't gotten trapped in the nu metal swamp, but for the long-term health of the band, they couldn't get trapped in *any* sound.

"We went into the album realizing that it was our opportunity to break outside of those expectations, what people thought the type of music we made was," Mike explained, "and delivering a song like 'Breaking the Habit' on the record was a big deal." According to Mike, the band played *Meteora* for their label and told them to do whatever they wanted for the first single or second single, "just as long as 'Breaking the Habit' is a single at some point," he said. "It doesn't have any heavy guitars, it doesn't have any screaming—it's mostly programmed drums and sound. We need this to be a single."

"Breaking the Habit" was designed to upend expectations, making radio listeners do a double take whenever it materialized on radio—*Wait, this is Linkin Park?* The track was originally written as an instrumental interlude for *Meteora*, with picked guitar notes and turntable spirals latching on to skittering beats to create a sort of sprinting, achingly beautiful electronica. The band agreed that the foundation was too promising to remain an interlude, that "Breaking the Habit" could sound like a riff on Depeche Mode, one of Chester's hero acts, if fleshed out correctly.

"And so Mike went home," Dave recalled, "worked on it all night and put these lyrics down that he's been working on for almost five years but never really got to finish." Mike handed over the finished lyrics the next day; Chester read them, then started crying. He felt like his bandmate had burrowed into his mind and written from his point of view. Each word hit devastatingly close to home.

"Breaking the Habit" animates the demons of addiction: Mike's lyrics linger on the irrationality of a user's actions, the base loneliness, the alienation from the rest of society, and—with lines like "'Cause inside, I realize, that I'm the one confused"—the blistering self-awareness, each mistake examined with startling clarity. Chester had been battling addiction long before he met the rest of the band, but Mike had watched firsthand as his co-frontman struggled on that 2001 tour, had witnessed the painful mornings that always followed the off-kilter nights.

In this context, "Breaking the Habit" reads as a message of understanding from a friend: as written by Mike and sung by Chester, "Breaking the Habit" demonstrates how much trust had grown in their relationship. The whole thing nearly proved too emotional for Chester. He fought back tears in the studio and delivered a fragile, determined vocal take. "Breaking the Habit" became another crossover smash—not quite to the level of "Numb," but still top 20 on the Hot 100—the cherry on top of a gigantic album cycle. Despite its success, Chester wouldn't feel ready to perform the song live until eight months and six tour legs after *Meteora* was released.

Joe envisioned the "Breaking the Habit" video as an anime re-creation of Linkin Park. He filmed the band performing in Los Angeles, then hired a team of Japanese animators—led by Kazuto Nakazawa, who had helped Quentin Tarantino create the anime sequence in *Kill Bill Vol. 1* a few months earlier—to turn the footage two-dimensional, frame by frame. The final product is even more ambitious than its medium, weaving in a police investigation, romantic betrayal told in reverse, and tomatoes hurled in fury to become blood-red explosions.

"It's really like watching a live-action movie," Brad gushed ahead of the video's release, and he was right. Unlike the faux-*Matrix* silliness of the "One Step Closer" clip, "Breaking the Habit" is among the band's most riveting visual moments, capturing the dynamism of the song in its stark, fluid movements.

In the same way that the sound of "Breaking the Habit" was designed to jar radio listeners, MTV viewers catching its video could conclude: Linkin Park was growing up. The final single from *Meteora* solidified their newfound maturity—in sonic aspiration, in visual presentation, in thematic purpose—wrapping up a sophomore campaign that once and for all avoided "nu metal flash in the pan" status.

While the sound of *Meteora* isn't markedly different from that of *Hybrid Theory*, its singles were different in all the right ways, an amalgamation of sounds that never lost the band's center. It was never going to be bigger than its predecessor: *Meteora* has sold 6.49 million copies to date, still around four and a half million short of *Hybrid Theory*. But if Linkin Park's debut album made them superstars within a specific moment in rock, their second album saw the future beyond that moment—and hinted at their longevity, their legacy. Ultimately, that might have been more important.

Projects like *COLLISION Course* were not ordinary in popular music in 2004, so when it was first announced, it sounded like a fever dream. Jay-Z and Linkin Park collaborating on an official multisong project? Two artists at the peak of their commercial power combining their biggest hits, Voltron-style, into new megahits? It was unfathomable, but somehow, it was happening.

Jay-Z had worked with rock artists before 2004, and *Reanimation* proved Linkin Park's bona fides as hip-hop interlopers. Yet even so—*Collision Course* was something different. This was Godzilla versus King Kong, a mega-wattage showdown that, worst-case scenario, would be a publicity stunt guaranteed to move a lot of units. Best case? It could upend the way listeners thought of popular music.

Timing is everything when the world's biggest rapper calls to collaborate on an extended project. In 2004, Jay-Z was the thirty-four-year-old king of popular hip-hop: the coolest artist in any room, on a years-long hot streak that had transformed him from a rap headliner into a crossover pop star. While mega-selling albums like 1996's *Reasonable Doubt* and 1998's *Vol. 2 . . . Hard Knock Life* were met with critical acclaim and produced multiple videos in MTV's hip-hop blocks, Jay turned into a Top 40 hit-maker in the early 2000s with singles like "Big Pimpin'," "I Just Wanna Love U (Give It 2 Me)," and "Izzo (H.O.V.A.)."

In 2003, a few months after Linkin Park topped the *Billboard* 200 album chart for the first time with *Meteora*, Jay-Z hit No. 1 on the Hot 100 alongside his girlfriend, Destiny's Child breakout Beyoncé, on the summer-ruling pop smash "Crazy in Love." Then, in November, Jay released *The Black Album*, a record stuffed with more hits as well as fond-farewell messaging. *The Black Album* was positioned as Jay-Z's final album: he was going to go out on top, relinquishing his throne to become president of Def Jam Recordings so that he could develop other artists (like his producer pal Kanye West and newly signed upstarts named Rihanna and Young Jeezy) into stars.

Jay-Z's "retirement" was always tenuous, a sentence that ended with an ellipsis instead of a period. That's because Jay didn't *really* go anywhere after *The Black Album*. He was making moves in the Def Jam boardroom but would still pop up on remixes and as a guest artist on songs by Mariah Carey, Snoop Dogg, Lenny Kravitz, and Mary J. Blige, among others. Jay-Z even released *Unfinished Business*, a second collaborative album with R. Kelly following 2002's *The Best of Both Worlds*, less than a year after supposedly hanging it up. So it was clear that, even though Jay-Z wouldn't be working on a new solo album imminently, he wanted to remain active in the recording studio as a complementary voice and collaborator.

As luck would have it, that period was exactly when executives at MTV called him up with a new show idea.

MTV Ultimate Mash-Ups was pitched as a taped concert series in which a rap artist and rock artist would jump onstage and rearrange at least one song together in front of a live audience—think *MTV Unplugged*, but as a genre-splicing jam session. Jay-Z, who had worked with The Roots on an actual *MTV Unplugged* in 2001, was one of the network's first calls, and they asked him point-blank which rock act he'd want to work with for the show.

At that moment, Linkin Park was headlining more North American arenas as "Numb" kept climbing the Hot 100 and *Meteora* trailed *The Black Album* on the *Billboard* 200. Jay pointed at them.

For the band, the call from Jay-Z's management not only came at a fortuitous time—nearly a year into the *Meteora* campaign, around the same moment during the *Hybrid Theory* album cycle that Mike began to plot *Reanimation*—but also came from the right artist. "There are six guys in our band who all grew up listening to different things," Mike explained. "There are very few artists I can say that we all like. Jay is one of them."

While the whole band were fans, Mike was the one who had worshiped Jay-Z growing up, an adoring teenaged producer as the MC ascended the NYC hip-hop scene. Prior to joining Xero, Mike had mashed up *Reasonable Doubt* songs with tracks by Smashing Pumpkins and Nine Inch Nails in his bedroom; the *Meteora* track "Nobody's Listening" opens with an adult Mike paying homage to Jay with a lyrical callback to his track "Brooklyn's Finest." So when Linkin Park received the offer to work with Jay, Mike wanted to ensure that—whatever this MTV show would eventually become—the collaboration would become more meaningful than a cable-series one-off. "I didn't just want to say, 'Hell yeah, let's do it.' I wanted to show him what it might sound like if we did it," Mike said.

The work itself was second nature to Mike. He had grown up watching artists like Public Enemy and Anthrax mash up their sounds into formative records as well as *literally making Jay-Z mash-ups* himself! So, before any deal was agreed on, he slipped into the recording studio in the back of Linkin Park's tour bus and fired up his laptop. Mike synced up Jay-Z's vocals from a few songs on *The Black Album* with Linkin Park instrumentals by matching the beats per minute (BPMs) of each: the hater-shedding anthem "Dirt Off Your Shoulder" aligned with the *Meteora* wall-rattler "Lying from You," and Jay's self-mythologizing curtain call "Encore" paired perfectly with "Numb."

For the latter, Mike chopped up his band's still-rising hit and reorganized the instrumental into a repeating pattern, similar to a DJ sampling part of an old rock song for a new rap track. He then added in the flourishes of "Numb"—the keyboard hook, the guitar, the piano, the bass—in ways that would support Jay's flow, before turning the back half of the song into a modified version of Chester's vulnerable showcase.

Stitched together, the mash-up of Jay's braggadocio and Chester's bare emotion isn't lyrically coherent, but somehow the tones make sense together. Jay-Z sounds more reflective spitting "As fate would have it, Jay's status appears / To be at an all-time high, perfect time to say goodbye," over brooding piano and splintered guitar chords, while the introduction of Chester's verse with "I'm tired of being what you want me to be" acts as a dramatic shift into the song's back half, his words driving comfortably over accented hip-hop beats.

Mike finished the demos for "Numb/Encore" and "Dirt Off Your Shoulder/Lying from You" in less than two days on the tour bus, then sent them to Jay-Z to see what he thought of the direction for the songs. "His reply was, 'Oh shit!'" Mike recalled. "Needless to say, we were off on the right foot."

———————

WHEN JAY-Z HOSTED LISTENING SESSIONS for *The Black Album* prior to its release, he often looked around the room and realized that some of his lyrics weren't connecting with listeners, his lines getting lost in the production. The solution was simple enough: he asked his main engineer, Gimel "Young Guru" Keaton, to play the songs a cappella.

As Jay watched the rooms absorb his unadorned words, he liked what he saw. So he asked Roc-a-Fella and Def Jam to release a *full a cappella version* of *The Black Album*, and it hit stores one month after the original. It was an outrageous request, but Jay wielded enough star power that the labels quickly acquiesced.

Mike had downloaded that a cappella album while making the demos to send to Jay-Z; without it, he couldn't have made such clean mash-ups and may not have gotten such a strong response from Jay. But then again, without the a cappella version of *The Black Album*, MTV might not have come up with the mash-up show idea in the first place.

Jay's secondary motivation for the a cappella edition of *The Black Album* was for other producers to "remix the hell out of it," according to Young Guru—to place Jay's voice over other instrumentals, share them online, play them at clubs, and help his legend grow during his "retirement." This was a stroke of marketing genius, and plenty of producers were happy to oblige. Producer Kevin Brown created a funk- and jazz-based remix album titled *The Brown Album*, for instance, and Minnesota DJ

Cheap Cologne placed Jay-Z's vocals over Metallica's own *Black Album* for . . . wait for it . . . *The Double Black Album.*

Most famous of all was *The Grey Album*, which fused Jay-Z's *Black Album* vocals with The Beatles' landmark 1968 self-titled double LP (aka the White Album), by the LA producer Brian Burton, who went by the moniker Danger Mouse. The concept was, at once, deceptively simple and musically brilliant: Jay-Z's "99 Problems" smacked even harder over The Beatles' "Helter Skelter" freakout, and "Public Service Announcement" became oddly blissed-out above the looped folk of "Long, Long, Long." Created over two and a half weeks in December 2003 immediately after the a cappella *Black Album* was released, *The Grey Album* became internet lore in early 2004, with bootlegged CDs selling like hotcakes and file-sharing sites swarmed with its twelve songs.

Mash-ups had existed for decades before *The Grey Album* as an integral part of DJ culture, but they became even more commonplace at the turn of the century. Chalk it up to the proliferation of music-swapping platforms and production software, like the Pro Tools that Mike favored or the Acid Pro that Danger Mouse used for *The Grey Album*. Artists like Richard X, Soulwax (with their 2 Many DJs project), and Freelance Hellraiser rethought the remix in the early 2000s by jamming songs together with creative panache and lighting up the early blogosphere.

Yet *The Grey Album* represented a critical turning point for the medium: the project was the sort of underground sensation that functioned like a viral YouTube video before YouTube even existed. Suddenly, Danger Mouse became one of the most in-demand producers of the mid-2000s—helming albums from Gorillaz, Beck, and The Black Keys, among others—but not before entering a legal quagmire over *The Grey Album*, as EMI, The Beatles' copyright holder, shut down distribution of the project. Obviously, the White Album samples hadn't been cleared; then again, Danger Mouse had never intended to get rich off of *The Grey Album*, only to make something cool.

Jay-Z, for his part, liked *The Grey Album*—which made sense, since he was the one pushing for his a cappella vocals to become natural resources for producers like Danger Mouse. "I champion any form of creativity," he said in a 2010 interview with NPR. "And that was a genius idea to do, and it sparked so many others like it."

Although *The Grey Album* wasn't legally sanctioned, MTV clearly saw the commercial potential of mashing up Jay-Z's rapping with the familiar sounds of a famous rock band. So, presumably, did Jay-Z, he of the "I'm not a businessman, I'm a business, man," credo. The music industry generally facilitates collaboration between artists, producers, and songwriters regardless of label or publishing info—it's how chart-topping duets and cross-affiliate tour pairings are born. But a mash-up album is different, with more legal obstacles involving rights clearances, even when both artists are on board. As Mike and Jay traded demos over email and realized that this collaboration could become more significant than an MTV special, both camps pushed to make sure that, whatever was created, it was able to go on sale. Then, after Linkin Park worked on the rearranged production, Jay and the band logged a total of four days together at NRG in West Hollywood in July 2004, rerecording the vocals of their existing songs to better fit the deconstructed tracks.

The result: a retail-ready EP, featuring thirteen songs combined into six mash-ups, with all label partners—Def Jam, Roc-A-Fella, Warner Bros., and the Linkin Park imprint Machine Shop—on board and an "MTV Ultimate Mash-Ups Presents" sticker slapped on the cover.

At the end of that week, on July 19, 2004, the two artists took over the Roxy in Los Angeles for a special joint performance that would double as the pilot of MTV's mash-ups show. Some fans at the Roxy sported LP tees, others held up the Roc for Jay symbol, and plenty did both. The mash-up project aired on MTV and showed up in big-box retailers by November, just in time for holiday shopping.

"To me, *Collision Course* is a landmark album," Mike said later that year, "because it's a first: two multiplatinum artists getting together, using their original masters and new performances and production to create an album of mash-ups—that's something that has never been done before."

Within a year of *The Grey Album* going viral, Jay-Z and Linkin Park had elevated its concept, jumped through all the necessary legal hoops, and primed it for big business. A couple years later, when Linkin Park and Jay-Z were standing on the Grammys stage together to collect a trophy for "Numb/Encore," Mike made sure to thank "everybody in management and legal teams that made this record possible, because it was a nightmare!"

———————————

WHAT STANDS OUT MOST TODAY about *Collision Course*, in both Linkin Park's and Jay-Z's respective discographies, is how *fun* it sounds.

Jay has made plenty of party hits over the years, but he's never been a party rapper, his flow authoritative and grounded in gritty come-up stories even as catchy melodies float around it. Meanwhile, Linkin Park's most up-tempo singles still focused on heavier themes, and their first two albums had been laboriously fine-tuned by Don. When set up side by side without a perfectionist producer lurking in the studio, however, both aesthetics relax, the lyrics freed of their intensity when placed in fresh, buoyant atmospheres.

Take "Big Pimpin'/Papercut": Mike's words about paranoia and stress from "Papercut" remain intact, but his rhyming is slightly slowed down and placed atop the opulent island boom of Timbaland's "Pimpin'" production. On "Jigga What/Faint," Jay re-creates the knuckle-bruising threats of 1998's "N—a What, N—a Who"—but really, the main attraction of that song is the introduction of the "Faint" strings under his rhyming around the thirty-second mark, which becomes the EP's purest rush of adrenaline.

By design, *Collision Course* is a stunt release, and the mash-ups can't possibly hold the artistic power of the original tracks. Yet the inherent looseness of those moments—the playful energy of two giant artists in their prime, tinkering together in the same room—makes *Collision Course* worth returning to in the years since its release.

Ultimately, it was the shared studio time, with Jay-Z arriving at NRG and dapping up the band before laying down his verses one-on-one with

Mike, that proved crucial to manufacturing the chemistry at the core of the EP. *Collision Course* gave Mike the opportunity to share space with, and produce, a childhood hero who had become a peer. Jay-Z had been a star for years before Linkin Park took off; it could have easily been a classic never-meet-your-heroes moment for Mike. But the recording sessions were full of bro-hugs and easy feedback, Chester clowning on Mike for working too hard and Jay uttering "That transition's mean!" while scrunching his face behind the boards.

"I *like* this shit—I *like* to do different things," an animated Jay-Z exclaims at one point on the *Collision Course* making-of DVD. He's speaking to Chester while huddled in the corner of a studio room, gesturing and breathlessly trying to keep up with his thoughts. "You just bring what you do to the table, I bring what I do to the table, uncompromising—you're not trying to be me, and I'm not trying to be you, that fusion, and just whatever happens happens. *I love that!*"

The casual tone provoked plenty of ad-libs that can be heard on the final cut of the EP: Chester muttering, "I ordered a Frappuccino, where's my fucking Frappuccino?" and garnering a Jay-Z belly laugh; Jay quipping, "You're wasting your talent, Randy!" to some guy in the studio Reddit users are still trying to identify. Even the decision to combine "Numb" and "Encore" was partially due to Mike just wanting to hear Chester bellow the "What the hell are you waiting *fo-o-o-r-r-r*?" line. Again: *fun*.

"There was no ego at all working with Jay," Mike reflected later. "If I asked him to perform something a certain way or put a vocal line here or there, he was happy to do it. He's really easy to work with."

As they were finishing up in the studio and preparing to perform at the Roxy, a goal formed in Mike's mind: he wanted the mash-up collection to be so good, so immediately effective, that MTV would never be able to make another one. And that's exactly what happened. *MTV Ultimate Mash-Ups* transformed from a series into a one-off concert show that aired on November 10, 2004, with the CD and behind-the-scenes DVD hitting stores three weeks later. To this day, no follow-up episode has ever been executed.

Collision Course debuted at No. 1 on the *Billboard* 200—a rarity for a six-song EP, in any era—but its true legacy is "Numb/Encore," which rose to No. 20 on the Hot 100 as the project's lead single and gave alternative programmers an excuse to sneak Jay-Z onto their airwaves. Beyond that early radio play, "Numb/Encore" has endured as an immaculate equilibrium of rap and rock—its melodies joined logically and wholly, soulmates that made their way to each other from different parts of the world. Although "Numb" has now crossed one billion Spotify plays on its own, "Numb/Encore" is not far behind it; rather astonishingly, the mash-up remains one of the five most-streamed songs on the platform across Jay-Z's legendary career.

"'Numb''s other dimension is 'Numb/Encore,'" Brad asserted. "You could love just one. However, I think about them in tandem. And when you think of *Meteora*, you think of *Collision Course*—that moment in collaboration with Jay-Z, which is really special."

Ultimately, *Collision Course* did not change popular music in a literal sense—officially released mash-up albums remain a rarity to this day, primarily because of the legal red tape. On a more abstract level, though, the project did foretell a future in which amateur and professional producers crashed songs into one another.

Soon after the release of *Collision Course*, hip-hop's mixtape era exploded: artists like Lil Wayne, Gucci Mane, and Clipse spent the mid-aughts hijacking other rappers' beats, freestyling over them, and releasing compilations for free online, one-upping the original artist and favoring internet buzz over commercial sales. Meanwhile, the release of mash-up songs and albums—from DJ Earworm's annual "United State of Pop" singles, featuring the twenty-five biggest songs of the year rolled into one, to Girl Talk's full-length pastiches of hundreds of samples, to a 2022 mash-up of Britney Spears's "Toxic" and Ginuwine's "Pony" that charted as "Toxic Pony"—became more commonplace in the years after the album's release.

And the advent of social media and streaming platforms further delivered that mash-up power into users' hands, with multimedia mash-ups constantly concocted and posted in ways that helped artists gain more listens—even today. Want to know why Lady Gaga's 2011 song "Bloody Mary" suddenly became a Hot 100 hit in 2023? That's because TikTok users synced up the song with a dance sequence from the Netflix series *Wednesday*, and the mash-up went viral enough to make "Bloody Mary" a belated sensation.

Collision Course was like a star-studded summer blockbuster that lived up to the hype upon its release, then proved sneakily influential in the years since. Its mainstream impact still reverberates today with every new spin of "Numb/Encore," but perhaps most importantly, *Collision Course* further legitimized Linkin Park in the moment. Jay-Z is widely considered the greatest rapper of all time—and he picked *this* band, out of any artist, to reimagine his biggest hits.

Linkin Park had entered rarefied air, the type of rock stratosphere that's reserved for only a few bands per generation. But they wanted *more*.

CHAPTER 15

O N JUNE 6, 2004, near the end of what is widely considered to be the greatest Linkin Park performance of all time, the band pulled a goofy kid onstage, asked him to say something in his language, and watched him scream something in their own instead.

During the bridge to "A Place for My Head" at Rock am Ring, the annual hard-rock festival held in Nürburgring, Germany, the band asked a fan to speak German to the rest of the crowd and pulled onstage an eager twenty-something with a sweatshirt tied around his khakis and a safari hat dangling on a string around his neck.

"My name is Benjamin!" the guy tells Chester, who gets the audience to roar for the fan.

"I want you to tell them that they're the greatest crowd ever, in German," Chester instructs him, then holds the microphone to Benjamin's lips.

Without hesitating, Benjamin turns toward the crowd and bellows in broken English, "YOU ARE ALL MOTHERFUCKERS THAT I'VE NEVER SEEN BEFORE, SO MOTHERFUCKING GREAT, PEOPLE IN THE WORLD! AND NOW GIMME A YEEEEEAHHHHHH!"

Benjamin did not understand the assignment. But he *did* unwittingly personify the spirit of the sixty-five thousand bouncing bodies in attendance.

That Rock am Ring show is the stuff of Linkin Park legend today, still eliciting feverish descriptions from those fans lucky enough to have been in attendance and the many more who watched the replay. And one name keeps popping up, forever a secret password in the Linkin Park community: Benjamin.

The setlist didn't deviate from the rest of the *Meteora* world tour—a few nights prior in Glasgow, Linkin Park started covering Nine Inch Nails' industrial freakout "Wish" in their encores—and the stage was familiar because the band had played Rock am Ring back in 2001. A large part of the lore around the 2004 performance is based on the quality and availability of the footage: the entire show looks crisp and riveting, even on a YouTube playback. Something about that show *was* different, though—some purified oxygen inhaled to turn every aspect a notch more special. Chester sounded like a chainsaw, his voice ripping every big chorus and tiny ad-lib to ribbons as sweat beaded his black mohawk, and Mike raced around the stage rapping, his black ball cap pulled low but never masking his wide-eyed grin.

Each song transition was handled masterfully, the interplay between Rob's drum fills and Brad's shredding was pristine, the crowd engagement didn't lag for one second across seventy-one minutes. Linkin Park had been playing arena-sized venues for years, but now, they finally had enough hits and stage experience to turn every single song into a highlight.

The nine-show European tour that included Rock am Ring had been preceded by a thirty-four-show North American trek across the first three months of 2004, dozens of US arenas leveled as "Numb" kept rising and *Meteora* kept selling. After Europe came the thirty-two-date Projekt Revolution 2004 tour, featuring Korn as the lead-in for Linkin Park on the main stage, nu metal students turned masters.

Then: exhaustion, again. By the fall of that year, as the band played the final *Meteora* show nearly eighteen months after the album's release, the breakneck pace of the past five years completely consumed Linkin Park. *Collision Course* was about to be released, marking the band's fourth studio project in five years (following *Hybrid Theory*, *Reanimation*, and *Meteora*), and by the time the mash-up project came out in November, Linkin Park had played well over four hundred shows since the turn of the century.

"At the end of that, we needed a break," Dave said. "By the end of 2004, we were about to burn out."

All six members, now in the second half of their twenties, had spent the years that most people take stumbling toward post-college career beginnings instead conquering popular rock music and arena crowds around the world. Mike married Anna in 2003, the same year that Brad wed Elisa Boren. Meanwhile, Joe was preparing to marry Karen Benedit in February 2005, a few weeks before Chester's son Draven turned three years old. They all needed time at home—to exhale, to focus on their families, to grow up away from the studio and the stage.

Linkin Park spent 2005 "recuperating," as Mike put it, and ended up playing only two shows that year. The first was the all-star benefit concert Music for Relief: Rebuilding South Asia, which was held in Anaheim that February. Following a devastating tsunami in Southeast Asia in late 2004, the band founded Music for Relief, a charity organization focused on raising funds to rebuild regions affected by natural disasters.

Since marrying Mike, Anna had become very active with the band's charity efforts, coordinating charity auctions and working with the foundation Projekt Charity, led by LP Underground. She directed Music for Relief efforts as the program became the band's primary nonprofit focus. The Rebuilding South Asia concert boasted performances from No Doubt, Jurassic 5, and The Crystal Method, as well as a twelve-song Linkin Park set—the back half of which featured Jay-Z, re-creating the six tracks from *Collision Course* in their entirety.

Jay-Z also joined the band at their other 2005 performance: Live 8, a string of international benefit concerts timed to the twentieth anniversary of Live Aid and set to precede that summer's G8 summit in order to raise awareness of global poverty. The US concert was held on July 2 in front of the Philadelphia Museum of Art, with Stevie Wonder, Destiny's Child, and Dave Matthews Band among the performers, and Linkin Park's set once again consisted of their own hits followed by their *Collision Course* material with Jay-Z.

Unlike the Music for Relief show, however, the band's audience was literally endless—an estimated one million onlookers for the eight-hour event in Philadelphia, and millions more watching from their homes around the world. There was no back to the Philly crowd, no way for the guys to find out the number of people actually watching one of their most-watched shows ever.

The reason Linkin Park was on the Live 8 lineup during an off-year and with plenty of other groups that would have taken their place? Bono, who was performing with U2 at the Live 8 concert in London, had personally phoned them to ask if they would perform in Philly. Such was the rarefied space that Linkin Park occupied at the time: even when they were staying at home, Bono was calling them and asking them to share the stage with Jay-Z in front of a million people. Even when they'd stopped traversing the world, the ground beneath them kept rising.

———————

No one reacts to fame identically, and once you're in it, you're never sure where it will lead. "There's always a new level," Mike said in 2006. "You go on tour and people recognize you. That's a level. You're driving through a city and hear your song on the radio. You turn on the TV, and you're on TV."

By the time of Live 8, the entire band—but especially Mike and Chester—had blown past those early markers of fame; being co-frontmen lessened each of their household-name statuses a little bit, but you knew their faces if you paid attention to popular music in the mid-2000s—and not just in the United States. "Some guy in Malaysia asked me to sign his baby," Mike said in another interview. "I was sitting at a shoe store, and this guy walks up and holds his one-year-old kid out, face-down, and hands me a marker. I felt like if I didn't sign the kid, he was going to be pissed, so I did it."

Mike admitted that global exposure felt strange. He had grown up dreaming about making music mostly as a producer and beat creator, not as a celebrity who signed babies. But he also understood that immense success translated into creative power, carte blanche to make whatever he wanted without the naysaying that he had experienced during the *Hybrid Theory* days.

So, while at home in 2005, with the majority of the band satisfied taking a breather, Mike used what was left of his juice to launch a passion project that had been simmering on the back burner for a few years: he was finally going to make a personal hip-hop solo album.

Mike worked under the name Fort Minor—a paradox of a moniker, one juxtaposing strong and soft in a manner that reminded him of the soldier with dragonfly wings on the *Hybrid Theory* cover. He produced and mixed all the songs on the project himself and described the album as a tribute to "organic" hip-hop, music that relied on live instruments at a moment when popular rap was dominated by crunk's booming strip-club anthems and backpack rap's chipmunk-soul samples.

"I've learned so much about production, songwriting, and people in the last few years," Mike said at the time. "I think Fort Minor started about two years ago when I began to wonder what it would sound like to bring it full circle, to get back to my roots but use all the tools I have learned since then."

He was no longer just a teen producing beats in his bedroom but a star with an insane Rolodex: Black Thought, John Legend, Common, and Machine Shop's Styles of Beyond all guested on the project, and its executive producer was none other than Jay-Z. Jay didn't actually produce anything, but along with Brad, he joined Mike in the studio and helped whittle down the songs into a cohesive project. He also provided a sampled spoken-word intro, during which Jay raves, "That's an underground hip-hop record! The richness of the music and everything!"

The Rising Tied, the lone Fort Minor album, might initially scan as a vanity project. Parts play out like a re-creation of the rap-leaning songs of Xero and early Linkin Park, now with a bigger budget and a self-righteous proof of concept. "He doesn't need his name up in lights / He just wants to be heard, whether it's the beat or the mic!" Mike raps on "Remember the Name," the quasi-motivational single that recalls songs like "High

Voltage" and "It's Goin' Down"—but with dramatic strings, arranged by the same guy who did "Faint" and "Breaking the Habit." Tracks like "Petrified" and "In Stereo" are skate-rap grooves with electroshocked beats that each would have been an enjoyable change of pace on a Linkin Park album but that aren't memorable enough to anchor a hip-hop record.

However, the Fort Minor album runs deeper than its most boastful moments. On "Back Home," Mike explores the nonstop hustle and cultural melting pot of the greater Los Angeles area alongside Common and Styles of Beyond, and on "Cigarettes," he prods at what it means to have rap cred over a spaced-out beat. Neither song fully leaves the ground, but their lyrical intent and point of view make them more admirable than ham-fisted.

Better still is "Kenji," a moving piano-rap portrait of a Japanese American immigrant in the 1940s who experiences Pearl Harbor, racial profiling, forced relocation, and postwar alienation. The story is that of Mike's family, of course—his father and aunt even recorded spoken-word interludes about their internment camp memories for "Kenji"—and simmers with furious details: "Some folks didn't even have a suitcase to pack anything in / So two trash bags is all they gave them / And when the kids asked mom, 'Where are we going?' / Nobody even knew what to say to them," he seethes. "Kenji" was an intimate look at a painful family history and unique enough that it became one of two tracks that Mike demanded make the final cut of *The Rising Tied*. "I've never heard a song, much less a hip-hop song, before or since about the subject," he said.

The Rising Tied debuted way down at No. 56 on the *Billboard* 200 albums chart upon its release in November 2005: the project wasn't preceded by a hit single, with "Remember the Name" only climbing to No. 66 on the Hot 100, and the Fort Minor name wasn't as bankable as Linkin Park. But Mike had accomplished what he had set out to do with the project—share more of his story and use his clout to work with his preferred sound and collaborators.

"Remember the Name" might have been a bit ahead of its time, in some ways; eventually, the song became a new-school jock jam, ubiquitous as an NBA-starting-lineup soundtrack, and earned hundreds of millions of streams. In 2006, Mike was awarded the Japanese American National Museum's award of excellence for "Kenji" and his various charitable acts. And that year, a song he wrote for his wife—the *other* song that he insisted make *The Rising Tied*'s track list—became one of the biggest hits of his career.

"Where'd You Go" takes place from Anna's perspective, as someone waiting at home while their partner travels the world for months on end. Mike fashioned the lyrics to capture a universal longing—waiting by the phone, remembering simple times together, the frustration of being apart, and ultimately the straightforward plea "Please come back home." The haunting piano of "Kenji" finds a gentler note progression in this track, and to balance out his rap verses and handle the chorus, Mike brought in Holly Brook, a nineteen-year-old singer-songwriter from Wisconsin whom Brad had just signed to Machine Shop. She knocked out the hook in a half hour and created a conversational balance that's genuinely affecting and not unlike a lot of Linkin Park's biggest dueling-vocal hits.

Although the sentimentality of "Where'd You Go" made the track an outlier on *The Rising Tied*, the song took off on both pop radio and MTV when it was released as the fourth single from the Fort Minor album, streaking all the way to No. 4 on the Hot 100 in June 2006. Holly Brook later changed her professional name to Skylar Grey and went on to score smashes as a collaborator and songwriter for Eminem, Rihanna, Dr. Dre, and Diddy. Meanwhile, with "Where'd You Go," Mike drew upon his fame and examined how it affected his evolving home life, turning his voice into a radio fixture outside of Linkin Park for the first time.

————————

THE TIMING WAS PERFECT FOR Mike to dedicate a year to the Fort Minor campaign, really: even if his bandmates weren't worn out in 2005, they certainly weren't going to put out another album that year, as Linkin Park spent most of it trying to get out of their label deal.

Warner Music Group had made plans to go public and earn a windfall of cash from the IPO, but none of their signed artists would be involved in the revenue share. Setting aside lingering resentments about how their identity was questioned after they signed to Warner Bros. years before, the band—which was a core artist on the label—believed they should be profit-sharing instead of just receiving royalties. They were concerned that cut costs prior to the stock offering had negatively affected label operations.

But when the label refused to budge, citing that *none* of its artists would be involved in the IPO profits, private contract negotiations turned into public demands for release. "We feel a responsibility to get great music to our fans," the band said in a May 2005 statement, days before the IPO. "Unfortunately, we believe that we can't accomplish that effectively with the current Warner Music."

The stalemate lasted for months, with the four albums left on Linkin Park's Warner contract in limbo. Finally, an agreement was announced in the final days of 2005: Linkin Park would remain at Warner Bros., with a reported $15 million advance for the band's next album and an increased royalty rate moving forward.

Still, the bid for profit-sharing had been unsuccessful, and a few months into 2006, band manager Rob McDermott asked to be released from his own contract with The Firm, the talent agency that had been enlisted for the battle with Warner. However frustrating it must've been at the time, in hindsight, the eight-figure advance and increased rate demonstrated the band's sway at Warner Bros., which continues to be their label home years later—all the other artists on the Warner roster, from Green Day to Faith Hill, had been in the same position as Linkin Park, and yet none of *them* received the same perks.

Mike launched Fort Minor during the prolonged label dispute, and Chester started tinkering with some music on his own. He wrote songs at home on his acoustic guitar, then sent them over to his friend Ryan Shuck, the rhythm guitarist for Orgy who had first gotten to know Chester when his band and Linkin Park overlapped at NRG Studios during the creation of *Hybrid Theory*.

For the first time since joining Linkin Park, Chester considered making his own solo album: the songs he was writing "were darker and moodier than anything I'd come up with for the band" and wouldn't have fit into Linkin Park's sound, he explained. For instance, "Let Down," one of the first songs he worked on with Ryan and his Orgy bandmate Amir Derakh, would eventually become a Soft Cell–esque synth-rock song and found Chester mixing anger and resignation: "All those years down the drain," he sang, "love was not enough, when you want everything."

The songs Chester wrote during that period captured the downward spiral he experienced once the *Meteora* tour ended. His marriage to Samantha had gone from strained to disintegrated, with neither party sure about why they were still together when Chester came home. Their relationship devolved into "a vicious and destructive cycle that we couldn't get out of," Samantha wrote in her memoir. The couple divorced in early 2005, and Chester moved out of their mansion and into a tiny apartment in Santa Monica, his ego bruised and his feelings bitter.

He had been smoking and drinking again on the road, a habit that caused friction with his bandmates, but at least he was able to use the stage as a form of release. Once he returned home, however, Chester started binge drinking and popping antidepressants, refusing to set foot outside of his home. "I'd shack up in my closet in the dark and shake all day," he recalled. "I'd wake up and have a pint of Jack Daniel's to calm down, then I'd pop a bunch of pills and go back in my closet and fucking freak out for the rest of the day." Chester also had regular seizures, which led to regular hospital visits. He hated himself but couldn't figure out how to turn things around, so he just kept drinking.

Unlike Chester's struggles with substance abuse during the *Hybrid Theory* tour, this period of self-described "absolute self-destruction" was coiled around his twisted perception of what his addictions had helped him gain. He had spent years pouring his agony from drugs and alcohol into his art, and the fame that Chester achieved as Linkin Park's singer had been fueled by smash hits, from "Crawling" to "Numb" to "Breaking the Habit," that chronicled that suffering.

Chester had won a Grammy for a song about the lack of control he felt as an addict; when he sang "Numb/Encore" alongside Jay-Z at Live 8, his half of the song bared his deepest scars in front of a million people. His pain had paid off for him, beyond his wildest dreams, time and time again. It was a reality that felt impossible to process.

Eventually, Chester asked for help, and as he put it, "everybody came to my rescue." He and his Linkin Park bandmates attended counseling sessions, where Chester was able to process their frustrations and concern for his well-being.

"They really opened up," Chester said of his bandmates, "and told me how they felt. I had no idea that I had been such a nightmare. I knew that I had a drinking problem, a drug problem, and that parts of my personal life were crazy, but I didn't realize how much that was affecting the people around me until I got a good dose of 'Here's-what-you're-really-like.'"

Once he again committed to sobriety, the tension he felt within the group rapidly dissipated. "We all hang out now because they actually want to be around me," he said in 2010 while looking back on that period. "That's a huge deal for me."

Meanwhile, Chester also quickly fell in love again: after Ryan introduced him to Talinda Bentley, a former *Playboy* model who had gone to school for veterinary medicine, he knew almost instantly that they would end up together, and the couple moved in together within a few weeks. Talinda soon became pregnant with their first child, and she and Chester married on New Year's Eve, a few hours before the calendar flipped away from 2005.

Chester was certain that the coming year would be easier than the last, and in fact, his family continued to grow in 2006: in addition to Chester and Talinda welcoming a baby boy named Tyler into the world in mid-March, Chester adopted Isaiah, the son of his high school girlfriend

Elka Brand and the half brother of Jaime, whom Elka gave birth to in 1998 during another relationship. By 2006, Chester had four children from three different relationships, and utilized the support of that blended family as a steadying force.

On February 8, 2006, five weeks before Tyler was born, Linkin Park reunited onstage for the first time in over half a year at the Grammy Awards. "Numb/Encore" won Best Rap/Sung Collaboration that night, and the band once again linked up with Jay-Z to perform the mash-up, this time in prime time from the Staples Center stage in Los Angeles.

Jay, rocking a black John Lennon tee underneath a white suit, exuded swagger from center stage, but Linkin Park appeared particularly invigorated. Chester crooned with renewed passion, his jet-black hair matching his unbuttoned suit jacket, and Mike grinned while intoning "Get 'em, Jay" from behind a grand piano. Meanwhile, Brad, Dave, Rob, and Joe, who had played each note plenty of times, sounded crisp as ever on national TV.

Just as Jay-Z closed out his last verse, Chester changed up the "Numb/Encore" formula. Instead of launching into his half of the song, he warbled the first verse of The Beatles' "Yesterday," his voice floating delicately across every classic syllable.

And then, a figure in a white linen shirt appeared onstage behind him.

Jay-Z's Lennon T-shirt was a subtle tip-off to the audience: Paul McCartney strolled out as a surprise guest during the performance and picked up "Yesterday" right where Chester left off, supported by the rest of Linkin Park and a small orchestra. Suddenly, Chester was harmonizing with Paul Freaking McCartney on "Yesterday," as Jay-Z offered ad-libs to Macca's right and a string section swelled behind all three. This was *The Grey Album* live, and out of anywhere in the world they could have been that night, the six guys of Linkin Park were the ones onstage, sharing a moment they knew immediately would be rendered immortal.

That performance would have been the pinnacle of any artist's career. But, really, the 2006 Grammys were just an exclamation point for Linkin

Park, extravagantly capping off one of the most remarkable five-year commercial runs in music history. In the months and years that followed that Grammys ceremony, the band would tear down their sound and identity and build them back up, bit by bit. They would enter a new phase—they had to. But that night, they were sandwiched between legends in front of the world. And they belonged.

INTERLUDE

"It's Something That Anybody Can Relate To"

Skylar Grey, who went by Holly Brook while singing the hook of the Fort Minor smash "Where'd You Go," looks back on the power of the single, the start of her career, and how Linkin Park helped inform her songwriting technique.

Linkin Park and I were both managed by people at The Firm, which was a big management company back then. My manager connected me with them, and Brad came to meet me at this hotel in LA, which is now called The London, but back then it was called the Bel Age. And there was this huge—I think it was a Ukrainian restaurant in there? With a piano in the corner. And I played for him, two songs at the piano. And pretty much the next day, I got offered a record deal with Machine Shop.

They had heard some of my demos, and then when I played those two songs for him, he seemed really excited. So then we locked in—I signed my first record deal with them, and actually, my publishing deal was tied to that and I'm still in the same publishing deal now. So they kind of got me off the ground in music in LA. I had only lived there about a year and a half when I met them and signed with them. I was eighteen, and I learned a lot. I was coming from Wisconsin and had no idea even what a record deal was when I was offered one. So the learning curve was really steep.

Machine Shop was a JV company under Warner Bros. So there was the support of Warner Bros. as a major, but I didn't have an A&R person at Warner—my A&R was Brad. So, initially, I started working with Brad the most on my own material, just trying to build an album, build a sound. And then Mike asked me to come in, because he was recording his Fort Minor album. And he was like, "I have this song that I really want you to sing the hook on." It wasn't that far into our relationship when I did this—I might have been signed to them for, like, six months at the time. And he had me come into the studio and sing "Where'd You Go." I didn't really think much of it. It was like, I sang the song, and I left!

And then suddenly, out of nowhere, he released the album, and then [later] put it out as a single, and it was a hit! It was my first time ever experiencing being on a chart, which was really exciting and really scary at the same time. I was like, "Ah, this is happening so fast! I don't know how to handle this!"

I was so young and inexperienced. I didn't know how to follow it up or how to turn it into something more. I was really shy at the time—I remember being super shy on the set of the music video. I was so green in the industry, and I didn't really know how things worked and was just learning as I went. We were being flown around to do TV performances—I remember doing one of the last *TRL* shows that ever happened, and then I got to do *Jay Leno*. And then I got thrown on tour, my first tour bus experience, and it was crazy, a total whirlwind.

The funny thing is, a lot of people think I wrote the hook, but I just sang it. [Mike] wrote the song from the perspective of his wife when he lives on tour. But it's something that anybody can relate to—missing someone. I think that the key to most hit songs is having a really universal message that everybody can relate to. And that was one of those.

He's super talented, and I learned a lot working with him and working with Brad. They taught me a lot about song structure. I came from a background of songwriting, without any formulas or any knowledge of what works. When I was a young songwriter—I started writing when I was, like, fourteen, and my songs were these epic, long, drawn-out, no-structure, free-flowing type songs, and they helped show me how to shape a song into something that was more accessible. That was a really important thing I learned from them, for sure.

After "Where'd You Go," we put out my album, and it didn't really take off the way that I hoped it would. But also I know that I made a lot of mistakes. I tried to rush it out, trying to follow up this "Where'd You Go" hit, and I don't think I was ready. I don't think the songs were necessarily there yet, but I still love the album, I was really proud of it. And [Machine Shop and I] ended up parting ways over creative differences. And then I ended up going broke and leaving LA and taking a break from the music industry for a while, so I lost touch with pretty much everyone. And then a few years later, I wrote "Love the Way You Lie," obviously got sucked back into the music industry, changed my name. I ran into them backstage at the AMAs [in 2017], when I performed with Macklemore. That was the first time I'd seen them since everything, and I gave them big hugs.

I love their music. I remember the first time I heard "Crawling" on the radio, when I lived in Wisconsin, and I loved it. It was an interesting, new, fresh sound at the time, and the emotion was all there. They had this way of taking these genres that were kind of niche and bringing them into the forefront, all together in one piece. It was really inspiring.

Also, I got my first tattoo backstage at a Linkin Park concert! I was eighteen or nineteen, and that was more Chester's influence than anyone. I really looked up to him and learned a lot about performing on big stages by watching him perform. I loved how he would put his foot up on the monitor and physically lean into the notes he was hitting. I kind of adopted a bit of that body language. My tattoo was a Pisces symbol. . . . Chester was Pisces, too.

PART IV

THE MESSAGE

IT STARTS WITH one simple beat, then another, falling into a steady rhythm. The programming kicks in like distant sirens after a few seconds, and the soothing bass undertone after that. Chester's voice arrives, unadorned.

> *I close both locks below the window*
> *I close both blinds and turn away*
> *Sometimes solutions aren't so simple*
> *Sometimes, goodbye's the only way.*

His voice often lilted into a confessional in the past—the first half of the "In the End" bridge comes to mind—but never before this tenderly or with such gentle movement. The most fragile edges of his tone drift downward in defeat, but then the song swells, his notes crystal clear and increasingly steady, the first gesture of what it will soon become. Chester sounds emboldened by the first chorus, his soul set ablaze once more:

> *And the shadow of the day*
> *Will embrace the world in gray*
> *And the sun will set for you.*

"Shadow of the Day" is about the inevitability and acceptance of death, but right around halfway through—after the fourteen-piece string section has begun its mournful sway, Mike's keyboard loop has assumed its ghostly role beside Joe's programming, and Rob's drums have ratcheted up from an unobtrusive start—the song sounds like a new beginning for Linkin Park. The hook widens its stance into full-blown stadium rock, intentionally designed for raised lighters and mass sing-along. After the second chorus, Brad bursts in with a searing, heartland-ready guitar solo—and back then, Linkin Park hadn't really *done* guitar solos. And then Chester brings the song home with one final, gigantic refrain, completing the most soaring vocal performance of his career.

Linkin Park had never made a song like "Shadow of the Day" prior to their third album, 2007's *Minutes to Midnight.* That was the point of making it. The risk was apparent: the millions of fans who had purchased *Hybrid Theory* and/or *Meteora* could have easily listened to a song like "Shadow of the Day," processed the sound of their favorite rap-rock band pivoting toward stadium grandeur, and shrugged off Linkin Park for good.

Yet by their third album, the band's fear of alienating their core fan base was far outweighed by their desire to shake things up. They had experimented with new textures on *Meteora,* and songs like "Faint" and especially "Breaking the Habit" suggested that the band could, and should, branch out sonically. But their second album had largely been a continuation of the sound created at their inception—and that meant their third album could not be. The idea of repeating the exact same formula to "make a trilogy," as Chester put it, incensed the band on a molecular level, regardless of the backlash they might face.

"We sold thirty-five million records of that old sound," Mike said. "Saying that we wanted to leave it behind and make something new and equally good was horrifying but thrilling." Dave added, "I knew that I wasn't going to be happy just doing a continuation of what we'd already done before."

Removing the band's rap-rock engine was the logical reset. "We're ripping that out," Chester said of their recognizable nu metal sound. "There's a common thread that people are going to expect, and we're trying to pull that out of the new music." What exactly would replace it, however, proved to be a more difficult question to answer. So the band brought in Rick

Rubin—a master of deconstruction and the natural producer for a drastic change of pace.

Not only had Rick helmed albums by Run-D.M.C. and Red Hot Chili Peppers that were indispensable influences on Mike, but also his entire process was different from Don Gilmore's painstaking behind-the-boards work; famously, Rick can't read music and doesn't really play an instrument. Instead, he works off of pure vibes and an impeccable ear. In 2006, when work on Linkin Park's third album began in earnest, a pair of projects that Rick had just finished—Red Hot Chili Peppers' *Stadium Arcadium* and Dixie Chicks' *Taking the Long Way*—would become two of the biggest albums of that year and earn Rick a Grammy for Producer of the Year in early 2007. Rick represented the gold standard of rock production, and fortunately, Linkin Park was notable enough to secure his time.

The band members were in a good place as they set forth on their third album. Mike felt more confident as a producer following *Collision Course* and the Fort Minor album, and for the first time, he was listed as the coproducer on a Linkin Park album, which he described as "a huge nod" from his bandmates. Meanwhile, Chester, sober and newly remarried, came into the sessions rejuvenated, cracking up his bandmates with silly voices and non sequiturs. All their physical features had deepened—Brad's brown curls had blossomed into an afro, and Dave had fully grown out his fire-red beard—and they felt older, more connected, with most of the band having played together for nearly a decade.

In March 2006, a few weeks after sharing the stage with Jay-Z and Paul McCartney at the 2006 Grammys, and a few days after welcoming his first child with new wife Talinda, Chester became the first Linkin Park member to enter his thirties. "As Chester put it really eloquently," Brad said, "at this point, we're not just idiots jumping around the stage."

BUT BEFORE THEY COULD LOCATE complex themes and a more mature sound, Chester and Mike had to sing gibberish.

"*Da-na-na-naaaaa,*" Chester mumbled in the vocal booth over a half-finished guitar track, scraping at a melody that may or may not exist while sounding like an Adam Sandler bit from the mid-nineties. On another day, Mike warbled over an incomplete drumbeat, "*Da-naaaaaaaa.*" Chester often joked with Mike: Who was this girl Donna, and why was the band writing so many songs about her?

Of course, it was all an exercise. When Linkin Park started working with Rick in early 2006, he wanted to first observe their natural workflow and then pointed something out to Mike: Linkin Park wrote songs like a production group instead of a rock band. For years, they had been completing production tracks and then placing vocals on top of those finished tracks, like icing on a fully baked cake, instead of gradually enmeshing music and lyrics.

"We didn't pitch the songs. We didn't change the tempos. We just put vocals on the songs," Mike explained of their first two albums. "And sometimes, songs didn't work because, truth be told, we needed to speed them up, slow them down, or change the key in order for the song to have a good vocal. But we just didn't do that."

Rick gently suggested trashing that process. Instead, the band should try incorporating their voices into tracks much earlier and not worry about perfecting the lyrics—sing nonsense, use *da-na-na*'s as melodic placeholders, to get a better sense of where the songs might go. So the guys began listening back to tracks with filler vocals, learned how "to just take the initial musical idea and put the vocals on it," Brad said, "and you could tell right away whether it's worth developing."

That was just one wrecking ball that Rick wanted to swing at Linkin Park's longtime process to help remodel it, brick by brick. "He would initiate conversations like, 'You want to do it this way. You've done that before. Why don't you think about doing it another way?'" Joe recalled.

That same attitude extended to how the song ideas originated. Instead of Mike leading one-on-one pairs and translating most of the early thoughts, or "seeds," into a multilayered track, Rick set up all six members with their own hard drives and Pro Tools rigs in their home studios. Once a week, the band would convene and play their individual seeds for the group—a musical show-and-tell that eventually amassed 150 song ideas for the new album.

Rick essentially gave all the members free-form time to go wild with their seeds and make whatever came to mind, regardless of what the final product would sound like. Some of those seeds leaned toward dance music or doom metal or eighties synth-rock—and the understanding was that most of them would never see the light of day. But through that process of "aimless wandering," as Joe put it, the band was chipping away at some previously unseen creativity. The question of what should replace the band's rap-rock sound was being answered, piece by piece.

After spending the first half of 2006 conjuring up ideas, the band decamped to Rick's mansion in Laurel Canyon to begin recording, even though they were nowhere close to finalizing the track list. With their first two albums, the band "never went into the studio until we were 80 percent done [with] the songs," Rob explained. "This process, we went into the studio about a year before the completion date."

Unlike Don's compressed boot camp at NRG Studios, however, The Mansion—a four-bedroom stunner built in 1918, full of tiny rooms and curving stairways that was incorrectly rumored to once have belonged to Harry Houdini—was full of space to let the guys' creativity unfurl at its own pace. The living room became the main tracking area, electronics were stored on the second level, the old library became a control room, and the vocal-cutting rig was set up on the top floor. The band toiled away on all three stories of The Mansion when they weren't playing basketball or Ping-Pong, tacking tapestries on the wall, or posing in front of the house's giant pirate flag. They had never worked like this before—so much freedom outside of the studio walls, ample time to screw around in a giant house!—and they worked slowly. Those hundreds of seeds and scatted vocals congealed over weeks, the thin top layer of whatever their third album would turn into boiling away.

"They really are reinventing themselves," Rick told the press about Linkin Park at the time. He kept pushing the band's process out of its comfort zone, identifying the guys' habits and then shaking them sense-less. Linkin Park's first two albums didn't have extended guitar parts or swear words? Their third could—*should*—have both. The band never recorded songs live together? They were going to set up in The Mansion's common area, with Chester and Mike in vocal booths on opposite ends of the room, and Brad and Dave with their guitars sitting in between them. The enclosed booths became so stifling that Chester staggered out of takes covered in sweat and stripped to his briefs—but then he'd hustle back in, willing to give it another go.

For Chester, much more agonizing than a hot vocal booth was Rick's suggestion of printing out all the song lyrics that he and Mike had written and having the rest of the band pick them apart. It was one thing for Don to pore over their lines during the recording process and then challenge the writers to turn in something more effective; it was a whole other thing to sit with Rick and their four bandmates in a corner of The Mansion, lyric sheets strewn across a circle of couches, and analyze their personal thoughts and feelings as a group project.

Chester's and Mike's lyrics had never been subjected to committee feedback before, and the vocalists immediately became defensive. "I appreciate democracy," Chester said, "but at the same time, I have very strong feelings when it comes to the kind of music that I want to listen to." He wanted to hear out his bandmates, but the words that he sang had always been *his*. Meanwhile, Mike had just written and produced a full album as Fort Minor—and was now getting more notes than he ever had before.

Eventually, the two frontmen realized that if Joe, Brad, Rob, and Dave all didn't like a particular line, that line probably wasn't any good. They inched toward a compromise with each song, evolving the lyrics so that every member would feel comfortable standing behind them, while also keeping the identity of the vocalist intact.

"It worked out for the greater good," Chester admitted. "But, man, it was like pulling your teeth out at some points."

"Yeah, here we go for the hundredth time," Mike raps to open "Bleed It Out," which would become a wiry rap-rock stomper on their third album. The line was Mike's updated version of Chester's studio-frustration growl, "I cannot take this anymore / I'm saying everything I've said before," from "One Step Closer" seven years earlier. "Bleed It Out" had gone through dozens of rewrites, to the point where the lyrics became a commentary on those rewrites. "Fuck this hurts, I won't lie / Doesn't matter how hard I try / Half the words don't mean a thing / And I know that I won't be satisfied," Mike spits later, and then Chester repeats with fury about his discarded thoughts, "I bleed it out, diggin' deeper, just to throw it away!"

That process of banging their heads against a wall in the studio was familiar to Linkin Park—and this time, it resulted in a writhing firehose of energy, a song full of drum thwacks, handclaps, live cheering, and exasperated adrenaline that Mike once described as a "death-party-rap-hoedown." "Bleed It Out" recaptured the sprinting-through-brick-walls spirit of the band's first two albums, but it was an outlier on their third, more of a callback to their bygone rap-rock era than anything reflective of their newly evolved sound.

Outside of "Bleed It Out" and the orchestral march "Hands Held High," Mike doesn't rap on *Minutes to Midnight*, a choice that was made after he tried adding some hip-hop verses into different tracks and heard them come out clichéd. Instead, Mike is singing more than ever, providing backing vocals on a handful of tracks, which he had done in Linkin Park's past, and taking lead on "In Between," which he had not.

Mike had dabbled with singing hooks on *The Rising Tied*, but in Linkin Park, he had a bandmate with a tsunami of a voice and, understandably, was used to ceding the floor. Yet while the band was working on "In Between," Mike warbled over the twitchy, apologetic campfire song, and after Chester recorded his own version of the track, he was adamant that Mike's tone sounded better over the understated production.

"I consider Chester one of the best singers of our time," Mike said in 2007. "I mean, that's not just being in the band with the guy. I would challenge anybody to sing the stuff that he sings, to cover the song and make it sound anything like him. You can't do it." So when Chester pushed for Mike to sing lead on "In Between," Mike was genuinely moved by the gesture. "For him to listen to something that I sang and say, 'Yours is better'? That was crazy for me," he said.

The experimental ethos of *Minutes to Midnight* sprawls across the entire album, the bag of studio tricks that Rick utilized to snap the band out of its self-diagnosed rut fully evident on the final product. On the album's first two proper songs, for instance, the band pivots from the mangy punk-rock assault of "Given Up," which features some all-timer Chester screaming, to the swaying pop balladry of "Leave Out All the Rest," which rests on a gentle bed of electronics and strings.

"In Pieces" on the back half of the album is even more startling: as Chester pokes at the wounds that his divorce inflicted, the song's ominous electronic skittering turns into . . . a ska riff? The steel drums and reggae influence produce one of the most truly surprising swivels in the band's entire discography, but damn if "In Pieces" doesn't make you as a listener want to dance a little by the time Brad's finger-flying solo arrives.

Even the first single sounds reasonably removed from every prior Linkin Park hit: "What I've Done" was the last song finished during the recording sessions and was chosen to lead the *Minutes to Midnight* campaign as a thematic link between albums two and three. "Lyrically, it's about recognizing the faults of the past and trying to move on with the future," Joe explained. "And that's what this album's about."

Although "What I've Done" is an accessible rocker with a throaty chorus, unlike "Somewhere I Belong," which preceded *Meteora* by directly recalling the biggest successes from *Hybrid Theory*, the song plows into a new direction as an obvious radio offering. The eerie piano riff, the uncluttered percussion, the raw guitar breakdown, the solitude of Chester's voice giving way to the harmonies in the final thirty seconds—none of it sounds like "Breaking the Habit," per se, but "What I've Done" still carries the fearlessness of the Linkin Park single that preceded it, an itch to recontextualize the band's mainstream appeal.

"What I've Done" soared to No. 7 on the Hot 100 chart, but outside of a soundtrack single soon to come, that single would be their final top 10 entry. The album title *Minutes to Midnight* was a reference to the World War II–era concept of the Doomsday Clock, a device for counting down to nuclear holocaust and the end of the world. The title might as well have been a meta commentary on their time being almost up as automatic hitmakers, though. Six and a half years had passed since *Hybrid Theory* was released, and a lot of the headbanging teens at their earliest shows had by then gone through college and leaped into early adulthood. Linkin Park's fan base had grown up, beyond the youthful angst that their early smashes had captured. So, on the same album where the band matured their sound to avoid stagnation, they realized their message had to mature, too.

For the first time, the band also wrote with what Chester described as a "political hint." The album was recorded at a moment in which the Iraq War was beginning to stretch on endlessly and President George W. Bush had become a punchline in his second term. In this regard, Linkin Park was following the lead of bands like Green Day, whose 2004 album *American Idiot* had been an anti-Bush blockbuster, and System of a Down, whose 2005 single "B.Y.O.B." excoriated those who had engineered the war. But the primary motivation for the guys dabbling in political messaging was that they were simply getting older and feeling their priorities shift in the process. "When we wrote *Hybrid Theory*, I was the oldest one in the band and I think I was twenty-three or something," Chester said. "And things that weren't important to us then are definitely important to us now."

Mike raps through his frustrations on "Hands Held High," delivering lines like "The leader just talks away / Stuttering and mumbling for nightly news to replay" with the same intensity he brought to "Kenji" on the Fort Minor album. The combination of the takedown rhymes and military drumbeat makes "Hands Held High" a little too ham-fisted; "No More Sorrow," a flamethrower against political greed where Chester sees red throughout, fares better as a straightforward ripper. Yet both songs pale in comparison to "The Little Things Give You Away," the album's monumental, six-minute-plus closing track that affects through its subtleties. The song comments on the Bush administration's disastrous response to Hurricane Katrina in 2005 and the human cost of their incompetence ("All you've ever wanted / Was someone to truly look up to you / And six feet underwater, I do," Chester sings on the chorus) but adopts a restrained tone throughout, slowly building around acoustic guitar and palm-pounded beats until the song title evolves into a full-group chant.

Chester described "The Little Things Give You Away" as "the pinnacle of what we can achieve as a band," and indeed, its grand scale, thematic ambition, and skin-rattling climax make the song one of Linkin Park's all-time achievements. But part of the reason why the band so successfully pulled off the Mature Third Album exists in the way their growth was reflected in their most personal songs as well as those about the state of the world. Which brings us back to "Shadow of the Day," the album's other epic.

The same grandeur that captured the devastation of a world event on "The Little Things Give You Away" is applied to Chester's personal devastation on "Shadow of the Day," and for the first time, he avoids anything resembling a scream to express himself. The lyrics—endlessly workshopped by the entire band before coming out the other side fully realized—are open to interpretation. When he sang them, Chester could have been thinking about his self-destructive period following the *Meteora* tour ("I close both blinds and turn away") or the band's struggles to reinvent themselves ("Sometimes, beginnings aren't so simple") or a host of other things. It could be about grief or depression, or a mix of both or neither. The song's power is in that very universality, though—the rejoinder that circumstances are always changing, that things are always falling apart, that the sun will set for all of us at some point.

"Shadow of the Day" eventually reached No. 15 on the Hot 100 as the third single from *Minutes to Midnight*. "What I've Done" was a bigger hit from the album and, along with "Bleed It Out," has become a bigger streaming hit in recent years. Maybe the world wasn't ready for the version of Linkin Park that "Shadow of the Day" created—the anthemic-rock field simply too crowded at that moment in time—so the song became a hit, but not a career-defining one. Yet "Shadow of the Day" is one of the most important songs in Linkin Park's journey, the one that fully, convincingly catapulted Linkin Park out of the rap-rock genre. "Shadow of the Day" was a huge risk, just like the rest of *Minutes to Midnight*. But because the band had grown into the song by the time they made it, that risk paid off.

I'T'S COOL TO be a part of recovery. This is just who I am, this is what I write about, what I do, and most of my work has been a reflection of what I've been going through in one way or another."

Chester said these words in July 2009 while discussing Dead by Sunrise's *Out of Ashes*, a project based around the solo songs that he had started working on in 2005. Back then, he was spiraling after the *Meteora* tour—divorce and relapse, followed by remarriage, counseling sessions, and sobriety. Four years later, Chester brought forward a new project that captured that chaotic period, and naturally, he was asked about the inspiration behind these lyrics when the press cycle began.

He didn't *have* to provide answers, necessarily—he could have shrugged off the questions or gestured at his past addiction issues (specifically, his battle with alcoholism). But that had never been his approach. Instead, he actively unpacked them in a condensed interview. Even in a succinct, on-the-record discussion, Chester identified an opportunity to be frank.

"I don't have a problem with people knowing that I had a drinking problem," he continued. "That's who I am and I'm kind of lucky in a lot of ways 'cause I get to do something about it. I get to grow as a person through it."

Linkin Park burst onto the rap-rock scene in 2000 when it was still dominated by brash, hedonistic stars like Fred Durst and Kid Rock, the ones blamed for turning Woodstock '99 into a total shitshow. Partially through their hijacked hip-hop swagger, those artists continued the myth of rock star as superhero: hassled by haters but ultimately indestructible, partying hard and damning the consequences.

When they debuted, Linkin Park positioned themselves as the antidote to that alpha-male posturing—no cursing, no hijinks, not a "Nookie" in sight—but the emotional honesty wasn't a strategic put-on, either. Both musically and aesthetically, Linkin Park examined their inner pain from the very beginning, holding up their findings to the audience for maximum relatability. And that process simply would not have worked if Chester held back who he was or tried to hide what he was fighting. From day one, Chester was molding his personal issues into sentences and melodies, for himself and others.

For as propulsive and catchy as *Hybrid Theory* was, the band's mega-selling debut album is, across the board, crushingly bleak. Consider its hit singles: "In the End" is a towering paean to dashed hopes, and "Crawling" climaxes with Chester bellowing, "I've felt this way before / So insecure!" Of course, Chester wasn't alone in setting the band's sorrowful tone—Mike raps about paranoia and self-doubt throughout the debut album, and the rest of the band create an atmosphere of cleanly produced sadness. But Chester's vulnerability is the straw that stirs the drink, a force of nature that immediately comes across as genuine. He was drawing upon the physical abuse he suffered as an adolescent and the substance abuse he fought as a teenager as inspiration. And the more he talked about his issues, the more he could pinpoint how to express them.

"Once I came out with being abused as a child, a lot of those doors opened for me," Chester said in a different 2009 interview. "It was like, 'Okay, if I can write about that, I can pretty much write about anything.'"

One thing is abundantly clear when you watch candid footage of Chester with the band, in practically any scenario from any time period: he wasn't moping around. If anything, Chester was often the quickest to crack a joke, throw out a silly voice, break a tense moment with a juvenile aside to get someone else in the room to smile. He refused to let his personal difficulties define his personality, but he also knew how to tap into those struggles for creative inspiration. And as Linkin Park's dominant run continued through the 2000s and their sound evolved, Chester's unguarded thoughts would often power the band's most visceral moments.

On *Meteora*, "Numb" was partly born of the exhaustion and substance abuse issues that Chester faced on the *Hybrid Theory* tour in 2001 ("It's kind of about those times when you've got no feeling left or you just don't care . . . which, funny enough, is how we felt after touring last year," Mike had explained), and Chester delivered those feelings as huge, outward-reaching catharsis. The music video, directed by Joe, helped make "Numb" more universal: the clip stars Briana Evigan as a student who gets picked on and shunned, depicts depression and thoughts of self-harm, and climaxes with the young woman angrily hurling paint at a blank canvas. The "Numb" video has nothing to do with Chester's specific issues but funnels them into an easily identifiable archetype: the outcast triumphantly turning their pain into art.

Meanwhile, the enduring importance of a song like "Shadow of the Day" on *Minutes to Midnight* rests in its even more plainly discussed portrayal of depression. Chester whittles down his phrases into short, declarative lines about blacking out the world when easy answers are nowhere to be found, then finally achieves a release within a major-key chorus and a cobwebs-clearing guitar riff.

Chester spoke often and eloquently about his long-term battles with clinical depression, using his platform to make the mental health disorder more understandable and relatable to the general public. "It's not like, 'Ah, man, I'm just bummed'—it's like, 'I don't want to do anything, and I don't feel like doing anything, and I don't like anything,' like, there's no sunshine," Chester said later in his career. "For me, I've always kind of dealt with that my whole life. I've always had this depressive side. And I think that's something I've never liked, but I've also never liked being *anything*. I don't like being happy—I want to be happy, but when I'm in it, I try to get out of it. I don't like being sad; when I'm in it, I try to get out of it. I've never been comfortable being . . . just *being*."

Stigmas around mental health discussion in popular music are drastically different today from when Linkin Park made their debut. Really, discussions about mental health barely even *existed* when Linkin Park made their debut. But throughout his career, Chester let it be known that the issues discussed in his lyrics were steeped in reality, that his demons were heartbreakingly real. Maybe, Chester thought, when someone going through a similar struggle would listen to him sing, that distinction would help them feel less alone.

———————

IN EARLY 2008, RIGHT AROUND the midway point in the *Minutes to Midnight* album cycle, Chester stated of Linkin Park: "After everything we've been through to get here, we're in the best place we could possibly be." Their third studio album not only was another hit upon its May 2007 release—*Minutes to Midnight* soared to No. 1 on the *Billboard* 200 chart, with 623,000 copies sold, the biggest sales week of 2007 at the time—but also confirmed that their audience had evolved with them, buying CDs in droves despite the group's different sound. As a declaration of reinvention, its success felt especially meaningful for the band.

The band also got to enjoy the fruits of their labor when it came time to promote *Minutes to Midnight*. They played both *Saturday Night Live* and *Jimmy Kimmel Live!* for the first time in May 2007, performing "What I've Done" and "Bleed It Out," two disparate-sounding singles that both studio audiences nevertheless gobbled up. They headed back to Europe that summer, returning to Rock am Ring and once again crushing it, then stopped by Japan in July for Live Earth, a climate-change-awareness benefit that Al Gore had asked them to play. All five of the singles released from *Minutes to Midnight* reached the Hot 100 chart—a feat that neither *Hybrid Theory* nor *Meteora* accomplished—and by the time Linkin Park wound down its 2007 touring slate in Australia and Asia that fall, "Shadow of the Day" had transformed into a real crossover radio hit and eventually hit the top 10 of Pop Airplay the following March.

Chris Cornell toured with the band on those Australian dates—he was promoting a solo album, *Carry On*, at the time—and Chester was elated to meet the Soundgarden legend that he had long described as "one of my heroes." Instead of being disappointed when he got to spend extended time with the voice on his endlessly played CDs, Chester discovered another artist he could speak with candidly and collaborate with easily.

"Sometimes you meet somebody and it's like you've known them forever," Chester said of Chris. They agreed that the Australian run together in the fall of 2007, which had lasted almost two weeks, had been too short, so Linkin Park invited Chris to be the main support on their 2008 Projekt Revolution tour.

Chester, a troubled teenager when Seattle grunge took over mainstream rock, grew up riveted by raw, open-hearted groups like Soundgarden; his own band Grey Daze practically tried to re-create that early-nineties movement, to little avail. To some degree, the lyrical sensitivity that gestured toward mental health issues carried over from the grunge scene to the alternative explosion as those eras overlapped—hits like Nirvana's "All Apologies," Pearl Jam's "Jeremy," R.E.M.'s "Everybody Hurts," and Red Hot Chili Peppers' "Under the Bridge" all carrying a similar base energy—and even to early rap-rock, within Limp Bizkit's and Korn's more brooding moments. By the 1990s, mental health discussions had picked up in the medical community, with Congress establishing the first week of October as Mental Illness Awareness Week in recognition of the National Alliance on Mental Illness (NAMI)—but at the turn of the century those discussions still weren't foregrounded anywhere in modern society, let alone in popular music.

When Linkin Park began its ascent, popular rock was experiencing a particularly macho period, not just with the chest-thumping nu metal stars but also with burly post-grunge stalwarts (Creed, Nickelback) and snotty pop-punk upstarts (Sum 41, Good Charlotte). Some of the bigger groups made the occasional serious turn—songs like Matchbox Twenty's

"Unwell" and Blink-182's "Adam's Song" addressed anxiety and teen suicide, respectively—but they were primarily released in between those bands' lighter hits.

Meanwhile, the garage revival coincided with the advent of the blogosphere, giving greater visibility to guitar-rock and indie music. Bands like The Strokes, The Killers, and Franz Ferdinand scored radio hits with casual, catchy flirtations, while mass media properties like *The O.C.* and *Garden State* made sweeping declarations in support of ultra-sensitive indie rock—screw the mainstream, bands like Death Cab for Cutie and The Shins will *change your life*.

If those cultural shifts poked holes in the hyper-masculine rock-star paradigm, the twin rise of emo music and MySpace in the mid-2000s actively worked to deflate it. Emerging from the punk and post-hardcore scenes, emo started as an outsider culture that turned far more commercially viable than anyone could have dreamed, with My Chemical Romance, Fall Out Boy, Panic! At the Disco, and Paramore doing big business in the middle of the decade.

The core tenets associated with emo music—intense emotion, confessional lyricism, gender fluidity, acceptance through shared societal alienation—also paved the way for more open discussions about issues like anxiety and depression from the leaders of the scene. Suddenly, artists writing about personal battles on the fringes of popular rock, just as Linkin Park was doing in the mainstream, were discovering a host of listeners who felt just like them and who wanted to see their bands in arenas. "Mental illness used to be a taboo and now it's not anymore, at least, I feel like it's not," My Chemical Romance frontman Gerard Way said. "I'm glad about that."

My Chemical Romance's theatrical misfit anthems took off from the New Jersey suburbs in part because of their early fan base on MySpace, a social media network launched in 2003 as a streamlined amalgamation of Friendster, AOL Instant Messenger, and early message boards. MySpace became closely associated with emo in a prestreaming music industry, as bands personally interacted with their fans online, embedded a few of their songs in the site's custom music player, and watched users post their favorite tracks in their own profiles.

Part of it was guerrilla marketing for millennials, but really, MySpace likely would have influenced the proliferation of mental health discussions regardless of its association with popular music simply because it was a means of greater connection for users. In light of the myriad problems that have resulted from social media becoming a universal norm over the past decade and a half, an early platform like MySpace fostered community with fewer strings attached. Subreddits about mental health issues, closed Facebook groups, Twitter threads, and viral Instagram posts were all preceded by MySpace users posting song lyrics that spoke to them on their profile, and other users—whether they be friends, acquaintances, or strangers—messaging them that they could relate, too.

All these cultural shifts impacted Linkin Park in subtle ways. As MTV's musical footprint shrank in favor of reality programming, Linkin Park partnered with MySpace for music-video premieres and sponsored concerts. Ahead of the 2009 release of Dead by Sunrise's *Out of Ashes*, Chester shared a series of short behind-the-scenes webisodes on the platform, clips the length of music videos in which he played a song, recorded some vocals, or set up a photo shoot. This was the new reality of the music industry—Instagram Reels before Instagram existed—and Chester adapted to give his fans what they wanted to see.

And on Projekt Revolution 2007—the year prior to Chris Cornell touring with the band—the main opening act was My Chemical Romance. The bill was a one-two punch of near impossible catharsis, different sounds converging for a night of understanding through screaming. Like Linkin Park, My Chemical Romance was unflinching in addressing mental health topics, in and out of their music. It's not a coincidence that they, too, would become a defining rock band of the early twenty-first century, much like Soundgarden had been before them.

THE FOLLOWING YEAR, CHESTER AND Chris continued to grow closer during Projekt Revolution 2008: during each stop of the twenty-four-date tour, Chester would join Chris's opening set to sing "Hunger Strike" (a Cornell–Eddie Vedder duet as Temple of the Dog), and Chris would come out to sing the second half of "Crawling" with Linkin Park. Chester's wife, Talinda, and Chris's wife, Vicky, immediately clicked as well, and the two couples stayed in touch even after the tour wrapped in August. "That developed into Chris and Vicky asking me to be the godfather of their son, Christopher," Chester said. "One of my favorite memories of our friendship was the baptism and the christening and taking on that promise to the family."

Like Chester, Chris had battled depression and addiction since he was a teenager—a child of divorce taking drugs and hiding away from the world up in the rainy Pacific Northwest a decade before a young Chester followed a similar path in the Phoenix heat. Chris had been able to fend off his issues as he found the ragged power of his voice and became a grunge superstar, but the 1997 breakup of Soundgarden was followed by his divorce from his first wife, which then catapulted him into an extended relapse and a serious bout with depression.

By the time Chris met Chester, both singers had a lot in common. They'd been sober and remarried for years and liked spending time with their families off the road, confiding in each other away from parties and hangers-on. Chris was a rock god in Chester's eyes, long before he got to know him, but as Chris opened up about his life and all its complications, Chester recognized a kindred spirit who had also broken down at times after achieving fame and fortune.

"The idea that success equals happiness pisses me off," Chester admitted. "It's funny to think that just because you're successful, you're now immune to the full range of the human experience."

That worldview ignited Dead by Sunrise's *Out of Ashes*, which Chester finished following the *Minutes to Midnight* campaign. He brought in studio veteran Howard Benson (who had helmed My Chemical Romance's 2004 breakthrough *Three Cheers for Sweet Revenge*, among other albums) to produce. What had begun as a handful of solo songs that Chester had noodled around with in 2005 became a full-blown side band over the years; Chester had executive-produced *Death to Analog*, his friends Ryan Shuck and Amir Derakh's debut album as the leaders of the group Julien-K, and wanted them to join him as a proper trio while he completed those shelved tracks.

Dead by Sunrise entered the studio in July 2008. As a proven front-man working within a new, smaller group, Chester found himself adopting a more hands-on approach to song construction, fleshing out the lyrics, melodies, and overall purpose of those years-old acoustic tracks. He was creating the musical identity of a band without Mike, who had largely been the architect of Linkin Park's sound; in turn, Mike was proud of what his bandmate was accomplishing on his own. Chester "played me nine songs, two of which had (amazing) vocals," Mike wrote as the Dead by Sunrise album was finished in February 2009. "It's going to be incredible!"

When *Out of Ashes* arrived the following October, the album did not sound like a derivation of Linkin Park; instead, grunge overtures define the project, from the dramatic vocal sweep of opener "Fire" to the sludgy undertones of "Crawl Back In" to the hazy, falsetto-scraping balladry of "Give Me Your Name." Chester explored other sounds that had inspired him over the years, like the roaring punk spittle of "Condemned" and the Cure-esque goth beauty of "Too Late"; the finished version of "Let Down," the first song he worked on for the project, is a straight-up new wave anthem, full of bleeping synths and programmed beats. But as a whole, *Out of Ashes* feels like Chester threading the needle between the sound of his pre–Linkin Park musical output and that of the grunge icon who had recently become one of his close friends.

Despite all the passion poured into the project, *Out of Ashes* was not an outright hit: the album debuted at No. 29 on the *Billboard* 200 chart, and "Crawl Back In" received minor rock radio play, but neither made a lasting chart impact. Looking back on 2009, part of the problem was that the Dead by Sunrise album had been commercially overshadowed by . . . the one song Linkin Park *did* release that year.

"New Divide" had been commissioned by the team behind *Transformers: Revenge of the Fallen*, the second installment of the big-budget robots-in-disguise blockbuster film series. Although Linkin Park had never released a one-off single in between albums before, they had an idea for a slightly futuristic soundtrack stopgap that could work for the closing credits. The result was a highly competent synth-and-cymbal rocker that sounded a lot like "What I've Done." It was placed as the lead song on a soundtrack that had giant mechanical beings overlooking the pyramids on its album cover.

"New Divide" didn't progress Linkin Park's formula or show off any sonic innovation, but it wasn't created for growth. A Hollywood franchise was investing in the proven Linkin Park brand, wrangling the guys to the premiere for a post-film performance. Because the band remained enormously popular and the members were consummate professionals, the bet paid off handsomely.

The song debuted at No. 6 on the Hot 100 upon its May release; as it stands, "New Divide" is Linkin Park's highest-charting hit outside of "In the End," and their final top 10 single, a chart anomaly for a largely forgotten song. In that sense, "New Divide" makes for a nifty trivia answer today—but compared to *Out of Ashes*, which was already finished by the time Chester sang the *Transformers* song, the level of artistic achievement between the 2009 releases is no contest.

As the lone Dead by Sunrise album and the closest thing Chester ever made to a proper solo album, *Out of Ashes* sounds like a transmission from a complicated soul at uneasy peace. The songs he composed during a particularly self-destructive period in his life ring out with brutal honesty; Chester's songwriting benefited from hindsight. "After I went through all of that, *that's* when I started writing very clear and very forward songs about what I went through," he explained.

"My Suffering," for instance, examines the ways addiction intertwined with his success and the depression triggered by reflecting on that dynamic.

"There's something crazy running wild inside my brain," Chester growls over a racing guitar–drum exchange; later, he murmurs, "I found salvation in a vial," his voice faded out. Meanwhile, "Crawl Back In" moves rapidly through its account of relapse, but processing the lyrics—"I can't deny it / I try to fight it / But I'm losing control"—makes for a devastating experience. Tracks like "Give Me Your Name," a love song for Talinda, offer tender rays of hope, but *Out of Ashes* largely serves as an open dissection of Chester's issues—even more frank than what he presented in Linkin Park up to that point and a not-so-subtle message to anyone who was feeling the same way.

In the summer of 2009, Linkin Park spent a month in Europe and Asia, an international run of headline shows and festivals ostensibly scheduled to promote "New Divide." Ryan and Amir joined the band on the road for part of the run, and at a few select dates, Dead by Sunrise played a three-song mini-set—"Fire," "Crawl Back In," and "My Suffering"— before Linkin Park started their encore with "New Divide."

However, there was a dramatic difference in the way the crowd responded to these various songs. The *Transformers* song was already a smash by the time of those shows, and the Dead by Sunrise album was still a few months away from release; consequently, everyone in the crowds knew "New Divide" and no one knew the Dead by Sunrise material. One song was written for a robot-heroes action film; the others, by a rock star who made clear that *no one* was impenetrable. Chester would sing a top 10 smash, but before that, he would share a more intimate piece of himself.

The guys in 2000
Mick Hutson/Redferns

Mike and Chester in November 2000
Al Pereira/Michael Ochs Archives

Chester performing in February 2001
Scott Harrison/Hulton Archives

Mike and Brad at Ozzfest in June 2001
Scott Gries/Getty Images Entertainment

Dave at the KROQ Weenie Roast
in June 2001
Steve Granitz/WireImage

Joe performing in 2001
Kevin Mazur/WireImage

The band posing at the 2001 MTV Video Music Awards
Dave Hogan/Getty Images Entertainment

Chester and Mike having fun at 2001 VMAs rehearsals
Frank Micelotta Archive/Getty Images Entertainment

Brad performing in February 2002
Scott Harrison/Getty Images Entertainment

The guys posing with their
Grammy in February 2002
Lee Celano/AFP

Chester commanding the crowd in July 2003

John Atashian/Getty Images Entertainment

The guys accepting a Moonman at the 2003 VMAs
Christopher Polk/FilmMagic

The guys hanging out in Hong Kong in June 2004
Peter Parks/AFP

Mike sharing the stage with Jay-Z in February 2005
John Shearer/WireImage

Jay-Z, Paul McCartney, and Chester ruling the Grammys stage in 2006

Kevin Mazur/WireImage

Mike posing with his *Fort Minor* album artwork at a gallery in 2006
John Shearer/WireImage

Mike and Chester goofing around in May 2007
Stephen Lovekin/WireImage

Rob performing in August 2008
Avalon/Hulton Archive

Chester singing at the O2 Arena in July 2017
Burak Cingi/Redferns

Mike reflecting during the Linkin Park & Friends
Celebrate Life concert in October 2017

Christopher Polk/Getty Images Entertainment

Chester performing in May 2017
Santiago Bluguermann/LatinContent Editorial

INTERLUDE

"It Was So Dark, but It Was Real"

Amir Derakh, a former member of Orgy who formed Julien-K with Ryan Shuck and Dead by Sunrise with Ryan and Chester, recalls the making of *Out of Ashes* as both a home for stray ideas and a healthy purging of emotion.

Ryan and I became good friends with Chester—the three of us really clicked, and we used to hang out a lot. I remember when he bought his first "fancy car," as he called it, and actually, I think it was a PT Cruiser? It was purple, and it had a skull on it. It was so silly, but that's just how he was. We'd go over to his house, and he was all excited about this car. We were just scratching our heads—"What is this thing, Chester?" He's like, "I don't know! It's fast! It's purple!" We could joke with each other, we could make fun of each other, we could just be super silly. And Ryan and Chester were exceptionally silly. I was a little older, so I would just stand back and laugh as the two of them would just go into some crazy nonsense.

When Ryan and I started doing the Julien-K stuff, we were still in Orgy, and honestly, we never planned on leaving Orgy—it just kind of fell apart.

So the Julien-K thing started to come to the forefront, and while we were doing it, Chester really liked it. We were kind of surprised that he liked it so much, because it was so different from what he'd do with Linkin Park, but he really loved it, and he wanted to be a part of it. At one point, he actually was like, "I want to be the singer for Julien-K," and we were like, "Uhh, wait, what? You want to sing on these disco, new wave, electro-dance songs?" We just didn't get it, but he was serious. And out of that started Dead by Sunrise. It seemed like he really wanted to do something else, something different.

He had a couple of ideas that he would noodle around with on acoustic guitar—maybe he would hum some melodies, maybe he'd have a couple words, but he was always doing this. At the time, I think Chester was actually living with Ryan, and he had lived with me for a short period of time, so we would work on music and hang out, because we were that good of friends. Eventually we were like, "What's happening with these ideas, Chester? Are these for Linkin Park?" And he's like, "No, no, these are just my ideas. I don't really know what to do with them." So Ryan said, "Well, why don't we try to develop these, to just see what happens?" It was based off of what he was doing—it really wasn't about us, these were not Ryan and Amir ideas, which would have been Julien-K, basically. That way, Chester can be the singer, and it'd be tailored more toward him.

I think the first song might have been "Let Down." We went in and Chester hummed some bits and played a little bit of acoustic and then we created the entire track that you hear. He walked in a couple days later, and we're like, "Okay, Chester, so this is what we did with that little idea that you had." And he just lost his mind: "Oh my God, this is so cool!" He was running around the studio!

As far as the sound and Chester's influences, he had this grunge and punk background, and that was what I always sensed from him. Even though he would start some of these ideas on acoustic guitar, the feeling I would get definitely had a lot of attitude and would be translated into the music. But he was also good at writing these ballady songs, and there's quite a few slow songs on the record. It was really based on Chester's roots and ideas and was very different from Linkin Park—we were never really trying to compete with that.

All of us went through some dark times, and part of the catharsis was creating the album. Listen to the lyrics—there was a lot of shit going on. And we just took to each other, and we were able to sort of get rid of all these demons through the music. It's a very dark record, all the way around. I was recently relistening to everything, and it was just like, wow—a lot of it was right there, in his lyrics. That's the thing with Chester and Linkin Park: the music and the words really took what they were trying to say to the level that people connected with it. And with Chester as the vocalist, his delivery was so real and so felt, and the subjects were so on the money, that it just completely connected with people. With the Dead by Sunrise record, I think in some ways, it's almost too much—what he was saying, the feelings, it was so dark, but it was real. When you go back and you listen to the lyrics of that record, especially, this is him telling everyone where he was at.

Making the record and actually being able to tour with Linkin Park— I mean, this tells you what kind of friendship we all had. Mike went to Chester initially and said, "Look, why don't you premiere your Dead by Sunrise stuff with us onstage every night?" And Chester came to [Ryan and me] and we're like, "Are you fucking kidding? Are you serious?" Mike was like, "I want you guys to come out on the encore and play a couple songs, and this way we can introduce the band and everything." I mean, we were just blown away. And it tells you what kind of band they are, to do that. Mike was always very supportive of Dead by Sunrise. He liked the record, and he was very supportive of Chester doing it. A lot of bands, that wouldn't be the case.

There's only one Chester. We used to call him Ol' Golden Throat. There was a magic there! And it didn't just happen once—lightning struck many times. That's because there was an insane amount of talent in that band. They wrote great songs and they're great performers and there was a lot of chemistry. To me, the most important part of it all is that they were there for all these people all over the world and I'm sure have helped so many people get through some really rough times. I know that Chester would be very proud of that, and I'm sure Mike is, as well, and the rest of the guys. Chester's talent goes without saying, and I'm just grateful that I got to be the smallest piece of any of that. And to just be his friend.

CHAPTER 18

I N 2010, TWO popular rock groups released statement albums six weeks
apart from each other. Both bands had existed since the early 2000s, had
garnered immediate followings with their debut albums, and had been
increasingly displaying time-honored rock ambitions—nodding toward
the established canon, while not-so-subtly trying to join it.

That year, they released their respective shoot-for-the-stars full-lengths,
each bursting with instrumental grandeur and apocalyptic dread. Both
albums were designed to challenge their audiences while still being accessible enough to top the charts—and both did, in fact, reach No. 1 on the
Billboard 200, one in August and the other in September.

But then, a few months later, one of those two albums shocked the
world by winning the Grammy Award for Album of the Year. The other
one—Linkin Park's fourth album, *A Thousand Suns*—did not.

A month and a half before Linkin Park returned with its towering
full-length, Arcade Fire had released its third album, *The Suburbs*, an
expansive meditation on its titular subject that harnessed the Montreal collective's artsier indie-rock and Springsteen leanings into a sometimes tense,
often sumptuous listen. On Grammys night in February 2011, when Bar-
bra Streisand opened the final envelope and confusedly announced, "And
the Grammy goes to . . . *The Ssssuburbs*," it seemed like a true underdog
story had come to fruition—after all, those plucky Canadians were far
from the favorites in a category featuring albums by Eminem, Katy Perry,
and Lady Gaga.

In hindsight, however, Arcade Fire's Grammys triumph actually represented a summation. That win was the flash point of an indie-rock boom that had kicked off a few years prior—beginning around the time Linkin Park released *Minutes to Midnight* in 2007 and reaching a fever pitch around *A Thousand Suns* in 2010—and that would spend the next few years poking its head into popular music. What was cool in rock had once again been redefined, with the word *indie* the new nomenclature for the underground sensations that were overtaking the discourse (regardless of whether an artist was actually, you know, independent). It was the alternative explosion of the early nineties for a new generation—this time with blogs instead of alt-weeklies and YouTube instead of MTV.

And, like the alternative movement, the indie takeover didn't have one identifiable image or sound. There were the mass-appeal bands like Arcade Fire and Vampire Weekend (the latter also topped the albums chart in 2010), bearded folk interlopers like Bon Iver and Fleet Foxes, commercial-friendly synth-pop groups like Passion Pit and MGMT, and scruffy experimentalists like Animal Collective and Dirty Projectors.

In 2009, some of these groups released albums that received good reviews, and those reviews then led to sprawling, nearly arena-level audiences. That was the same year in which the bedroom-pop artist Owl City scored a No. 1 smash, "Fireflies," by making a song that sounded vaguely like the cult indie-pop duo The Postal Service; that was *also* the year in which Jay-Z, longtime friend and champion of Linkin Park, showed up at Grizzly Bear's Brooklyn show to groove to some art-folk jams, then said, "What the indie-rock movement is doing right now is very inspiring."

So much of that movement was influenced by *Pitchfork*, the Chicago-based online music publication (originally called *Pitchfork Media*) that regularly coronated left-of-center artists with its "best new music" album ratings. *Pitchfork* had even famously helped launch Arcade Fire by championing their 2004 debut *Funeral*, long before other publications had sniffed out a classic. *Pitchfork* became a mighty force concurrent to the rise of indie—launching its own music festival, issuing feverishly debated year-end lists, inspiring countless spinoffs and parodies—and did it all by telling music fans what was cool. If *Pitchfork* endorsed an album with a glowing review, a whole lot of people in search of the Next Big Thing were guaranteed to give it a listen.

So, what did *Pitchfork* think about Linkin Park? Well, it's not that Linkin Park were poorly reviewed by *Pitchfork*. It's that they weren't reviewed *at all*.

The site's hipster ethos clashed with anything too mainstream, including the major pop artists and rock bands of that period, whose albums came and went without critical assessment by the site. That stance shifted a bit over time: following its acquisition by mass media corporation Condé Nast in 2015, *Pitchfork* has more recently started reviewing albums by previously ignored megastars such as Taylor Swift, Adele, and Rihanna. Less common are reviews for major rock bands, though, which means that none of Linkin Park's albums were ever reviewed by *Pitchfork* upon their release.

Even if *Pitchfork*'s dismissal could be chalked up to brand maintenance by an indie-leaning publication, Linkin Park had long been shrugged off or downplayed by critics across the board. When *Hybrid Theory* was released, *Rolling Stone* bemoaned its "corny, boilerplate-aggro lyrics," the *Calgary Herald* waved it off as "trodden ground," and the *Indianapolis Star* dismissed the band as "derivative pretenders." Reviews of future releases were not much nicer: according to the review aggregator site Metacritic, Linkin Park's studio albums never earned an average rating higher than a barely okay 66 out of 100.

That high-water mark was achieved by *A Thousand Suns*, which, on paper, could have been the project to prime Linkin Park for long-overdue critical reappraisal and possibly give the band their first major-category Grammys nod since Best New Artist in 2002. These things can take time for arena-level rock bands: Coldplay received their first Album of the Year nomination with their fourth album, Foo Fighters did with their sixth album, and U2 did with their fifth album.

Linkin Park had successfully followed the U2 blueprint with "Shadow of the Day" from their previous album, a top 20 hit that served as their version of "With or Without You." It was a belt-along ballad, broad and undeniable enough to win over any unconvinced masses. And *Minutes to Midnight* was, in some ways, their *Joshua Tree*—the sonic leap forward with plenty of hits, a grown-up tone, and even an album cover where the whole band thoughtfully looks off into the distance.

To continue the metaphor, that made *A Thousand Suns* Linkin Park's *Achtung Baby*, the dark, image-destroying experiment that would wow listeners after confounding them. Whereas U2 became Grammys darlings with those projects—*The Joshua Tree* actually won Album of the Year, and *Achtung Baby* was nominated for the same award—Linkin Park was stuck on the outside looking in, watching bands like Arcade Fire enjoy the spoils of the indie explosion. What should have been a second, more critically appreciated phase of the band's career never came to be. After they scored a lone Grammys nod for "What I've Done" from *Minutes to Midnight*, Linkin Park earned zero for *A Thousand Suns* and were never nominated for a Grammy again.

"I'm not on some 'What I've Done' shit."

Mike's voice is even-tempered as always as his defeated bandmates sit around him in the studio, Rick Rubin hovering in the background and red string lights shining down on their shared exasperation. Mike's face is obscured during this key sequence in a making-of documentary for *A Thousand Suns*—blocked out by the giant computer monitor that he's parked behind in the studio—as the band and Rick try to come to an agreement on a first single for the album.

Brad doesn't hear a hit on the album, so they're considering writing more songs expressly for that purpose. Dave doesn't want to water down a bold project and shoehorn something "Linkin-Park-ified" onto the track list. Rick is staying Zen about the ordeal—"If it doesn't happen, then it's not meant to happen, because the songs we have are the songs that should be on the album," he offers—but Mike is hyperaware of looming deadlines. He knows that Linkin Park has a deal with video game juggernaut Electronic Arts to incorporate their new single into the trailer of an upcoming *Medal of Honor* game, and they have to deliver something soon.

"Just so you know that I know what you're talking about," Mike tells Dave, to acknowledge and subtly cosign his concerns about scrambling for a radio hit, "the kind of sounds that I was starting on, when I was trying to play around with this, was stuff like *this*." He then clicks the computer mouse, and a snippet of what sounds like an electrified sitar rings out in the studio. He clicks again, and the next snippet is a menacing industrial wipeout.

Mike's point is clear: they might have scored a top 10 hit a few years ago with "What I've Done," and then scored another with the similarly drawn "New Divide," but there would be no more carbon copies of that straightforward radio-rock sound. Linkin Park were about to get weirder—and whatever business partners they had were going to have to accept that.

Ironically, a lot of the sounds Mike was pulling from while conceptualizing Linkin Park's fourth album came from *Pitchfork*-approved instrumental electronic music of the late 2000s: British noise specialists Fuck Buttons, avant-garde hip-hop producer Flying Lotus, and dream-pop auteur Caribou were all in rotation for him at the time. He wanted to marry that hardware experimentation with the large-scale fearlessness of his favorite progressive rockers—Radiohead, Nine Inch Nails, Tool—who had never been afraid of alienating their audiences by shaking up their sounds.

"If we do it right," Mike said as the album was coming together in 2009, "it'll have a cutting-edge sound that defines itself as an individual record separate from anything else that's out there."

Encouraged by Rick, who signed up for a second go-round to coproduce with Mike after *Minutes to Midnight*, the band dismantled their sound to an even greater degree on their fourth album, toying with bongos, harmonica, vocoders, tambourines, shakers, and megaphones in their familiar studio home at NRG. All six members shared space to record gang vocals for the first time, bellowing *"NO!"* and *"WHOA-OA"* in unison on the song that would become "The Catalyst." Mike was the mad scientist mixing up a unique sonic concoction—picking through other tapes and

CDs, listening for uncommon drums, hunting for bangs and slams that intrigued him. At one point, the band recorded a broom being clanged onto the studio floor, hoping the sound would help unlock . . . something.

Ultimately, the band settled on a shadowy, industrial-influenced electronic rock undercurrent for the album and paired it with themes of nuclear paranoia, mass destruction, and technological dread. The album title came from J. Robert Oppenheimer, the father of the atomic bomb, quoting the *Bhagavad Gita* following the 1945 obliteration of Hiroshima and Nagasaki: "If the radiance of a thousand suns were to burst at once into the sky, that would be like the splendour of the Mighty One. . . . Now I am become Death, the destroyer of worlds."

Oppenheimer's voice is sampled on *A Thousand Suns*, as are famous speeches by Martin Luther King Jr. and Free Speech Movement activist Mario Savio. The band contorted the political righteousness of *Minutes to Midnight* into a type of social consciousness: instead of buying into the optimism of the early Obama era, Linkin Park tapped into the fear that America—amid a bitter recession and the endless war in Iraq—was experiencing in communities around them, the personal anger of their early albums now assigned to public service.

Linkin Park originally considered making *A Thousand Suns* a *concept album*, often using the phrase in press hits before the album was actually completed. Eventually, however, they pulled back on that tag. "This doesn't have a narrative; it's more abstract than that," Mike explained prior to the album's release. Similarly, there were early talks about incorporating the music from the album into an original standalone video game—the band's songs would have soundtracked the story of a mental institution patient developing superpowers—but plans were abandoned while the game was still in early development.

Considering all the audibles called during its creation, *A Thousand Suns* could have been crushed under the weight of the band's ambitions. In their mission to create a truly innovative fourth album, Linkin Park ended up with a project that had its "concept album" status nixed halfway through creation, that was almost the soundtrack of a goofy-sounding video game, that featured civic-minded spoken-word interludes and zero surefire singles.

And in spite of it all, they pulled it off.

A Thousand Suns is a bit too messy to be considered a full-blown masterpiece, but every inch of the album is buzzing with purpose—each synth line, drum fill, and group harmony shaking the listener with flexed muscles. MTV described *A Thousand Suns* as "Linkin Park's *Kid A*," with good reason: the juxtaposition of the mechanically rendered music and the human themes of fear and hope serves as a familiar through line, and like Radiohead did a decade earlier, Linkin Park took a sledgehammer to their sound without sacrificing the strengths of the band members' identities.

After rapping in small doses on *Minutes to Midnight*, for example, Mike comes alive on tracks like the vibrant reggae/rock/hip-hop triptych "Waiting for the End" and the cacophonous, Public Enemy–quoting "Wretches and Kings," while Rob's tribal booms bolster his rhymes on "When They Come for Me." "Burning in the Skies" offers some of Dave and Brad's smoothest interplay, with a swiveling bass and fingerpicked guitar (which later morphs into a showy solo), and the whole band reaches skyward on "Robot Boy" and "Iridescent," a pair of rousing chant-alongs with enough song craft to sidestep any bluster.

Then there's "Blackout," which can reasonably be described as "'March of the Pigs,' if Trent Reznor had added in a dancefloor breakdown." A gargantuan synth line gets teased in the intro and propels Mike's singing over a club thump in the second half; in between, Chester sings like he can't stop moving and shrieks like he wants to blow your house down, as Joe samples his screams and then loops them into a fidgeting bridge. "Blackout" could have feasibly been a single from *A Thousand Suns* if not for one of Chester's all-time blistering vocal takes. Instead, the song became one of the boldest in the band's catalog.

What *did* end up becoming the lead single, though, was "The Catalyst," which is about the furthest thing from "some 'What I've Done' shit" that the band could have possibly chosen. Instead of scrounging for a last-minute radio hit, the band opted for a five-and-a-half-minute electro-prog anthem with DJ scratching, plinking synths, doom-metal metaphors ("Like memories in cold decay / Transmissions echoing away / Far from the world of you and I / Where oceans bleed into the *skyyyyyy!*" Chester declares), and a second-half collapse into a sing-along refrain ("*Lift me uuuuup, let me gooooooo,*" Mike croons).

If "What I've Done" upended expectations for Linkin Park's rap-rock sound ahead of *Minutes to Midnight*, "The Catalyst" doused those expectations in gasoline and lit a match. The band's label was hesitant to service the song as the album's lead single, and it's not hard to imagine the Electronic Arts brass being dumbfounded when "The Catalyst" was delivered for the *Medal of Honor* trailer.

Yet somehow, just like its host album, the song works—propulsive in its tempo, absorbing in its intent, genuinely moving in its swelling finale. And that's ultimately all that mattered to Linkin Park.

"Let's stop trying to do things that other people want us to do, and let's get back to just being fluid and writing songs and coming up with ideas," Chester told his bandmates before deciding on "The Catalyst" as the lead single. And although the song only peaked at No. 27 on the Hot 100, it reached the top of the Rock Songs chart, with the *Medal of Honor* trailer helping spread the word. Today, "The Catalyst" stands as one of the band's most indispensable singles. It ended up being the right choice to lead their most adventurous album.

———————

TRY AS THEY MIGHT, ARTISTS do not have control over their acclaim—whether their work is appreciated in the moment, in a few years' time, in another generation, or never at all. *A Thousand Suns* earned Linkin Park some of the best critical reviews of their career upon its release on September 13, 2010, with *Kerrang!* crowing that the album "plots a remarkable course" and *Entertainment Weekly* nodding to its effect on "the kids who clamor for their headphone catharses," but other reviews were not as kind.

"They sound like a killer Linkin Park tribute band," *Rolling Stone* noted of "Wretches and Kings," and AllMusic's review begins: "Continuing their slow crawl toward middle age, Linkin Park opt for moody over metallic on *A Thousand Suns*." The mixed reviews doomed the album from ever becoming an awards contender; meanwhile, their contemporaries, Arcade Fire, crashed the Grammys in early 2011 a few months after *The Suburbs* earned raves across the board.

The lack of critical approval and awards recognition around *A Thousand Suns*—and Linkin Park, in general—can partly be explained by long-standing associations with rap-rock. Critics had pigeonholed the band into a movement, even as they waved their arms and shouted that they didn't belong to that movement. "We came out with *Hybrid Theory* at a time when nu metal was a thing," Mike said, "and every single chance I got, I told people, 'Don't put that flag in my hand—because I'm not going to hold it.'"

Linkin Park's fourth album is by no means a rap-rock album (at least, not in the traditional sense of their *Hybrid Theory* sound), but for some faction of the music industry, the band was inescapably associated with nu metal, despite protests from the band members themselves. Even now, as many forms of once-ignored popular music have undergone a critical reevaluation over the past decade, nu metal largely remains a punchline. In recent years, some of the bands that were once lumped into that movement, like Deftones and System of a Down, have been accepted by the critical consensus because their songs transcended that era, but many more artists have been frozen dismissively in that era, only to be revisited through snarky music-writer tweets and Woodstock '99 documentaries.

The nu metal tag was a hurdle for Linkin Park in their quest to be taken seriously, but in previous iterations of the music industry, they could have overcome it. Plenty of huge rock bands have transcended their original scenes—the Grammys didn't care about the "scenes" that U2 and Coldplay came from; they just wanted to herald their big, mainstream albums!

Yet a key factor in the indie explosion at the end of the 2000s was the transformation of the music industry itself, away from bands that could represent the monolith of pop culture. At a moment when Linkin

Park released a major rock opus, music listeners were pivoting away from major-opus albums altogether.

The advent of the MP3, with Apple's iTunes Store launching in 2001 as a means of legitimizing the illegal downloading wave that Napster had helped unleash upon the industry, gradually changed the way music was presented by labels and processed by consumers. Suddenly, listeners didn't have to buy a full album or physical single to hear their favorite song on demand—they could download tracks à la carte for ninety-nine cents each, create custom playlists, and tote them around in a clunky-looking device called an iPod.

In 2005, with physical single sales plummeting, the *Billboard* Hot 100 started incorporating digital download sales; by 2011, on the eve of the streaming revolution, digital album sales topped physical album sales for the first time. The indie boom was undoubtedly accelerated by these technological shifts as independent artists and catchy singles broke through in digital download stores without any radio or MTV support. Music was becoming more personalized—song collections accrued via word of mouth, then track lists were tailor-made with a few clicks—and that level of intimacy did not favor full-lengths by mainstream bands that were designed to be experienced as a whole from start to finish, like *A Thousand Suns*.

"When we were making the album," Mike recalled following the release, "in the very early stages, management suggested to us, 'Could you make something that we would release in smaller chunks? Because everybody's consuming music by the song. Couldn't you make EPs, where it was like three songs, and then do that a few times, every few months?'" Such artists as Lady Gaga, Usher, and Ke$ha were all doing the smaller-song-chunk releases around that time, but automatically, Mike and the rest of the band felt allergic to the idea. "It kind of felt like, that's what everybody else was up to," he explained. "People don't make albums anymore, and we grew up on albums. I love albums! So let's try to make space for it."

A Thousand Suns debuted at No. 1 on the *Billboard* 200, but with overall album sales greatly deflated and "The Catalyst" not as big a lead single as "What I've Done," it bowed with a little over one-third of the debut sales number (241,000 copies sold) of *Minutes to Midnight* (623,000 copies sold). As the band embarked on another international tour, another single, "Waiting for the End," performed well on the rock chart but didn't eclipse "The Catalyst," and *A Thousand Suns* effectively receded from popular culture. Linkin Park was still a giant brand name playing arenas around the world, but their most outside-the-box album had failed to produce smash singles, widen their fan base, or provoke critical respect.

The truth was, before *A Thousand Suns*, Linkin Park could have just remade "What I've Done" eight more times and probably scored eight more hits. "New Divide" was proof positive that they knew how to fashion an inconsequential rock-radio hit. They could have swallowed their creative restlessness, catered to fan expectations, and easily acquiesced to the industry's shifting tectonic plates.

Instead, they raged against the machine. *A Thousand Suns* represents a rejection of what they had already accomplished and a message of gut ambition—one that would remain prevalent with every album that followed.

"It's going to take people some time to figure it out and know what to do with it," Dave said of *A Thousand Suns* prior to its release. That's proven true in the years since: once the shock of its sound wore off, the album developed a cult following, with many fans championing songs such as "The Catalyst," "Blackout," "Waiting for the End," and "Iridescent" as some of the band's all-time high points. Although the way that Linkin Park moved forward with their fourth album was jarring in 2010, as more time passes, the album sounds increasingly essential to their journey overall.

A Thousand Suns "sold [fewer] copies than our other records," Mike said in 2012, "but it wasn't necessarily about selling copies—it was more about taking people on a journey and expanding the possibilities of what the band could do." That mission was summarily accomplished. Critics and award shows were not kind to *A Thousand Suns* at its release. Hopefully history will be.

CHAPTER 19

I T'S JANUARY 2012, the guys are back in NRG Studios, and Chester and Brad are piecing together Linkin Park's next hit single, so deep in concentration that barely a word is spoken between them.

Chester taps the side of his headphones with his middle finger, motioning to the control room that he needs sound, and Brad is behind the boards, noodling with a chord progression and trying to whistle through an in-the-works hook. He brings that melody into the live room with Chester, who closes his eyes and slightly bows his head as Brad whistles the "*Da-na-na-naaaaaaa-naaa, da da daa-daa-ba-na-na-naaa*" melody and taps his foot to keep time.

After a few seconds, Chester opens his eyes and grunts—he's got the melody. Suddenly, they move toward their respective positions—Chester to the vocal booth humming in falsetto, Brad to the control room to record him—like figure skaters darting through a choreographed routine. As Chester belts in the vocal booth, back in the control room, Dave taps a pencil against the boards, Rob leans against some equipment, and Joe polishes up what looks like a dragon in a sketchbook.

Brad's voice materializes in Chester's ear: instead of ending the melody with "*ba-na-na-naaa*," he suggests making that part a single escalating syllable, "*ba-aa-aa-aaa!*" Chester immediately understands and sings the new version back to Brad, whose hand instinctively flutters up alongside the rising voice. The other band members look on, teammates watching Brad hoist up an alley-oop to Chester in separate rooms. Brad points at Chester across the studio in appreciation. He nailed it.

The largely wordless action—captured in a 2012 episode of LPTV, the long-running web series that depicts the band's studio process and lifestyles in short video bursts—is nothing that the guys hadn't completed hundreds of times in the past, a series of tiny studio gestures that would someday result in a fully formed anthem. Linkin Park still had weeks to go before finishing the song that would become "Burn It Down," the lead single from their fifth album, *Living Things*; the melody that Brad and Chester were molding together would anchor the song's verses, but at that moment, it didn't yet have any words to match.

Chester and Mike still needed to sit side by side in front of a laptop at NRG, strengthening the song's themes of toxic cycles and inevitable destruction while finalizing the lyrics over a Mexican takeout lunch. Mike would suggest, "A little more-defeated sounding!" to Chester; later, Chester would eyeball Mike's scribbled rap verse while crunching on an apple and point out the lines where his cadence sounded rushed. Then they'd both listen to multiple vocal takes and distinguish the minuscule differences in delivery, both nodding at the slight uptick in emotion, before Chester ultimately declares, "That's the one."

There is magic in this mundanity. After more than a decade of working as a collective unit with zero lineup changes, the six members of Linkin Park had developed such an understanding of each other's artistic tendencies that songs were constructed through a fine-tuned shorthand.

Like any successful long-term relationship, communication was key: by understanding how to plainly navigate each other's skill sets and idiosyncrasies, the guys had long since solidified their individual roles within the larger group dynamic. That type of balancing act needs constant tending and often erodes in musical groups—there's a reason why so many of Linkin Park's musical influences, from Public Enemy to Red Hot Chili Peppers to Rage Against the Machine to Korn, have either reshuffled their lineups or taken long breaks away from each other.

Once Dave rejoined Linkin Park on bass right before the release of *Hybrid Theory*, however, the guys knew what they had. At all costs, they protected that chemistry, personal biases be damned.

"I think it's really important for young musicians to understand that this is the type of shit that usually breaks bands up," Chester said, referring to individual egos warring within a group dynamic. Mike added, "When we've got a problem—and believe me, we do—stuff's always coming up for any band—we can look in each other's face and say, 'This is a problem, let's fix it.' We like what we do as a band, and we don't want to be bummed out about any facet of it."

At the start of their second decade together, these roles were down pat: Brad, who was increasingly part of the production process, would bounce ideas back and forth with Mike in seamless bursts, while Rob, Joe, and Dave all understood how to ensure that the song was rhythmically secure. Rick Rubin, back for his third straight album coproducing with Mike, would offer up a fresh perspective in feedback on the song pieces that the band felt were ready for presentation.

And no one knew the contours of Chester's voice, the way to capture his timbre to best exemplify each of his words, better than Mike. "I love vocal producing—I didn't even know it was a job until I had done it for ten years," Mike explained later. "At some point, somebody asked me if we wanted a vocal producer on a track. I was like, 'What does that mean? That's specific to just vocals . . . ?' Chester was like, 'Why would we hire someone? I just do that with Mike.'"

Together, the band members' creative approach had evolved by the early 2010s. Beginning with *A Thousand Suns*, Linkin Park was "no longer making albums and then touring and then starting from scratch and making new albums," as Mike put it. Instead, the band was constantly writing, cobbling ideas together over weeks and months, and when those ideas started to congeal, they'd hit the studio and chip away at a new album. That change in the band's songwriting process ignited Linkin Park's most prolific stretch as recording artists: after making fans wait over four years for the *Meteora* follow-up and over three years after

Minutes to Midnight, the band knocked out three albums between 2010 and 2014.

That period began with *A Thousand Suns*; its follow-up, *Living Things*, arrived in June 2012, a scant twenty-one months later. The band knew that they needed something more like a back-to-basics album—they were proud of *A Thousand Suns* but also recognized the album represented a journey into the sonic wilderness. Linkin Park wanted to create a project that built on their recent songwriting forays while dialing down the production bombast, so they literally stripped away a lot of their recording equipment from *A Thousand Suns*. The goal, Mike explained, was to use only the most crucial sounds available: "If you can cut down on the number of pieces of gear," he said, "you can create a signature sound for the record."

New technology was on the band's side. Digital audio software had progressed enough over the previous decade, to the point where Linkin Park could piece together songs for their fifth album while hitting the road in support of their fourth. Instead of requiring an enormous studio rig in the back of their tour bus, as they did during the *Hybrid Theory* days, the band members could whip their laptops out of their backpacks and plug away just as efficiently. "We're working on new music as we're driving in the car to a venue or in our hotel room," Chester said in the middle of the *Thousand Suns* tour in 2011, "and when we come home, everybody works in their homes."

That's how "Burn It Down" came together: as the stems of a vibrant electro-rock workout under the working title "Buried at Sea" in 2011, unveiled as the band's most radio-friendly single in years in April 2012, and perfected with muted studio convergence in between. The lead single of Linkin Park's fifth album centers on an inability to resist taking something intricate and tearing it apart ("We're building it up / To burn it down / We can't wait to burn it to the ground," Chester roars on the chorus). It's a song about false idols in society as well as the lead singers' personal demons. It's an ode to destructive tendencies made by a group that avoided its own.

THE BAND'S PERSONAL PRIORITIES HAD evolved by the early 2010s, too. Linkin Park loved presenting their new material in concert but had grown to loathe the never-ending road life. "Touring for two years is excruciating," Chester said in July 2011, a few months after the band canceled a week of their North American arena run when he got sick and couldn't muster the strength to hit the stage. "When we would tour for two years, even the most resilient person in the band, at the end of that, was fucking miserable."

After plotting a grueling tour schedule in support of *Minutes to Midnight*—eighty-eight total shows in 2007, an additional seventy-four in 2008—Linkin Park pulled back a bit during the following album cycle, with a total of eighty-five performances spread between 2010 and 2011. At that point, the six members were in their mid-thirties—no longer young men built to withstand the grind of bus sleeping and road food for consecutive seasons.

At that point, the majority of the band were fathers: Brad and Elisa's son Jonah was born in 2008, and the following year, Mike and Anna welcomed their son Otis. While Linkin Park was touring behind *A Thousand Suns* in the first half of 2011, Dave and his wife, Linsey, were preparing to welcome their third daughter that October; the following month, Talinda Bennington gave birth to twin daughters, Lila and Lily. When the band wrapped up their 2011 touring in September, the baby boom ensured that their next album would be created in the midst of more dirty diapers than wild nights out.

With their family lives expanding, less time being spent on the road, and more songs being tinkered with in their respective home studios, it was only natural that Linkin Park's fifth album adopted a more intimate lyrical focus than its predecessor. "We chose the album title *Living Things* because it's more of a record about people," Mike said ahead of its release. "On the last few records, we've had an interest in global issues and social issues, and those things are still around, there are certainly traces of them, but this record is far more personal."

Gone are the spoken-word interludes and global meditations of *A Thousand Suns*, replaced by lean, single-length self-examinations about broken promises ("In My Remains") and ill-fated relationships ("I'll Be Gone"). The album's first offering, "Lost in the Echo," sets the tone immediately as a compact, electronically charged rap-rock song in the vein of *Hybrid Theory* opener "Papercut" on which Mike raps, "I can't fall back, I came too far / Hold myself up, and love my scars." The one-two wallop of "Victimized" and "Roads Untraveled" ushering in the album's second half is even more revealing. The first song finds Chester purging his past abuse by screaming, "VICTIMIZED! VICTIMIZED! NEVER AGAIN, VICTIMIZED!" and the second song ebbs from that unsettling catharsis, as the two frontmen sing in delicate unison and Chester croons, "May your love never end, and if you need a friend / There's a seat here alongside me."

Linkin Park's fifth album attempts to split the difference between the densely packed energy of their first two and the songwriting experimentation of their third and fourth, which results in a collection of songs with ample electronic textures between their many hooks. There is, notably, a *lot* of synthesizer here: "Burn It Down," another Hot 100 Top 40 hit for the band, is the album's sharpest moment, with the words that Chester and Mike ironed out together slicing through the thicket of programmed melodies and guitar blasts. On "Lies Greed Misery," Mike spits and Chester sings in battle together against a faceless bully as keyboard chords transform into an electron cloud of programmed fuzz.

Unfortunately, the step down from the grand scale of *A Thousand Suns* requires a barrage of hooks on par with that of *Hybrid Theory* or *Meteora*, and the songs on *Living Things* simply can't reach that level of immediacy. "I'll Be Gone" and "Powerless" more recall Chester's grunge-adjacent work with Dead by Sunrise than forge a new path forward, and "Until It Breaks" seemingly tosses Mike's sneered rapping, Chester's theatrical bridge, and an extended outro sung by Brad (!) into a haphazard rap-metal blender.

"Castle of Glass" arrives in the middle of *Living Things* as a red herring: a zapped tangle of synths, sampling, and programming, the imagery and structure resembling something closer to a country single, and Mike and Chester sell the grief-stricken metaphors about river bends and glowing novas. "Castle of Glass," which originated during the *A Thousand Suns* sessions, doesn't function like anything else on *Living Things*. It's both goosebump-inducing and frustrating—a fascinating rabbit hole that the band identified but didn't fully jump down on the album.

In fact, early in the creative process the band *had* briefly considered making their fifth album a full-on electronic project: 2012 was the apex of the electronic dance music (EDM) movement, when major dance acts such as Swedish House Mafia, Skrillex, and Avicii were headlining festivals and influencing the turbo-pop strain of the mainstream. The thought of a Linkin Park EDM album wasn't so outrageous—after all, a few months earlier, in late 2011 Korn had released *The Path of Totality*, a foray into dubstep and drum-n-bass that featured three Skrillex collaborations and several other notable DJs.

Mike was a fan of a lot of those producers and revealed in a May 2012 fan chat that management had suggested some EDM artists for the band to work with in the first few months of writing *Living Things*. Ultimately, those collaborations never came to pass. Although Mike was interested in further exploring that sound, he didn't want Linkin Park to feel like they were jumping on the "electronic bandwagon" and chasing a trend.

Instead, he scratched that itch on *Recharged*, Linkin Park's second remix album, which *was* released in October 2013. Like *Reanimation* a decade earlier, *Recharged* featured different artists spray-painting their artistic graffiti over the original tracks of the band's most recent album; unlike their first remix album, which was squarely a hip-hop project, *Recharged* was full of the dubstep wobbles and bass drops that defined popular EDM at the time. Rappers Pusha T and Bun B did pop by, but their flows were placed over fist-pumping dance tracks courtesy of producers Vice and Rad Omen, respectively.

Recharged also features one original track, "A Light That Never Comes," a big-tent dance collaboration with A-list producer Steve Aoki that sounds like the propulsive remix of a Linkin Park song that doesn't exist. The song was unveiled as an unlocked prize in *LP Recharge*, a free action-puzzle video game that launched on Facebook one month before the release of the *Recharged* album. In a futuristic setting when Earth's supply of natural resources has been depleted, players need to work together as Resistance fighters to battle evil robot oppressors and mine new forms of sustainable energy. Four days after the game launched in September 2012, Linkin Park's new single became available to users who had collected a certain amount of energy in the game, while a message on the LP Recharge website told those special players, "The Resistance still needs you."

The big drops of "A Light That Never Comes" are perfect for both bedroom headbanging *and* rhythmic club swaying. Linkin Park had never released a straight-up dance single like it before, but its intensity, with Mike's rapping matching the production's thump before Chester launches into a canyon-sized chorus, fits snugly into the band's oeuvre. With a song like "A Light That Never Comes," which reached the top 10 of the Hot Dance/Electronic songs chart, Linkin Park's hard-rock fundamentals were almost unrecognizable. Mike was continuing to push the band into unknown creative territory, and the rest of the group continued trusting him to do it.

LEADING UP TO THE RELEASE of *Living Things*, Mike noted that the album launch was the band's most rigorous since *Meteora*, as the band prioritized expanding outward onto new platforms. The release cycle included a multiweek, five-continent scavenger hunt aimed at the most hardcore fans; an NBA partnership, through which "Burn It Down" soundtracked that year's playoffs on TNT; deals with Formula 1 racing and the Euro Cup that brought the band overseas for sporting events and festivals; and an extensive, multi-playlist campaign with a rising Swedish streaming site named Spotify.

The marketing campaign helped *Living Things* debut at No. 1 with a first-week sales number comparable to that of *A Thousand Suns*, and another global tour (albeit one with even fewer total shows than the last) followed. Writing for the band's sixth album was already underway by the time the band returned home in August 2013, but a handful of passion projects would take precedence before it could be completed.

While Mike was working on *Recharged* and helping orchestrate its release with the video game tie-in, Joe was finishing *Mall*, his full-length directorial debut that he'd filmed during an eighteen-day down period in 2012. Based on the novel by Eric Bogosian and starring Vincent D'Onofrio, the film unleashes surrealist hell at a shopping center, as a violent addict, troubled college students, an adulterous businessman, and a bored housewife bounce off each other in a haze of drugs and sex.

Mall could have been a tired thriller with straight-to-video shock value, but Joe imbues the movie with the same distorted sense of reality that he'd picked up from helming Linkin Park's grittier visuals, from "Numb" to "Shadow of the Day." "The music videos, they're all experiments in themselves," Joe explained. "The songs themselves indicate some kind of structure that you're able to easily follow—you can choose to construct a concrete narrative or an abstract narrative, then experiment with some visual techniques to help punctuate the emotion. So, I took that attitude into the filmmaking, where the script has to be really solid, just like the way a song has to be solid for the videos to be even greater [than] what the song is by itself."

The band served as a support system for Joe as he forayed into feature films: Mike, Chester, and Dave all helped him compose the music for *Mall*, alongside Deadsy drummer Alec Puro. The soundtrack features a few older Linkin Park demos and a bunch of short experiments that Joe worked on with Alec to flesh out the score for the film; it mostly exists for completist fans, but the forty-seven-minute project is hardly slapped together. Songs like "White Noise," an opening-credits metal scorcher built around toy piano plinks, and "It Goes Through," a spooky electronic flicker that would have fit on *Living Things* (and might have originated during those sessions), function as fleshed-out Linkin Park tracks. The promise of new music from Linkin Park also helped draw interest in the film from the band's fans when *Mall* was released in theaters worldwide in October 2014.

Actually, Chester could have costarred in *Mall* if he had wanted to—he had dabbled in bit acting parts over the years, popping up in *Crank* in 2006 and a *Saw* sequel in 2010. Remember: he'd grown up believing he would find a life on the theater stage before he pivoted to a musical one. But as Joe was working on *Mall*, Chester had his hands full with a different sort of dream project.

In a move that left the rock world flabbergasted, Chester became the new lead singer of Stone Temple Pilots.

"Madness, I tell you! Madness is happening! I know, it's crazy, but it's true," Chester said in October 2013, a few months after taking over for longtime STP frontman Scott Weiland, who had helped the San Diego band become an alternative-radio stalwart in a post-grunge world. The long-tumultuous relationship between Scott and the rest of the band had unceremoniously ended with the singer's firing that February, and in May, Chester joined guitarist Dean DeLeo, his brother Robert on bass, and drummer Eric Kretz during a surprise performance at the annual KROQ Weenie Roast, which benefited the Recording Academy's MusiCares MAP Fund for musicians in need of addiction recovery treatment.

The assumption was this: Chester was doing the STP guys—whom he had known dating back to Family Values 2001—a solid, filling in with a spot performance for a good cause. Nope: Chester and Stone Temple Pilots soon debuted a new single, the deliciously aggressive rock track "Out of Time," at the Weenie Roast and announced that they had booked studio time together.

The Weiland-for-Bennington swap was startling: STP's iconic frontman had drenched his hooks in winking grooves and sex appeal in a way that Chester had never traded in throughout his career. But for Chester, Stone Temple Pilots' decade-long run beginning with their 1992 debut *Core* ranked high "on my list of music that defines big chunks of my life," he said, so the unlikely side hustle was too personally meaningful to pass up. And although abruptly taking over singing duties from a beloved front-man like Scott—while also serving as the frontman of your *own* best-selling band—sounds like a political minefield, Chester insisted that all parties involved approved of the move, including his Linkin Park bandmates.

"I wouldn't be doing it if I didn't get the blessing of my friends, you know?" he said. "It's the respectful thing to do; those guys deserve an opinion in it." For Mike, who was busy finishing up *Recharged* as Chester and Stone Temple Pilots plowed through an EP and plotted tour dates, his understanding of the side project was founded on the same level of trust that Chester had always extended Mike when he would nudge their band's sound away from its comfort zone or tackle a side project like Fort Minor. Plus, Chester had grown up adoring Stone Temple Pilots; Mike wasn't going to deny his friend and bandmate such a special opportunity. "We understand that's, like, one of his childhood fantasies coming true," Mike said of Chester, "and we knew he was going to come back."

High Rise, the debut EP of Chester Temple Pilots, was released three weeks before *Recharged* in October 2013, a hard-charging, likably scuzzy five-song collection in which Chester adapted his voice to the leather-jacketed whine befitting an STP record. The EP was supposed to be an appetizer for a more robust studio project, and Chester ended up leading the band on multiple relatively short tours over the next two years. But at the end of 2015, Chester formally bid adieu to Stone Temple Pilots, thanking the band for allowing him to live out a dream but explaining that he needed more time with his family as well as with Linkin Park.

There would be no Stone Temple Pilots full-length featuring Chester, just as there would be no second Dead by Sunrise album. As of this writing, Joe has yet to direct another feature film, and Mike has yet to helm a third remix album. In the end, these side projects were not as commercially viable for the band members as their work in Linkin Park, but they were fun and creatively fulfilling, and that was the whole point. A band less secure in its chemistry might not have made allowances for such extended detours. But the center always held for Linkin Park, a home that the six members could always return to after time away.

"You know, these guys have played such a special role in my life," Chester said of Linkin Park in 2014. "And not just in my career. When you grow in a relationship, you find out that the band [itself] doesn't matter. What matters is that we all get through life in the most productive situations we can possibly be in."

INTERLUDE

"They Took a Chance on Us"

Travis Stever, lead guitarist of progressive-rock greats Coheed and Cambria, reflects on opening for Linkin Park on their 2008 North American tour—which included the band's first performance at New York's Madison Square Garden—and how the live run changed his perception of their stage show.

With Linkin Park, I learned from touring with them—I think we all did—how much of a force they truly were. We were very lucky to be touring with them because we had never done a tour like that. We had done some opening slots here and there, but I feel like Linkin Park was one of the first really big bands in that world to ask us to come and support them. And when I say "in that world," I mean that had broken through, that's a household name. As far as I remember, that was the first big production like that that we had ever been part of. We weren't sleeping on our amplifiers anymore, and we were no strangers to the fact that success was possible as a musician, but we had never seen it at the scope that Linkin Park had yet. They chose Coheed to support them. They took a chance on us, and that was a big deal.

Showing up, I believe Brad was one of the first people we met, and he was so warm and seemed genuinely excited to have us. And then we met Mike, and then Chester; we met everybody throughout the day. And just that warmth and the genuine excitement—if you want me to be fucking honest, it was a relief. When you're dealing with big beasts like that, you're [worried] that it's like, "Hey, management set this up . . . ," you know? They had chosen the band, and they made us feel comfortable right away. Being an opening band is always going to feel a little weird because you're coming into somebody else's show. They're the reason why you're there. So the fact that they did that for us was a lesson in early touring. We looked back and could say, "How Linkin Park treated us really helped in knowing how you should treat everybody."

There are a lot of artists, especially in the metal community, who are like, "I've had to live this, I've been in the grind to create this." And these guys are bringing in this hip-hop, and they were all really good-looking, really neat and polished, and some people would be like, "Well, is it a boy band?" And I'm sure within the metal community they got a lot of shit, and with Coheed—with our catchy songs but also writing weird things, having concepts with our records, all a little socially awkward—we were no strangers to people canceling us out before they understood us. And of course, you [spend time with] Linkin Park, and it's like, "Wow, this band is very serious. And they're all so talented—individually, and as a unit."

So, like I said, we had never seen production like this. We had a backdrop and our lighting guy, and they had an incredible setup and production up the wazoo. We go up to do our soundcheck, and we're looking around like, "Holy shit." It's one of those, "I hope we get to do this someday!" kinds of thing. And so you get that edge to you—"Well, they're gonna rely on all this production!" Guess what? No. They got up there, they played their hearts out the same way we were, but they *also* had that production. And it just was one of those lessons—you don't need the production, but, damn, does it heighten the show. They could play just bare-bones, but they were bringing a whole other aspect with that production, and it was a sight to behold.

As far as the crowd, [Linkin Park] would play those early hits, so you have a rabid crowd who's just singing every word of those songs, and they already had digested most of the new material, too. So it's like, from production to performance to crowd, we were like, "Okay, this band is never going away."

Another time, they offered to have us jump in after [Hurricane Katrina] in New Orleans, and they were rebuilding there, and we went after they invited us to do a day with Habitat for Humanity. And both bands donated, and we all showed up, and we worked on a house that day. Granted, I don't think that the nails I was putting in—I think people were looking at us like, "You know what, we can do a lot better without your ass here," ha ha. But we wanted to help, and [Linkin Park] was like that. That was also a lesson—that if you're able to be up here performing, and all these people really care about your art, and you're actually making a living doing it, well then, give back. That's something they clearly stood behind.

I get frustrated when bands get thrown into whatever their era is or labeled whatever is the "in" thing at the time. Linkin Park being labeled as just nu metal is a disservice to all the art that they created because they've been all over the place. It would be the same as taking certain bands and saying, "Oh, they're just indie rock," or "They're just an emo band." Linkin Park created a certain sound, and they actually are a band that's transcended quite a few different sounds, so to me, the proof is in the pudding with the fact of how long they've stuck around.

If you go back to a song like "Numb"—that song was for that time period, and that was what Linkin Park was then. But if you go through the process of all the years that band's been around, they evolved, they changed. They had all these different sounds, but they still were Linkin Park. And that was a lesson to me about evolution—that you can't jump to a conclusion, that you can't have assumptions about what you're dealing with or where an artist might go. I personally was impressed by this band and realized how extremely talented they were, but really, talent wasn't even part of it. It was all about how innovative they were.

CHAPTER 20

F OR YEARS, CHESTER never stopped to consider Linkin Park's influence on the world of rock music. He had always been too busy moving on to the next show, album, and/or side project to sit still and stew on their big-picture cultural significance.

But then one afternoon, after the band had performed on a smaller-than-usual stage at an unfamiliar festival, everything snapped into place—and the realization barreled into him at full steam. It was less of a light bulb going off in his mind and more of a deluge of voices that finally gave him pause.

On June 22, 2014, Linkin Park played a surprise set at the Vans Warped Tour, the annual traveling fest that had served as a mecca for dozens of rock acts every summer since 1995. The band had never performed at Warped before—they had blown up so quickly with *Hybrid Theory* that they instantly outgrew a supporting slot, and anyway, the festival had always leaned more pop-punk and emo than rap-rock. That year, however, they agreed to hop aboard for one show at the date outside of their LA residences in Ventura. Warped Tour was built for up-and-coming bands young enough to play gigs for forty straight days in sweltering heat; for Linkin Park in 2014, a special one-off was more their speed.

The band played a seven-song set on the relatively tiny stage they had brought to Ventura themselves, in front of a packed crowd that was made aware of the unlisted appearance the day before the show. During each song, Linkin Park welcomed a different Warped-affiliated artist to join them onstage: Yellowcard's Ryan Key tenderly crooned the opening verse to "What I've Done," Finch's Nate Barcalow hurled his guts out on the "One Step Closer" bridge, Issues' Tyler Carter and Michael Bohn harmonized on "Faint," and for the finale, Machine Gun Kelly mashed up "Bleed It Out" with his song "What I Do."

When Linkin Park looked out into that Warped Tour audience, they viewed a ton of teens and twenty-somethings—crowd members who'd been little kids when the band first started out and maybe even a few young onlookers who hadn't even been born before *Hybrid Theory*. Then, before and after their set, the band heard a similar refrain from their stage guests and other Warped artists in their orbit, all day long, over and over: they've always listened to Linkin Park, their music had been influenced by Linkin Park, they learned how to exist in the industry thanks to Linkin Park.

"I always felt like we were the new guys, even after five records," Chester explained later. "Because it doesn't really seem like it's been *that* long. We've just been working and working, and so it's gone by really quickly."

But it finally hit Chester at Warped Tour, hearing all these artists speak about Linkin Park's long shadow: fifteen years had passed by in the blink of an eye, and now they were the veteran group, the ones who had influenced the new generation. "Literally every kid, every adult, every parent—every grandparent!—that I met that day was like, 'I grew up listening to your music,' and 'I wouldn't be up here, in this band, if it wasn't for you guys.'"

The funny thing was, five days before that surprise performance, Linkin Park had released an album designed for the thrashing young bodies of the Warped Tour mosh pits—part of the reason they wanted to play the festival. *The Hunting Party*, their sixth album, casts aside the softer edges and electronic impulses of their previous two albums for an avalanche of guitars, but it's less of a back-to-basics rock record because Linkin Park had never made a record this punishingly heavy.

The follow-up to *Living Things* started coming together while Mike was working on *Recharged*: the album was initially going to feature an electro-pop sensibility, continuing the natural progression the band was making over multiple full-lengths. Then, Mike panicked, realizing that everything was too close to what the band had already made. "I'm doing the exact same thing!" he realized, and felt compelled to snap himself out of the creative rut. So he started sketching a hard turn toward aggressive guitar rock, full of visceral darkness and full-blooded alt-metal.

Linkin Park left behind longtime West Hollywood studio home NRG for the album, decamping instead to Larrabee Sound and EastWest in the greater Los Angeles area. They also decided, for the first time since *Meteora*, not to make the album with Rick Rubin (who was already plenty busy with projects from Black Sabbath, Eminem, and Ed Sheeran, among others). Instead, Mike would coproduce with Brad to keep everything in-house. Dave explained that, when the band got to a point on *The Hunting Party* where "traditionally, we've taken it this far, let's bring a producer in now to get an outside ear to see what they think," they just kept going with the six of them, comfortable enough with the material to forgo another perspective. "Brad stepped up a ton in the studio," Dave added, "not just in playing but also in producing the record and helping to organize the process as well."

All the band members needed a change of pace like *The Hunting Party* was. Brad had long been losing interest in playing guitar while immersing himself in producing electronics-based tracks, and Mike pushed him to instead rekindle the fire that he had developed as a teen marveling at the technical wizardry of Metallica in his bedroom. Meanwhile, Dave was reminiscing about the post-hardcore giants At the Drive-In and wanted to deliver bass movements that listeners could obsess over, like he had with the ones on their 2000 classic, *Relationship of Command*.

Chester certainly felt at home on a pummeling rock project: "For me, heavy music is the easiest to write to, because that's what I grew up on," he professed. And Rob wanted to challenge himself as a drummer in general; recording the speed runs of *The Hunting Party* ended up being so physically taxing that he needed to lift weights and work with a trainer to keep up with each song. "He eventually went to a chiropractor," Mike said with a laugh, "because he threw his back out playing drums."

The end result is a Linkin Park album that plays out like the type of detour usually reserved for their side projects. The band is clearly having a blast battering the grimy, neck-snapping songs on *The Hunting Party*, even if the songwriting never rises to the level of their strongest work.

Some of the shots taken on *The Hunting Party* are downright daring. There's a purposely disorienting metal jab with robo-voice effects ("Keys to the Kingdom"), a two-minute punk shredder about global atrocities ("War"), and a vaguely defensive closer with virtuoso guitar and drum work that sprawled into the band's longest song ever ("A Line in the Sand"). There are also, for the first time, featured artists on a Linkin Park album. Rage Against the Machine's Tom Morello, System of a Down's Daron Malakian, and Helmet's Page Hamilton all show up as guests on *The Hunting Party*, as a means for the band to both honor and have fun with some of their most talented idols and peers.

The one-for-us indulgence of *The Hunting Party* is encapsulated by lead single "Guilty All the Same": Linkin Park chose to precede their sixth album with a jumbled, nearly six-minute-long thrash song about corporate greed, with an extended body tremor of an intro and an out-of-nowhere guest verse from NYC rap god Rakim. "Guilty All the Same" makes "The Catalyst" look like "Jessie's Girl"—that's how unapologetically anti-commercial it was as a lead single selection.

But at that one Warped Tour, when the band was joined by members of metalcore band the Devil Wears Prada, "Guilty All the Same" rang out with pit-ready riffs and stormy intensity, placed, as it was, in the middle of a set full of older hits. It was as if the band was declaring, in front of young fans and young bands, *Hey, we can keep up with the kids, too.*

———————

"Guilty All the Same" "was too ROCK for radio," Chester tweeted in 2017, long after *The Hunting Party* cycle had unceremoniously concluded and the album became Linkin Park's first failure to produce a single Hot 100 hit.

The band understood from the beginning of the campaign that such a raw, pop-allergic album would be a hard sell commercially, but even with a marketing rollout as robust as the launch of *Living Things*, *The Hunting Party* was Linkin Park's first album since *Hybrid Theory* to miss the top of the *Billboard* 200 chart, debuting at No. 3. Although "Guilty All the Same" predictably didn't catch on at rock radio, its slightly catchier follow-up singles, like the atmospheric yell-along "Until It's Gone" and the rap-metal stomp "Wastelands," didn't fare any better.

In a career full of mind-boggling success, particularly when it came to radio, *The Hunting Party* was Linkin Park's first time being shut out in all formats. You'd be hard-pressed to catch "Guilty All the Same" while tuning in to your local rock station in 2014. But oddly enough, you'd probably hear a couple of bands that sounded a whole lot like classic Linkin Park.

A few months before the release of *The Hunting Party*, "Radioactive," by the Las Vegas rock quartet Imagine Dragons, made history. After being released on their 2012 album *Night Visions*, the single logged seventy-seven weeks on the Hot 100 by early 2014, surpassing the record previously set by Jason Mraz's "I'm Yours" to become the longest-running hit in the fifty-five-year history of the chart (and eventually reaching eighty-seven weeks on the chart).

Imagine Dragons broke through to the mainstream with their folk-leaning hit "It's Time," but "Radioactive" was a total game-changer—reaching No. 3 on the Hot 100 by crossing over to pop radio, turning *Night Visions* into a multiplatinum smash, and eventually growing into one of the forty biggest songs of the entire decade. And Linkin Park's influence on "Radioactive" is unmistakable.

As an electro-rock anthem with a heavy smattering of dubstep wobble, postapocalyptic imagery, and an oversized pop hook, "Radioactive" accumulates the sounds and themes that Linkin Park was exploring on *A Thousand Suns* and *Living Things* and constructs them into a muscular, undeniable howler instead. "Radioactive" wasn't a rap-rock song, but it became one at the 2014 Grammys, when Imagine Dragons performed alongside an up-and-coming rapper named Kendrick Lamar and mashed up their hit with his song "m.A.A.d city." The team-up was made available as a remix after the awards ceremony, a "Numb/Encore" for a new generation.

Throughout Imagine Dragons' commercial run over the next decade—as singer Dan Reynolds began rapping more on hits like "Believer" and "Whatever It Takes," and their collaborators ranged from hip-hop artists such as Lil Wayne and J.I.D to electronic producers including Kygo and Avicii—the band's ability to stream disparate elements into their accessible rock brand helped them unlock new audiences and kept them omnipresent on different platforms. Linkin Park had informed this ability because they were part of Imagine Dragons' sonic DNA. "Linkin Park has been and always will be one of the greatest bands of our generation," Reynolds acknowledged on Twitter in 2018. "Got me through many dark years growing up."

While Linkin Park were hopscotching across North America, China, and Europe in support of *The Hunting Party* during the summer of 2015, another rock group that prioritized rapping was transforming into the biggest new band at alternative radio. Twenty One Pilots, a duo from Columbus, Ohio, who took four albums to develop a grassroots fan base and top the charts, aren't direct descendants of Linkin Park's sound—there's rap-rock on their 2015 breakthrough *Blurryface*, to be sure, but also emo vocals, pop-punk refrains, and even some grooving dub production. And unlike Imagine Dragons' Reynolds, whose clear delineation between burly singing and nimble rapping recalled Chester's and Mike's split approaches, Twenty One Pilots' Tyler Joseph raps in a more conversational manner, as if his melodies need to speed up into rhymes so that he can convey more thoughts per minute.

Yet it's hard not to hear Linkin Park's lyrical impact on Twenty One Pilots' biggest hits, which absolutely dominated rock formats over an eighteen-month period and turned the duo into arena headliners. "I just wanna stay in the sun where I find / I know, it's hard, sometimes! / Pieces of peace in the sun's peace of mind," Joseph sings to open "Ride," a reggae-infused smash whose themes of finding purpose amid thoughts of death harken back to a song like "Somewhere I Belong." "Heathens," which exploded in 2016 off of the *Suicide Squad* soundtrack, is a moody outsider's anthem in which the emotional trauma that Linkin Park had been exploring for over a decade becomes a show of understanding and then solidarity. "Please don't make any sudden moves," Joseph croons in a downcast singsong, "you don't know the half of the abuse."

"Stressed Out," the most ubiquitous of Twenty One Pilots' hit singles, focuses on personal anxieties—not surprising, given its title—and was emblematic of the type of explicit mental health discussions that could suddenly exist in mainstream rock music and leap over to pop radio in the years after Linkin Park songs broke through. Twenty One Pilots had been singing about mental health long before breaking big with *Blurryface*, and with the days of alpha-male post-grunge and nu metal long gone, that unguarded songwriting helped turn them into stars. Even though Twenty One Pilots were addressing different kinds of personal issues than Linkin Park, their truthful examinations of self-doubt and loneliness similarly connected with listeners of all ages.

Really, a direct line can be drawn from Chester scream-singing on "Crawling" in 2000, "I've felt this way before, so insecure," and Joseph rapping on "Stressed Out" in 2015, "I was told, when I get older, all my fears would shrink / But now I'm insecure, and I care what people think." These were highly vulnerable sentiments, but they were not uncommon feelings for listeners, and they have resonated across generations—combined, those two songs have been streamed more than two billion times.

So, although *The Hunting Party* may have been a megaphone shriek that didn't impact the mainstream, one need only look at the biggest bands in rock music around the time of its release to see that Linkin Park's influence was very much thriving.

To THEIR CREDIT, LINKIN PARK were not trying to mimic the perspectives of bands like Imagine Dragons and Twenty One Pilots in the mid-2010s.

There was no point to being "aggressive for aggressive's sake," as Mike put it, and chasing the next millennial-angst anthem.

"We're thirty-seven-year-old adults making a loud record," Mike explained prior to the release of *The Hunting Party*. "And what makes a thirty-seven-year-old angry is different than what made us angry back in the day."

The most complete song on *The Hunting Party* serves as the perfect example of what Mike meant. "Mark the Graves" successfully pairs the heavy rock aesthetic that the band aimed for on the album via an extended thrash intro that never flags in energy with a poignant Chester performance in which he struggles between leaving trauma buried in the past and painfully exploring it to better inform the future. "No trace of what remains / No stones to mark the graves / Only memories we thought we could deny," Chester laments, guitar buzz cutting through his conflict before the song opens up into the throaty wail of the chorus. It's a mature brand of fury: whereas Twenty One Pilots' "Stressed Out" gets clammy when considering an uncertain future, "Mark the Graves" tries to process an uneasy past and pangs of regret, like a therapy session that lets the listener scream along.

"Mark the Graves" was not released as a single, never really cracked the band's setlist during their tour in support of the album, and is one of the least-streamed songs from one of the band's least-streamed projects. But still, like every Linkin Park song, it has its staunch defenders.

In 2020—during one of Mike's many midpandemic Twitch streams, when he'd spend hours tinkering with new tunes and live-chatting with fans—Mike noted that he had listened to "Mark the Graves" recently. That's because "a bunch of Peruvian Linkin Park fans did a playoff bracket of Linkin Park songs," he explained. A few people in Peru were outraged that "Mark the Graves" hadn't been included in that online bracket, so Mike clicked play on the song six years after its release. After another listen, he confirmed: yup, still one of his favorites from that record.

The fan bracket in Peru demonstrated just how far Linkin Park's reach had stretched, but in many ways, the band never lost the connection with fans that had formed in 1999, when they were sending MP3s of their rough sketches to kids in chat rooms and mailing merch out of Rob's apartment. Since 2001, Linkin Park Underground grew alongside Linkin Park as a forum to dissect every second of music, pore over and archive tour minutiae, zoom in on the meaningful details, and then pull out to the overarching themes that united the fandom.

The *LP Underground* albums, which were sent out for sixteen straight years, have functioned as a sort of secret handshake for hardcore listeners: fans who have dug deeper into Linkin Park's discography can compare the demos and different versions and can debate the live oddities and crate-dug remixes with like-minded obsessives. And to their credit, there are plenty of meaningful moments across the *LPU* albums, many of which are fairly accessible on YouTube today.

"Primo," a nearly six-minute version of "I'll Be Gone" from *Living Things* that was released on *LP Underground XIII* in 2013, remains a beloved demo thanks to the extended propulsion of its delicate features. But there's also "Pale," a haunting instrumental recorded during the *Minutes to Midnight* sessions; "Symphonies of Light Reprise," a poignant acoustic reinterpretation of "The Catalyst"; "Chance of Rain," a shuffling electro-pop song with a lovably restrained vocal performance from Chester; and countless others to mine and embrace.

Beginning in 2010, fans planned meetups during the band's tour dates: dubbed LPU Summits, these informal conferences reached London, Sydney, Tokyo, and Chicago, among other cities, and Linkin Park would join in, toasting the group hangs with one-time-only acoustic performances designed for completists. The LPU remains a robust community today, with an active Discord server, newsletter, merch store, and over a decade of exclusive tunes for new and longtime members to enjoy.

Yet, like any hardcore fandom clustered within a mainstream listenership, Linkin Park Underground remains just one faction of a much wider base—countless admirers and appreciators in every corner of the planet, many of whom only know the biggest hits, many others who love to vocally rally around an esoteric project like *The Hunting Party*.

Linkin Park fandom has naturally evolved over the years with the band, their sound, and the world around them. Some skeptics that initially dismissed *Hybrid Theory* as nu metal became converts within a few albums' time; the "What's your favorite song on THIS album?" discussions leaped from AOL instant message boxes to MySpace forums to Reddit threads over the years. Communication has been crucial in every iteration of Linkin Park's fandom, just as it has been within the band. Debates, recommendations, experienced remembrances, and general fits of passion still course through online and IRL discussions. Questions like "What song means the most to you?" receive dozens of comments on the official LP Reddit forum, and statements like "I relate more to Linkin Park in my thirties than I ever did as a teenager" garner hundreds of upvotes.

As the band members grew from crowd-surfing twenty-somethings into adults and fathers, Chester, Mike, Brad, Dave, Rob, and Joe always understood that maintaining a respectful relationship between artist and fan was a sacred balancing act. After all, they had spent their pre–Linkin Park days on the other side of the fence, finding purpose in the songs they played on repeat and the bands they watched from the crowd. They inherently knew the power of that bond and took great pains to preserve it, both across the internet and in person. Linkin Park's message has fundamentally helped every type of fan in some way, whether for a few seconds of headbanging euphoria or a lifetime of feeling seen.

"We've done meet-and-greets with our fans every night, every performance we've ever done," Chester pointed out in August 2014, a few days before Linkin Park's North American tour in support of *The Hunting Party* and a few weeks before the 10th LPU Summit. "For us, honestly, meeting our fans is pretty mellow, so when we're out on the street in our daily lives, we meet people all the time, every day, who are fans, and us being accessible to a certain degree is really important to us. We've been able to thankfully keep our private lives private and share our professional lives with our fans, and everybody's been really respectful of all that.

"And it's really cool to be in Linkin Park," Chester continued, "and kind of be a normal person at the same time."

PART V

THE LEGACY

CHAPTER 21

I T STARTS WITH one clear-eyed admission: "I don't like my mind right now."

Linkin Park struck the match that lit the song "Heavy" one day in 2016 when Chester walked into the studio, joining Mike and Brad as well as songwriters Julia Michaels and Justin Tranter. Mike asked him how he was doing.

"Oh, I'm fine," Chester answered. A few minutes passed, and suddenly, Chester piped back up. "Y'know what?" he told the room. "I have to be honest. I'm *not* fine. I'm *not* okay. Too much stuff is just happening to me. I just feel underwater."

What began as a dialogue among friends about destructive thoughts and crushing anxieties stretched outward to include the band and their new collaborators and eventually anyone who could listen and relate. And this conversation would start to form the lead single to the band's seventh album.

In another era, on another album, Chester's studio confessional might not have been immediately translated into a new track, but Linkin Park were once again trying something different with the follow-up to *The Hunting Party*. Typically, the band would start a song with a musical foundation and melodic structure, then retrofit the lyrics to match the production. With this project, however, they wanted their lyrical ideas to inspire their musical decisions.

"We've focused almost exclusively on songwriting," Brad said when the album was still in the works, "not on sound, not on genre, not on arrangement—on words and melodies."

So the band translated Chester's blurted frustrations into a song about feeling stuck in an unwanted cycle of thoughts and overcoming that sequence by identifying those fixations as self-imposed, just like Chester had done in the studio that day. Chester needed that first line to really pop: "To me, an opening lyric is so important," he explained. Unlike the band's biggest singles—"One Step Closer," "In the End," "Numb," "What I've Done," all of which include a table-setting instrumental intro—"Heavy" essentially begins with Chester's voice, alone and a bit wobbly, like a video that opens on an extreme close-up. He arrives two seconds into the song, after a production whoosh snaps into silence; it's all noise that his opening decree, "I don't like my mind right now," wishes to drown out.

Within those words, Chester specifies his anger—he doesn't like his *mind*, not himself, as if his brain is waging war with the rest of his being—and exhales on the word *now*, cautiously breathing an inner battle into reality. Chester wanted to hook the listener immediately, to speak as directly into their ear as possible. "What makes it a challenge on a song like this," he clarified, "is that you have a lot fewer words. So every word counts more. And if you get the words just right, I feel like there's a poetry in them in a way to portray your train of thought that's bigger than the sentence that you would have said, you know?"

The reason for each word's significance: every line of the song has been sanded down into a compact pang about feeling trapped with unwanted thoughts. "Heavy" is, above all, a pop song. The irony of Linkin Park following their most blistering hard-rock album, *The Hunting Party*, with arguably the softest-sounding single of their career—and then naming that single "Heavy"—goes without saying.

But, of course, the emotional weight of that single more than justified its title: sculpting the deeply personal into the unabashedly universal is what Linkin Park had always done, but never with this combination of undecorated pain and Top 40 catchiness. As "Heavy" progresses, Chester offers more plot points in the story of his mental struggles: he wishes he could slow things down, he drives himself crazy, he keeps dragging around what's bringing him down. And he does so with pillowy melodies over atmospheric programming and finger snaps. In the spring of 2017, hearing "Heavy" on pop radio and feeling bowled over by the devastation of Chester singing "I'm holding on / Why is everything so heavy?" felt like an effective jostle.

Perhaps *One More Light*, the band's seventh album, was always destined to be far more hummable than the *Guitar Hero* theatrics of *The Hunting Party*. Linkin Park committed to the lyrics and hooks guiding the album more than to the riffs and beats, but then, according to Mike, the guys had been in the habit of "reinventing the band, to some degree," with each successive project since *Minutes to Midnight* a decade earlier. *The Hunting Party* had been a course correction from the chewable electronica of *Living Things*, which had in turn been a change-up from the sprawling sonic tapestry of *A Thousand Suns*. "In order for each album to feel really interesting and fun to make, for me, I wanna go in learning something," Mike elaborated.

After the *Hunting Party* tour concluded in the fall of 2015, Mike spent some time in London meeting with a few British songwriters, such as Justin Parker, who had cowritten "Video Games" with Lana Del Rey, and Eg White, who had co-penned Adele's "Chasing Pavements," and he picked their brains about their processes. Linkin Park had always written their songs in-house, aside from the handful of guest artists on *The Hunting Party*; the band had long resisted trends, but in the back of their minds, the thought of working with new-school hitmakers and receiving a commercial jolt might have been intriguing. But Mike was also genuinely excited about craft more than results—to hear these expert studio minds describe their methods and to imagine how such techniques could contribute to the band's aesthetic. "It's just, like, having more ideas in the room," he explained.

As a result, more than a dozen outside songwriters and producers are credited on *One More Light*, including some of the industry's most prolific pop scribes—JR Rotem, Jesse Shatkin, RAC, and Ilsey Juber, in addition to Parker and White. The presence of Michaels and Tranter as cowriters on "Heavy" represented a harbinger of the album's hard turn away from hard rock in favor of a more commercial, accessible sound. While Michaels scored a pop hit of her own with the similarly self-lacerating single "Issues" in January 2017, she and her writing partner Tranter were credited in the liner notes of albums by Britney Spears, Nick Jonas, and Fifth Harmony prior to working with Linkin Park. On May 18, 2017—one day before the release of *One More Light*—Selena Gomez unveiled the kicky single "Bad Liar," cowritten by none other than Michaels and Tranter.

As if their behind-the-scenes contributions didn't scream "mainstream" loudly enough, "Heavy" also featured a guest alongside Chester: Kiiara, the alt-pop singer-songwriter who had scored an unexpected top 20 Hot 100 hit with her 2015 single "Gold" at the young age of twenty. Instead of having Chester wrestle with his thoughts on his own, the band constructed "Heavy" as a duet, the first in the band's entire run with a female vocalist and one who, when *Hybrid Theory* was released, had been five years old.

Maybe "Heavy" would have turned into a jump-the-shark jumble, with so many cooks in the kitchen and such blatant crossover aspirations, following the disappointing performance of *The Hunting Party* if Chester's studio outpouring hadn't served as its bedrock. At that point, however, he and his bandmates were veterans of translating that raw spirit into a song that millions of people could see themselves in. They would do so again with an approachable, and genuinely affecting, pop single.

"Heavy" played to listeners on rock, alternative, pop, and adult Top 40 formats in addition to racking up hundreds of millions of streams. The song became Linkin Park's biggest hit in a half decade. It also set the stage for what was arguably their most audacious musical foray and their most personal album yet.

IN FEBRUARY 2017, A FEW days after "Heavy" was released, Chester was asked about what inspired the opening line of the song during a KIIS-FM radio interview with JoJo Wright. The video of the interview shows Chester, head shaved down to a patch of black stubble and red flannel shirt buttoned up to the top, searching for words in the brightly lit radio studio, trying to convey the circumstances that make him overthink things, and coming up short.

Finally, he points both index fingers at his temples, taps the tips on his head, and leans into the microphone. "This place right here?" Chester says to the radio DJ, finger firmly on the side of his forehead. "This skull right here, between my ears? That is a *bad* neighborhood, and I should not be in there alone!" JoJo chuckles heartily as if his guest is telling a self-deprecating joke, but then Chester puts his hands down and keeps talking, and the DJ stops laughing. "I don't say nice things to myself," Chester continues. "Like, there's *another* Chester in there"—finger back on forehead—"that wants to take me down."

Chester was struggling prior to the release of *One More Light*, and he was candid about the darker pieces of himself that inspired the album. "This time last year, I was a mess—a total wreck," he tells JoJo later in the same interview.

Actually, roughly two years before the *One More Light* album cycle kicked off, Chester was physically incapable of taking the stage. On January 18, 2015, the band was in Indianapolis on the third date of their North American tour in support of *The Hunting Party*, and while playing basketball with members of the opener Of Mice & Men on the day of the show, Chester went up for a layup, and on the way down, his right foot landed on a water bottle. He was writhing around on the hardwood within seconds and left the basketball court in a wheelchair.

"My ankle's broken," he told Brad a few hours later, propped between crutches backstage at Bankers Life Fieldhouse in Indianapolis. With folded arms and thoughts likely on the month left of their tour, Brad asked, "What's the recovery time on that?" Chester replied, "A long time!" and laughed at his own misfortune.

Chester gave it a go that night in Indianapolis, arriving to the LPU meet-and-greet in a boot and on a scooter and heaving himself onstage in crutches, which Mike had painted black. But the next day, it was determined that his ankle required surgery. The sixteen remaining dates on

Linkin Park's nineteen-date tour were canceled, and the band chose not to make up the scrapped shows. After Chester wrapped up his final tour with Stone Temple Pilots in late 2015, Linkin Park stayed off the road for the entirety of 2016—the first year in their history with zero full-band performances.

Although Chester had previously suffered midtour injuries—his wrist needed stitches following an ill-advised platform jump during a 2007 show in Melbourne, and shoulder surgery forced the band to cancel a 2011 festival gig—the broken ankle occurred as he was creeping closer to forty and feeling tired of constant physical therapy. He was medicating to reduce the aftereffects of the injury and "having issues with that, kind of falling back into old habits," he later admitted.

As the recovery for his ankle dragged on—his right foot sporting plates and screws post-reconstructive surgery—Chester, irritated, worried that all his personal and professional relationships were becoming strained. Only one part of a multileg tour had been canceled, but that injury made Chester feel as if a load-bearing wall in his life had been removed, and everything else felt more difficult. "And that," he said, "took me into a depression that was really hard to get out of."

Chester's problems had multiplied by the time Linkin Park hunkered down on their seventh album in 2016. By then, his stepfather had passed away from cancer, and so had Amy Zaret, a twenty-five-year Warner Bros. Records veteran who had shuttled the band between Midwest radio stations in their early promo days. He was also struggling with his guilt for leaving Stone Temple Pilots without a singer, especially after Scott Weiland passed away from an accidental drug overdose in December 2015. At the start of the writing process for *One More Light*, Chester even had a song on his phone titled "I Hate the World Right Now." He knew that a lot of his suffering was self-inflicted, but still, he wanted to be left alone.

In August 2016, Chester suffered a three-day relapse in which he blacked out from alcohol. He continued drinking through the following months, trapped in a nihilistic spiral. "I even told one of my therapists at one point, 'I just don't want to feel anything,'" he said.

What pulled Chester out of that murkiness and helped him recommit to sobriety as the *One More Light* era kicked off were the same resources he had previously maintained for years: professional treatment (in this case, an outpatient program), the love of Talinda and his kids, the support of his bandmates and friends, and the focus that a new Linkin Park project instilled in him.

This time around, he reached out for help despite his instinct for solitude and found the conversations helpful. He was reminded to center his thoughts not on his flaws but on the fullness of his life: "I have a beautiful wife, great kids, awesome job," Chester enthused in April 2017. Before he talked about being a "total wreck" a year earlier on KIIS-FM, Chester had begun the interview glowing with pride describing his five-year-old daughter's current penchant for dropping F-bombs after her very first word was *shit*.

When Chester started talking publicly about *One More Light*, the physically and emotionally broken pieces of himself had begun to heal—but those wounds naturally made themselves visible throughout the songwriting process, particularly as Linkin Park prioritized lyrical expression during the album's creation. In the song "Talking to Myself," which empathizes with Talinda, Chester adopts her perspective as she tries to get through to an addiction-ravaged husband ("Tell me what I gotta do / There's no getting through to you / The lights are on, but nobody's home," he sings). "Sharp Edges" and "Halfway Right" both touch on Chester's refusal to follow easy advice, with the latter begging his adolescent self to slow down on the night he was so high that "I woke up driving my car."

For Chester, documenting those thoughts and memories could have made *One More Light* sound like a harrowing journal, one that would've been particularly excruciating to flip through over and over again across a months-long promo cycle. Instead, he embraced the opportunity to share his experiences and connect with even more listeners; as he tweeted in early 2017, "The new record is my favorite to date!"

———————

IT'S EASY TO UNDERSTAND WHY so many Linkin Park fans and hard-rock listeners disagreed when they first heard it.

One More Light is not just a pop album. It's a brightly colored collection of sing-alongs, with "*na na na*" refrains, chipmunked vocal hooks sprinkled throughout the warm production textures, layered guitars pushed into the background, and not a single Chester scream. Its hyper-catchy coziness functions as the antithesis of *The Hunting Party*'s thrash wizardry—in a way that an A to B comparison would make unfamiliar listeners conclude the albums were made by two totally different bands.

It was one thing for Linkin Park to whirl away from an old sound on a new album. It was another to make a record that anyone who loved the last one was seemingly guaranteed to hate.

"We're not trying to pick fights with those fans," said Mike, who acknowledged that the arena crowds who were watching Linkin Park play metal shows eighteen months prior might feel bewildered when they got their hands on *One More Light*. "Just like everybody, we've got different moods. There are times that you want to *listen* to different music, and there are times that you want to *make* different music."

At the time, Mike was emphatically declaring that "genre is dead"— and the music industry was changing in a way that just so happened to agree with him. By 2017, streaming had established itself as the dominant form of music consumption: on-demand audio streams totaled over four hundred billion, up 58 percent from the previous year. Meanwhile, digital album and track sales continued to plummet, as the iTunes model gave way to the on-demand streaming of Spotify, Apple Music, and YouTube Music.

Different types of music were still subcategorized on those streaming platforms, but genre lines were evaporating: instead of being relegated to different sections of a record store, different sounds were available at everyone's fingertips. And rock radio, which had helped catapult Linkin Park to stardom at the turn of the century, was not as crucial for audience engagement as it had been back then, so why not color outside the lines a bit on *One More Light*?

Linkin Park knew that their fans could appreciate both body-crunching hard rock *and* feathery pop music and had the ability to click and drag both sounds into a single, customized playlist. And anyway, it's not like they hadn't already been toying with genre and appealing to the mainstream since they first broke out. "'In the End' is a *pure* pop song," Chester asserted. "That was on the first record and is the biggest song of our career. It's been this way for twenty years."

Still, the sound of *One More Light* proved such an extreme pivot toward pop that, even as "Heavy" was performing well on radio and streaming platforms and the album was headed toward the top of the *Billboard* 200 chart after *The Hunting Party* failed to hit No. 1, the immediate reaction to the project involved a lot of recoiling.

Critics savaged *One More Light*, giving it the worst marks of the band's career, with *NME* describing it as "a contrived commercial move" and *Consequence* declaring that Linkin Park had "completely abandoned any sense of identity." By now, the band was used to low-score reviews, but the fan backlash, with some longtime supporters mystified by the album's sound and others downright angry over it, provoked hurt feelings from the band in turn.

"By now, if people don't know that we can throw a curveball, then fuck them!" Chester declared in an interview during the album's release week. Mike said in the same interview, "Somebody who's, like, trying to work out in their head, 'The band is making these decisions for marketing reasons, or monetary reasons, or whatever,' and if that's your thing, then yes, take a hike. That's not how I operate."

Getting defensive about the motivation of *One More Light* and telling confused fans to kick rocks was decidedly *not* the best look for the guys. They had just taken a major chance—forsaking the sound of their last album and letting their most intimate feelings drive the new album took a whole lot of cojones, after all—and as they heard heaps of rejection, regrettably, they lashed out. Linkin Park believed in this revamped sound and their ability to operate within it, but more than that, they believed in these particular songs and what they'd worked so hard to communicate.

And as more time passes, it's increasingly clear that they weren't wrong. Is *One More Light* saccharine at times? Absolutely. Is its brand of pop a little too contented instead of cutting-edge? Most definitely. But Linkin Park's seventh album also boasts some of the most undeniable hooks and moving lyrical passages of the band's discography. Their day-one investment in the album's songwriting paid off, with compositions that hum along efficiently before delivering a haymaker to the gut.

Even if the giggling chipmunk voices in the mix of "Battle Symphony" are too sugary for a listener's taste, for example, that same listener couldn't help but marvel at the anthem's airtight melodies and Chester's superhero promise, "If my armor breaks, I'll fuse it back together." Linkin Park also brings in Pusha T and Stormzy for "Good Goodbye"—a change-of-pace rap track, until it becomes clear that Chester's hook ("So say goodbye and *hi-i-it* the *ro-o-oad* / Pack it up, and *disappe-e-ear*") is the type of earworm that lodges itself in the mind for days.

Elsewhere, a pair of reflections on fatherhood—the *One More Light* album cover features a photo of children playing at Venice Beach, an ode to the band members' family lives—feature unflinching singing performances from Mike, who leans away from the sentimentality of the subject matter on "Invisible" and "Sorry for Now" to discuss his fears and anxieties as a parent. "This is not black and white, only organized confusion / I'm just trying to get it right, and in spite of all I should've done," he sings over cymbal taps and guitar vapors on "Invisible," his voice rising but never cracking as it heads toward the monster chorus.

Listeners' mileage on the album's various hooks may vary, especially considering that they were all written with different collaborators offering their own variations on Linkin Park's presentation. Yet the snapshots of the band members' inner lives, from the marital tumult of "Talking to Myself" to the parental concerns of "Invisible" to the inner demons of "Heavy," are delivered with truth and precision, their lyrics capturing deeply personal moments but designed to extend far beyond them.

The title track of *One More Light*, which the band wrote in honor of the late Amy Zaret, crystallizes that idea. With elegant electronics hovering around his voice, Chester sings about a light that flickers out and why, in "a sky of a million stars," that single dying light still matters.

Years after the release of *One More Light*, trying to remove its title track from its greater context is a fool's errand. That holds especially true for the album's opening song, "Nobody Can Save Me." After the song's vocal samples gently blink awake, Chester's voice parts through the muted production, singing about gathering storm clouds and answers that have yet to come. The song begins with Chester singing the line "I'm dancing with my demons"—an intentional choice to open the album with that line, according to Mike ("That's a really key part to what the album's about," he explained during a listening party on *One More Light*'s release date).

Instead of nervously scraping at his feelings, however, Chester belts them out proudly, fearlessly. The song crescendos into a rousing chorus:

> *You tell me it's all right*
> *Tell me I'm forgiven, tonight*
> *But nobody can save me now*
> *I'm holding up a light*
> *I'm chasing out the darkness, inside*
> *'Cause nobody can save me.*

"Nobody Can Save Me" is a piece of blinding pop songwriting, beautiful enough to make you cry. It was impossible to listen to a few months after its release, and it's still difficult to listen to today. *One More Light* was always going to have a complicated legacy—the members of Linkin Park knew that while they were creating it. When it became the band's final album with Chester, however, its most triumphant moments instantly turned all the more heartbreaking.

CHAPTER 22

I N THE SPRING of 2017, as Mike was sitting next to Chester on a couch, he asked for the microphone that they had been sharing so that he could explain what kind of guy Chester was.

They were in Berlin conducting an interview together during the *One More Light* promotional run, and Chester was talking about how he had to dig deep to overcome his struggles during the album's creation—about having "just enough things to keep me wanting to go," he said. Mike wanted to give an example of what his friend was talking about. So when Chester passed him the mic and leaned back on the couch, Mike told the story of the time Chester broke his wrist onstage, back before the shoulder that required surgery in 2011, and way before the busted ankle in 2015.

This was in Melbourne in October 2007, while Linkin Park were touring Australia in support of *Minutes to Midnight*, with Chris Cornell as their opening act. That night, Chester jumped off the top of the stage as the guitars kicked in on "Papercut." His foot got caught, he landed awkwardly, and his whole body slammed hard into the stage—but two and a half seconds later, Chester sprang up like nothing had happened. By the time Mike started rapping the song's opening verse, Chester was bouncing around in front of the crowd.

The band huddled minutes later. They were only five songs into a twenty-song set, and Chester was pretty certain that his wrist was broken. Mike and the guys presumed that they'd cancel the rest of the set, but Chester did not. "He's like, 'Well . . . it's gonna be as broken in an hour as it is right now,'" Mike recalled. "And we were like, 'What?!' He's like, 'Yeah, I mean, let's just play! It fucking hurts, but let's just play.'"

That's simply who Chester *is*, was Mike's point. He was not going to let something as pesky as a broken wrist push him off that stage. He was going to overcome every new hurdle because that's what he had done his entire life. "He's the kind of guy," Mike concluded, "that's gonna just power through anything."

To the ones who knew him best, and to the world that had embraced his voice, Chester Bennington seemed indestructible. And then, somehow, he was gone.

On the morning of July 20, 2017, Chester died of suicide by hanging in his Palo Verdes Estates home in Los Angeles County. The news felt incomprehensible when it broke online that afternoon, as if the thread of reality had unspooled. Chester was only forty-one years old, and his spirit was the size of a skyscraper; he should have been halfway through his life, if even that. When the unconfirmed rumors became verified fact, the loss felt like a total, unfathomable gut punch. "Shocked and heartbroken," Mike posted at 3:03 p.m. Eastern time that day, "but it's true."

Chester's death stunned and shattered those closest to him, including his bandmates. "The shockwaves of grief and denial are still sweeping through our family as we come to grips with what has happened," Linkin Park said in a joint statement a few days after Chester's passing. The individual messages in the immediate aftermath were considerably more raw. "Heartbroken," Dave wrote on Twitter, while on Instagram, Joe posted a performance shot of Chester, a warm glow of light around his head. "Always shining," Joe wrote. "I miss my friend."

Mike had just seen Chester a few days earlier at a recording studio: Chester had introduced him to the indie rapper and poet Watsky, after hyping up the artist for a while. Watsky and some of his friends left the studio, but Chester and Mike lingered together—spending a few hours talking, kicking around song ideas, game-planning their upcoming shows. It was nothing special or notable; it was just what they had always done.

In the days before his death, Chester had been in Arizona with Talinda and the kids, taking a family vacation at their cabin in Sedona ahead of what was to be Linkin Park's sprawling North American tour in support of *One More Light* later that month. Chester traveled back to Los Angeles by himself—he said that he needed to work, and the band had a photo shoot scheduled for the morning of the twentieth—but before he left, Talinda snapped a photo of Chester and their children gazing into the woods off their deck, grinning from ear to ear.

"He was happy," she said in an early 2018 interview. "He gave me a kiss goodbye, he gave the kids a kiss goodbye, and I never saw him again."

Chester had been candid about his substance abuse issues during the making of *One More Light*, including an extended period of drinking in the second half of 2016. According to Talinda, Chester "had been sober for almost six months" prior to his death. In his final months, however, while publicly discussing his general difficulties with life during the *One More Light* press run, he was privately telling loved ones about a specific problem: the urge to drink had consumed his thoughts once again. "He was describing an hour-by-hour battle with addiction," said Ryan Shuck, Chester's close friend who had helped turn one of his bleakest periods during the 2000s into the lone Dead by Sunrise album and who had been texting with him about his alcoholism in the weeks leading up to his death.

When an autopsy and toxicology report later confirmed that Chester had a trace amount of alcohol in his system at the time of his death—he had been discovered with an empty bottle of Stella Artois in the room as well as a glass of Corona that was less than half full—Talinda was not surprised. She had immediately understood that those beer bottles represented a relapse. "I knew instantly that that drink triggered that shame," she said, "triggered a lifetime of unhealthy neural pathways."

The timing and nature of Chester's death also led to widespread speculation that the recent passing of Chris Cornell, who had died by suicide two months earlier, was connected, as some sort of tragic catalyst. Both artists hanged themselves, and July 20 would have been Chris's fifty-third birthday.

Chris's death in May 2017 devastated Chester, who had lost a childhood hero turned close companion. "You have inspired me in many ways you could never have known," Chester wrote to Chris in an open letter posted online after learning of his passing. "I can't imagine a world without you in it." The day after Chris's death happened to be the release date of *One More Light*, and Linkin Park were scheduled to perform a short set on *Jimmy Kimmel Live!* that evening. Instead of opening with lead single "Heavy," however, the band played "One More Light," and a visibly shaken Chester—seated on a stool in a black suit, black shades covering his eyes—dedicated the song to the friend he had lost less than forty-eight hours earlier.

"We love you, Chris," he said into the microphone to begin the remarkably raw TV performance: Chester gasped out some of the lyrics, screamed in a song that contained no screams, and repeated with purpose, "Who cares if one more light goes out? / Well, I do." Mike later revealed that Chester couldn't make it through the song during the *Kimmel* soundcheck earlier that day, too overcome with grief over Chris's passing. And although the *One More Light* title track had been written in memory of their friend Amy Zaret, fans quickly adopted the just-released song as a Chris Cornell tribute.

A week later, Chester sang a tender version of "Hallelujah" at Chris's funeral at the Hollywood Forever Cemetery in late May 2017, urged on by Vicky Cornell and with Brad accompanying him on guitar. The *Kimmel* performance of "One More Light" had been so cathartic that Chester felt more prepared to sing in front of Chris's family and friends; "Hallelujah" was Chester's all-time favorite song, and Chris had been friends with Jeff Buckley, so the performance felt like a fitting tribute. Afterward, Chester spoke with Chris's daughter, Lily, who told him that she, her half sister Toni, and their father would all regularly sing "Hallelujah" together. "I didn't know that until after I'd performed it," Chester said, "but it turned out to be a very special moment."

Following Chris's funeral, Chester seemingly moved forward. *One More Light* debuted at No. 1 on the *Billboard* 200—the negative reviews and fan response hadn't dulled the commercial power of the band's catchiest album in years—and Linkin Park headed to Europe in early June for a month-long victory lap. "The fact that it debuted even beyond what we predicted is a great starting point," Brad said at the time, "and now we get to bring those songs on the road and share them every night."

At that point, Linkin Park were a well-oiled arena machine: they knew how to make years-old hits sound exciting to crowds that had heard them live several times over, whether through a somber piano version of "Crawling," an extended guitar solo on "What I've Done," or a fans-only second half of the "In the End" bridge. Meanwhile, some of the *One More Light* songs had been bulked up for the concerts, with Brad's guitar work foregrounded more than it had been in the studio on songs like "Battle Symphony" and "Heavy." Those European performances showcased the most sonically diverse setlist in the fired-up veteran group's history; according to a band statement from later that year, "Chester shared with us that he felt this was the best tour we had ever done."

Sounding invigorated during the European leg of the tour, Chester began to make plans for the rest of 2017, both within and outside of Linkin Park. The *One More Light* North American tour was scheduled to last for three months and would kick off with a pair of stadium dates alongside Blink-182 in late July, so both bands made a Funny or Die comedy video as "Blinkin Park" to promote the shows in advance.

In June, Chester announced that Grey Daze would be getting back together that fall for a twentieth-anniversary reunion show. He and Sean Dowdell had remained close over the years—Chester was even a co-owner of Sean's tattoo parlor, Club Tattoo, which had expanded beyond its Tempe location into a multistate chain—and Chester, Sean, Mace Beyers, and Cristin Davis had reunited earlier in 2017 to record some of the early Grey Daze tunes for a planned rerelease. Meanwhile, Chester had also been in touch with Guns N' Roses' Matt Sorum about rejoining Kings of Chaos, the covers-only supergroup that had been active with a rotating lineup since 2012, which Chester had joined for a few spot shows at the end of 2016.

Linkin Park's European tour ended on July 6, 2017, at Barclaycard Arena in Birmingham, England. The show was actually supposed to be the next to last stop of that leg of the tour: the band was originally scheduled to wrap up in Manchester, England, the following night, but the Manchester Arena bombing—a terrorist attack following an Ariana Grande concert in May 2017—closed down the arena for months, and Linkin Park couldn't find a replacement venue for that particular tour stop.

In Birmingham, Chester's voice sounded as sturdy as ever, ripping through the pre-encore run of "Somewhere I Belong," "What I've Done," "In the End," and "Faint" with precision and poignancy in front of thousands of fans. Midway through the show, Chester dedicated "One More Light" to the victims of the Manchester bombing, which had claimed twenty-two lives, and got off the stage and right up to the audience to perform the song.

"The one thing that can't be defeated is love," Chester declared, clutching the microphone as fiercely as he always had. He began walking up to the barricades and shaking hands, hugging people between lines of "One More Light," letting fans grip his arm and pat his shoulder as he sang the chorus. No one knew then that the performance would be Chester's last.

In the aftermath of Chester's death, multiple blog posts and message-board threads tried to construe *One More Light* as a cry for help that had fallen on deaf ears. Many of the interviews that Chester had given leading up to the release described his constant battles with depression and difficulties with day-to-day life. But then again, those same interviews often portrayed the most fraught moments in the past tense, tempered by professional aid and the support of those around him. "At the end of the process, I was surprised I was ever in this place," he said in April 2017. "I was like, 'Wow, I can't see myself getting in that place again because I have such good friends.'"

One More Light was certainly filled with lyrical documents of Chester's struggle, from "Nobody Can Save Me" to "Battle Symphony" to "Heavy."

The latter was a pop-radio hit at the time of Chester's death, his voice cracking on the hook "I'm holding on / Why is everything so heavy?" Yet Chester had *always* turned his personal pain into lyrical inspiration. He turned crushing admissions—from "Crawling in my skin / These wounds, they will not heal," to "I've become so numb / I can't feel you there," to "Sometimes solutions aren't so simple / Sometimes goodbye's the only way," to "I've tried so hard and got so far / But in the end, it doesn't even matter"—into widespread catharsis over the course of dozens of songs, long before *One More Light*. He had never tried to hide the reality his words were steeped in.

"We're trying to remind ourselves," the band wrote to Chester following his death, "that the demons who took you away from us were always part of the deal. After all, it was the way you sang about those demons that made everyone fall in love with you in the first place."

No one will ever really know why the darkness Chester battled his entire life consumed him on July 20, 2017. The light that Chester exhibited in the prior weeks around family and friends, the strength that he demonstrated onstage, the musical endeavors that he was plotting, the answers he seemed to have found—they all waged war against years of deep-seated trauma, struggles with addiction, physical injury, severe depression. The belief that certain factors definitively contributed to his death or that musical decisions served as warning signs suggests an unrealistic cause and effect, a logic that didn't exist. There are no easy answers, and there never will be.

What is clear, however, is that Chester's world was not defined by that darkness at the end of his life. In addition to Talinda and the band sharing warm memories of his final weeks, stories of Chester's good humor stretched far and wide following his passing, particularly across the music community.

Thirty Seconds to Mars' Jared Leto, Chester's close friend who had toured with Linkin Park in 2014, recalled going to the Benningtons' house for dinner one night and finding a home "just jam-packed with the biggest family you've ever seen," Chester happily serving up dishes in Dad Mode. ZZ Top's Billy Gibbons, who had played with Chester in Kings of Chaos, shared memories of talking shop with him for hours about Club Tattoo, the parlor that had asked Billy to design some silver jewelry. Metallica's Lars Ulrich called him "gracious, kind, and humble," while the Mountain Goats' John Darnielle zoomed out on Chester's artistic importance by recalling his time working as a psychiatric nurse: "Linkin Park meant a LOT to a lot of kids I used to take care of in treatments & placements & therefore to me, too," he wrote.

More of those tributes were shared by over five hundred family members and friends on July 29, 2017, when Chester was finally laid to rest during a private service at the South Coast Botanic Garden in Palos Verdes Peninsula. Mike, Joe, and Ryan Shuck delivered eulogies, KROQ DJ Ted Stryker led the service, and "Amazing Grace" was performed by Ours' Jimmy Gnecco, Bigelf's Damon Fox, GN'R's Matt Sorum, and STP's Robert and Dean DeLeo. Mourners were given lanyards and wristbands, as if those hundreds in attendance were all VIPs in Chester's life.

As Chester's loved ones joined together to celebrate his life, both hardcore fans and casual listeners banded together to process his death through his music. Linkin Park's listenership exploded in the wake of Chester's passing: the band's sales grew more than 5,300 percent immediately after news broke, and their daily streams earned a 730 percent increase on July 20, rising to 12.6 million on-demand audio streams, according to Luminate. "Heavy," the band's current single, ballooned in plays and reached a new peak of No. 45 on the Hot 100 following Chester's death. But the most-streamed Linkin Park song in the aftermath was "In the End," followed by "Numb," as listeners returned to the words that Chester had yelled into their minds over and over for decades.

One More Light instantly gained a grim new significance as the band's final album with Chester, and so did Linkin Park's entire catalog, their biggest hits and albums all charged with an underlying sadness. From that

moment forward, the sorrow imbued in so many of Linkin Park's defining musical moments would now have to be viewed through the prism of
Chester's passing, the anguish in their lead singer's voice and words turned
tragically real.

Yet that uptick in Linkin Park streams and downloads was only one
piece of a much larger fan reaction. "If you have pictures from any memorials or events you've attended in memory of Chester, please send your
favorites, I'd love to repost them," Dave tweeted on the day of the memorial service. Within a few hours, Dave received photos of a pictures-and-
candles shrine in Bratislava, Slovakia; a collection of handwritten letters
scattered around a photo of Chester in Modena, Italy; a public memorial
surrounding an enlarged performance photo of Chester in Johannesburg,
South Africa; and a poster board on the streets of São Luís, Brazil, on
which fans could write messages and song lyrics in black marker.

Some tributes were more despondent, as fans grappled to find somewhere to place their grief. "Dear Chester Bennington, It hurts all of us to
know that you saved so many lives, yet we couldn't save you," read one note
placed outside of Chester's home, which was encircled by homemade tributes in the days after his death. One photo that Dave shared showed the
back of a pickup truck with decals of Chester's name and the National Suicide Prevention Lifeline's phone number; the hotline reported a 14 percent
increase in calls on the day after Chester's death.

However, other tributes resembled something more like a rallying
cry: one video showed a vigil at Citi Field in New York City on the night
that Linkin Park had been scheduled to play the stadium, voices singing
"One More Light" and dozens of candles thrust high into the air, fans
refusing not to appreciate their favorite band on that summer evening
in Queens. And in one photo, a crowd stood in the shape of a heart in
a Russian town square, the words "WELL WE DO" inscribed on the
bricks between their feet as an answer to the question that Chester had
posed ("Who cares if one more light goes out?") with *One More Light*'s
title track. That song, which Chester had sung in honor of Chris Cornell

just two months prior, was now an ode from the fans to its singer, its lyrics penned onto balloons that were released into the sky in gatherings around the globe.

Even so, the full scope of Chester's influence couldn't be contained to a single tribute, fan meetup, or part of the globe. Per Warner Bros. Records—which had its own shrine pop up outside of its label offices in Burbank—over three hundred band-endorsed public memorials had been organized around the world in the weeks after Chester's death. LPU members and Linkin Park fans created a Google Docs document of past and upcoming gatherings during the summer of 2017—and the doc grew so massive it had to be organized by continent. And of course, the online tributes far outnumbered the in-person events, as millions of words were spilled on Chester's importance across thousands of social media posts, vlog clips, and long-form remembrances.

Like the rest of the world, Linkin Park fan communities erupted in shock and sadness when news broke of Chester's death. Yet as messages of disbelief poured in from all corners of the world, stories of a first Linkin Park album purchased, a first Linkin Park concert witnessed, a memorable vocal tic on a smash hit, a favorite performance on a deep cut were all shared as well. Testimonies about Chester's words and music helping fans wrestle with their own depression or substance abuse or insecurities became commonplace across the internet, the communal gatherings complemented by personal anecdotes. Type the words *Thank You Chester* into Linkin Park's official Reddit page or search the phrase in the comments of their YouTube videos and you'll find years of thoughts and memories, DIY performances and song recommendations, fan art and tattoos. You can scroll and scroll, but you'll never be able to reach the end.

Grief does not work like a timer; for many, including Chester's family and friends and fans, a bell will never go off denoting an acceptance of his death. Yet the outpouring of love and appreciation following his passing illustrated exactly what Chester, once a troubled kid hacking around Arizona and ready to give up on music, had accomplished during his too-short life. The personal turmoil that Chester overcame to transform into a rock star and the means with which he became a hero to those with their own private battles made him nothing short of an inspiration—a singular voice that millions, regardless of their devastation over his passing, couldn't help but celebrate.

Chester gripped a microphone harder than anyone, and in so doing placed his fingerprints upon the world. His death was shocking, but his impact was, in fact, indestructible.

CHAPTER 23

DON'T WANT TONIGHT to be sad," Mike declared prior to arriving onstage at the Hollywood Bowl on a clear Friday night in Los Angeles. "I want it to be uplifting and hopeful. Chester wouldn't have it any other way."

Fourteen weeks after Chester's death, Linkin Park had one more show to play: "Linkin Park & Friends Celebrate Life in Honor of Chester Bennington" would be an all-star tribute concert in the band's hometown on October 27, 2017. After the event was announced in mid-September, tickets to the 17,500-capacity venue sold out immediately; YouTube announced a free global livestream of the show, but fans still traveled to LA from all around the world. Some even camped outside the Hollywood Bowl in the days leading up to the concert—this was a one-of-a-kind performance, and the fans in the pit needed to be as close as physically possible to their favorite band, who may never do anything like this again.

Meanwhile, Linkin Park had spent weeks leading up to the concert in rehearsals, fine-tuning song arrangements with a double-digit list of special guests that included more than just vocalists. The show—Rick Rubin had recommended the band work through their emotions onstage—would require a mix of musical agility spanning multiple hours, artist coordination on the level of a mini-festival, and both mental and emotional fortitude, as Linkin Park's first-ever show without Chester.

Three months had gone by since the band lost its voice, and the grief wasn't as blindingly raw as it had been in the first days and weeks. Yet stepping onto a stage as a five-piece—and playing songs without Chester

271

present to sing them—was always going to be an entirely new proposition, regardless of how much time had elapsed since his passing.

The nerves weren't immediately visible when the band arrived to screams from the Hollywood Bowl audience. The guys were awash in blue light, with Mike positioned center stage in front of a collection of keyboards and wearing a ripped jean jacket and black Dodgers cap. Artwork from different Linkin Park eras and tours adorned the platforms underneath Joe's setup and Rob's drums, Chester's eyes peeking out from a poster behind Brad's wide stance to Mike's right.

The band began with a medley of particularly soaring songs from *A Thousand Suns*, harmonizing wordlessly on "Robot Boy" before Brad unleashed a chiming guitar line and Mike sang part of "The Messenger": "When life leaves us blind / Love keeps us kind." His voice slightly trembled and threatened to crack as he sang Chester's words, overwhelmed by the moment as he was. He was still hurting; it was obvious in every note. Mike looked like he was about to lose it a few times, but he soldiered through, into the sweep of "Iridescent" and the hope of "Roads Untraveled," a bit more intact with each new minute.

"Doing this show is one of the hardest things I think that we've ever decided to do," Mike admitted to the audience moments later, his eyes looking upward into the rafters. "And I think you're part of the only reason that we are even able to stand up here and do this."

The first of the special guests arrived to celebrate Chester and alleviate some of the pressure on the band while Mike continued playing master of ceremonies. Yellowcard's Ryan Key started things off by duetting with Mike on a mash-up of "Shadow of the Day" and U2's "With or Without You," encouraging the audience to "remind these guys up here how much all you out there and all of us up here love and respect each and every one of them." Bush's Gavin Rossdale popped out for a growly version of "Leave Out All the Rest," and later, Sum 41 frontman Deryck Whibley and drummer Frank Zummo joined for a committed take on "The Catalyst."

A six-song segment was dedicated to *One More Light*, the album Linkin Park never got to perform in the States, and it featured Julia Michaels and Kiiara on "Heavy" and singer-songwriter Ilsey Juber on "Talking to Myself," among others. And there were nods to that canceled tour, too: Blink-182, who were set to join Linkin Park for some stadium shows, came out to play "What I've Done" and their own version of "I Miss You." And Takahiro Moriuchi—the singer of post-hardcore band One Ok Rock, who were set to open for Linkin Park in their native Japan that fall—flew all the way to LA just to rip through "Somewhere I Belong" with the band.

Across the board, the guest artists performed admirably—the extensive rehearsals had clearly gotten the revolving door of voices comfortable with Linkin Park's onstage timing and approach, while allowing for enough movement and spontaneity to keep each collaboration feeling fresh. Yet a recurring theme for the evening emerged: many of the most memorable moments of the all-star tribute show came when it was just the band onstage.

Prior to the encore, for instance, "In the End" became a call-and-response between the band and the crowd, with Mike rapping his verses and the thousands in attendance at the Hollywood Bowl hoisting up Chester's choruses, bridge, and interjections. For "New Divide," near the end of the evening, the band played alongside archived footage of Chester leading Linkin Park through the song at the Hollywood Bowl in 2014, the pre-recorded footage acting as a soothing balm after a night of missing his inimitable voice.

"One More Light," which had fully morphed into a fan anthem in honor of Chester, felt even more intimate. As the entire audience held up their phone lights, Mike leaned over his keyboards and sang Chester's lyrics slowly and carefully, while Dave and Brad sat at his sides, cradling their instruments. When "One More Light" ended, Mike began talking to the crowd about the "roller coaster of everything" that he and his bandmates had been feeling over the past three months—the lightning strike of grief that would hit them regularly, the one that was always impossible to predict.

Then, in perhaps the most detail he's ever talked about publicly before or since, Mike shared his perspective on the day of Chester's death. "We were doing, like, a photo thing when I found out about Chester," he said, "and the first, for hours, I was just in disbelief, it didn't . . . I wouldn't believe anybody, what anybody had to say about anything." At some point, Mike continued, when reality finally sank in, he realized that music would help him cope—"not only listening to music but actually playing music," he pointed out. "I sat down in my studio, and I wrote something. It was about eight days after, and I want to share it with you guys tonight, if that's okay."

Mike started playing a pleading ballad titled "Looking for an Answer," which imagines a better reality for his lost friend ("Is there sunshine where you are? / The way there was when you were here") while examining his own feelings of defeat for not being able to save him ("Was I looking for an answer, when there never really was one?"). Keyboard chords cut through the silence, then Mike's voice would quiver and rasp with sadness; for most of the song, the crowd at the Hollywood Bowl could hear a pin drop. The performance epitomized the sorrow in Mike's soul, laid bare center stage for the world to witness.

The tribute concert felt harrowingly personal to the band, and yet, it also belonged to everyone. A few songs into the show, Linkin Park played "Numb" with no artist filling in for Chester's lead vocals. Instead, the thousands in attendance, and many more watching from home, sang out the words. A single microphone stood center stage at the Hollywood Bowl, shining under a pair of spotlights, and nobody approached it as Chester's five bandmates played on.

"I've become so numb, I can't feel you there / Become so tired, so much more aware," every onlooker cried out, the livestream capturing several crowd-reaction shots in the moment of mass harmony. Tears fell. Fists were clenched. The pain was still fresh, but an acknowledgment of that pain was shared in the Linkin Park community—as it always had been. As it turned out, the other most powerful performance of the evening occurred with no one behind the microphone either.

NATURALLY, MENTAL HEALTH AWARENESS WAS a common theme throughout the show. Multiple graphics flashed on the screens and the band mentioned the One More Light Fund, which they established in honor of Chester as an extension of their long-running nonprofit, Music for Relief. The fund was created to support We Care Solar—a Music for Relief program that Chester was especially passionate about, which provided solar electricity kits to health clinics in remote areas—and partnered with 320 Changes Direction, a mental health initiative spearheaded by Talinda Bennington and named in honor of Chester's birthday, March 20.

"It is time that we recognize that mental health is as important as our physical health," Talinda said onstage at the tribute concert. In between the main set and the encore, Chester's wife delivered an extended speech expressing gratitude to family and friends for the past three months of support, paying homage to the band's global fan base ("Chester always said, 'Linkin Park's fans are the best,' and you know what? He was absolutely fucking right"), and speaking about how 320 Changes Direction would assist those struggling with any number of personal issues, including addiction and depression, as her husband had been. "It is my mission," Talinda continued, "to make it easier to have access to mental health resources."

Following Chester's passing, Talinda worked with Music for Relief, having as many discussions with as many mental health groups as possible. She eventually joined the wide-reaching "Change Direction" mental health awareness campaign, which had been launched by the nonprofit Give an Hour in 2015 and was supported by hundreds of organizations. What those early conversations taught Talinda, she explained during the launch of 320 Changes Direction, is that enough high-quality mental health programs *do* exist—people just need access to them, and the shame around needing those resources had to be erased.

"We need to change the culture of mental health," Talinda wrote on the 320 Changes Direction website, "so that those in need—and their family members—are able to speak openly about their struggles so that they can seek the care they deserve."

Chester had always been comfortable discussing his mental health—using words and lyrics to describe issues that were less tangible than physical ailments—especially at a time when the music-star archetype was not as open with their emotional state. When Linkin Park took off at the turn of the century, many of their musical peers were silently battling while smiling for the cameras. Those who *did* speak up were often mocked for outlandish behavior or brushed off because of their professional success.

This was the era when Mariah Carey turned into a punchline when she was hospitalized for "extreme exhaustion" in 2001; she revealed many years later her exhaustion was due to a bipolar disorder diagnosis. This was also when Destiny's Child star Michelle Williams, at the height of the group's early aughts fame, told the band's manager that she was suffering from depression, to which he allegedly replied, "Y'all just signed a multi-million-dollar deal; you're about to go on tour. What do you have to be depressed about?" The mid-2000s ushered in TMZ and Perez Hilton and a new breed of invasive tabloids with celebs (most often women) in their crosshairs. The toxic misogyny underscored a general lack of sensitivity—the consensus seemed to be, if a famous person was unhappy or wrestling with demons, *boo-hoo*, they could wipe their tears with their wads of cash.

Since that problematic moment in pop culture, the level of collective understanding around mental health issues has evolved dramatically. Stigmas existed in 2017, when Chester passed away, and they still exist today. Yet the music industry has reached a point at which several of its biggest superstars have spoken out about their private struggles and methods of finding support, a chorus of A-list voices making commonplace what was once a source of derision.

In recent years, Ariana Grande has openly discussed her anxiety and advocates "normalizing asking for help"; Kid Cudi has admitted to using drugs to cover up his depression before seeking professional treatment; Doja Cat has opened up about how her ADHD has impacted her creative perspective; and Ed Sheeran has gone on the record about his social anxiety—a stadium headliner who admits to feeling claustrophobic in the wrong situations. Songs ranging from Kendrick Lamar's "U" and Kacey Musgraves's "Rainbow" to Julia Michaels and Selena Gomez's "Anxiety" have centered mental health issues over the past decade while sounding nothing like one another. And in the rock world, such artists as Bruce Springsteen, Paramore's Hayley Williams, Guns N' Roses' Duff McKagan, and Fall Out Boy's Pete Wentz have all become increasingly candid about their respective issues and how they experience highly relatable problems in between entertaining stadium and arena audiences.

These conversations did not all start happening at once; no flash point caused these artists to step forward or these songs to be written. Instead, each new voice chipped away at long-held beliefs around mental health issues, little by little. With greater representation among the most visible stars, popular culture gradually shifted over the past fifteen years—the music industry evolving concurrently with mental health discussions in sports, politics, film/TV, and books—as did the cultures within US education systems, government, workplaces, and homes. A new generation feels less hesitant to reach out for help than the last.

Circumstances are very, very far from perfect, and even as conversations become more mainstream and social media amplifies #mentalhealth stories, stereotypes, particularly of severe mental illness, remain prevalent. Modern society's comprehension of the value of mental health awareness and resources is improving every day, though. The more people speak up, the more normal speaking up becomes. And Chester—the lead singer of one of the biggest rock bands of the century, who always spoke his truth aloud, fearless of what anyone else might think or say—indisputably contributed to that change.

The money raised for the One More Light Fund during the tribute concert was critical: in early 2018, when Music for Relief joined forces with the long-running Entertainment Industry Foundation to become its official crisis relief program, Linkin Park's humanitarian fund had raised a whopping $11 million since its 2004 inception. Yet the stigma-busting words shared onstage that night were just as important.

"There's been a lot of vilification of people with depression and addiction," said Alanis Morissette, in between grooving through "Castle of Glass" with members of No Doubt and performing an unreleased song that she had written for Chester, "and being troubled and being in the public eye and being made fun of for the challenges that we, as a huge community of people with notoriety, have gone through. And it's an extremely isolating, challenging journey to go through. And so for me, I just want to offer empathy to all people in the public eye, to all of you here tonight."

During a video package featuring the band that ran in the middle of the concert, Rob also opened up, noting that Chester obviously wasn't the only member of Linkin Park who had experienced mental health issues. "I've had a lot of moments in life, many breakdowns," he confessed, "and I think some of the most creative and most healing and inspired thinking and actions come out of those moments."

In a night-long celebration of the music of an artist gone too soon, those sentiments honored a large part of Chester's legacy: the bravery he displayed in his openness with his thoughts and feelings, which compelled others to do the same. "Chester would have loved this," Talinda confirmed during her speech. "He would have loved to see us lifting each other up."

Then she ended with, "Fuck depression. Let's make Chester proud."

———————

A LITTLE UNDER TWO HOURS into the tribute show, Mike paused to catch his breath. "You having fun?!" he yelled into the crowd. He'd just jumped into the front row during the "One Step Closer" bridge, joined on the song by Korn's Jonathan Davis and Dead by Sunrise's Ryan Shuck and Amir Derakh; torn through "A Place for My Head" with A Day to Remember's Jeremy McKinnon; and brought out System of a Down's Daron Malakian and Shavo Odadjian for the *Hunting Party* headbanger "Rebellion."

"It's a weird thing to say," Mike continued after wiping sweat from his forehead and refitting his cap. "When it comes out of my mouth, it's like, are we *supposed* to have fun? But I think we *are* supposed to have fuckin' fun! That's what I think! I think about Chester, and I think, 'That guy would want us to have fun.'"

Ultimately, the Chester tribute functioned less as a melancholic celebration of Linkin Park's music and more as an unadulterated catharsis after the loss of their lead singer. It was sometimes heartbreaking but often pretty joyful, with interspersed moments of levity, like the Hollywood Bowl crowd singing along to a fan-favorite YouTube clip projected onscreen of Chester backstage warbling a silly tune called "Unicorns & Lollipops" while strumming an acoustic guitar. Later, when the band mistimed the opening to "Battle Symphony" with songwriter Jonathan Green, Mike earned a laugh by calling out the false start: "Chester would not have this shit!"

And the end of the concert was fittingly raucous, with Steve Aoki and Bebe Rexha turning "A Light That Never Comes" into a dance-pop anthem, Avenged Sevenfold's M. Shadows adding his possessed croon to "Burn It Down," and Mike rapping through "Faint" so deliriously fast that Machine Gun Kelly, rhyming along in the audience, had to work hard to keep up. On the final song, "Bleed It Out," Mike, Brad, Dave, Rob, and Joe were joined onstage by several of the evening's guest stars. As they extended the outro, bouquets of flowers were tossed up by the front row amid the crowd's deafening cheers.

"We don't know where we're going from here," Mike admitted over the "Bleed It Out" riff. The band finally left the Hollywood Bowl stage. Linkin Park's last performance was complete.

The tribute concert ended up crossing the three-hour mark, and Mike later described it as "exhausting"—after all, the band's previous longest show had lasted only around ninety minutes. When the band came off the stage, they fell to the floor of the dressing room and just lay there for a while.

"I was onstage for almost the whole thing, singing most of the time," Mike said. "I had to compartmentalize and be out of my body for some of it in order to get through the whole thing. But I really loved how it came out."

However, a by-product of an evening filled with other singers performing Chester's parts across the Linkin Park catalog—some famous artists,
some widely respected hard-rock vocalists, and some both—was the con-
firmation that, unequivocally, there would be no replacing Chester's voice.
Part of it was personality, and part of it was technical skill. The week after
the tribute show, when Mike listened to the performances, he heard a lot of
great singers, and even so, none of them came close to capturing Chester's
range. Someone like Julia Michaels could tackle one song, and Jonathan
Davis could tackle another—but one voice that could span the difference
between those two artists was no longer findable.

That realization "led to conversations about what to do next," Mike
said. "It became obvious that you can't just hire some schmuck to get up
there and sing with us, 'cause they won't be able to hit half the stuff."

Before the end of 2017, Linkin Park released *One More Light Live*, an
album capturing Chester's final shows with the band during their European
tour earlier that year and a means of showcasing that tour to the countries
that never got to see it. The band could have supplemented the live album
with some unreleased material from the *One More Light* sessions—which
apparently produced seventy songs, with only ten making the track list,
according to Brad—but chose to forgo any type of posthumous release.

"I would say the vast majority of those songs fortunately will never
see the light of day," Brad affirmed. They had also floated releasing the
tribute show as a live project, but because the entire concert was already on
YouTube (with twenty-four million views to date), the idea didn't generate
much interest. "I think from here," Mike said, "everybody wants to kind of
look forward."

How do you look forward, though, when you lose a voice as irreplace-
able as Chester's? In January 2018, Mike wrote that he had "every intention on continuing with LP, and the guys feel the same," but he admitted
a few months later that he was "unable to say what will happen with the
band." The five band members were checking in with each other regularly, meeting up in the Los Angeles area, and even playing music every
now and again. That time spent together didn't make the vision of Linkin

Park's future without Chester any more clear, though, and band operations slowed to a halt.

"I think we will do music again," Dave said in late 2018. "We all want to. We all still enjoy being together and being around each other. But we have a huge process to figure out what we wanna do and what that's gonna look like, and I don't have a timetable for how long that will take."

Seventeen years had passed between the release of *Hybrid Theory* and the Chester tribute show, almost to the day; some of the songs performed in his honor that night would've been old enough to drive. During a few of them, Chester materialized in Mike's head: throughout the tribute show his voice appeared in Mike's in-ear monitors to help with the song cues. Mike was used to hearing Linkin Park's biggest hits in a specific way, and that was with Chester on them. "When you think about some of my parts," he explained, "we would go back and forth, so I would want to hear that other voice."

Really, Linkin Park was feeling around in the dark for a new normal, just like anyone who's suffered an immense loss is forced to do. The tribute concert was a rousing success that offered a sense of closure to fans around the world, but the band itself was still searching for balance—a way to perform, to move into the future, without relying on Chester's voice for the cues.

INTERLUDE

"I Will Never Forget That Experience"

Ryan Key, frontman of pop-punk mainstays Yellowcard, describes the surprising ways his career has crossed paths with Linkin Park, from a Warped Tour performance to the 2017 tribute show.

We toured with Linkin Park in Japan in 2007—that was the first time that we connected. This [show] was a surreal, out-of-body experience. You walk out in front of twenty thousand people, and just the scale of what you're doing is overwhelming. Watching their production and their performance—I mean, they're absolute professionals, and when you watch them live, you start to take in the scope of their body of work, and how their songs can go from these gut-wrenching ballads to these just mental metal songs.

And then you add to that the experience of meeting Linkin Park. This is a diamond-selling artist, one of the biggest recording artists of all time—and they made an effort every day of that tour to swing by—"How are you guys doing? How have the shows been?" A genuine sense of care about our experience playing their shows. There was this feeling of warmth and wanting to invite you into their space. There was no gatekeeping of the Linkin Park world. And when you do this for as long as I've done it, you're around a lot of people that aren't that way. I mean, I wasn't that way—it took me the better part of twenty years to figure out how to solve my reactivity problem and how to be more open and more inviting to people. I had a lot of anxiety about being an artist and being a singer and a lot of insecurity that I had to work through for many, many years. And so seeing artists at that level have the ability to be so open was confusing to me, and also inspiring.

Minutes to Midnight was probably the first Linkin Park album that I was really invested in as a listener. I always liked the band, I knew they were incredibly talented songwriters, but I've never been a huge heavy-rock fan, you know? So with *Minutes to Midnight*, I recognized in them a thing that resonated with me, where I wanted to try something different as a songwriter. I wanted to branch out and step outside of the box of where the media and the fans and everyone had put the band and myself. *Minutes to Midnight* was a little bit polarizing among fans and critics because it was a very different experience, but that was the record where I connected with Linkin Park on a personal level, as a listener and an artist. So when they approached me about singing at Warped Tour [in 2014] with them, and they said, "We want you to sing 'What I've Done'"—that was extra special for me as well, because it's not like I sat down with them and had a conversation about how important *Minutes to Midnight* was for me.

I was terrified to get up there and sing with them. And just before the show, myself and Jeremy from A Day to Remember, and all the other artists that were going to sing with them, were stepping into their trailer to talk about how the show was gonna go, just run over the songs really quick. And I'll never forget, while I was in their trailer, it was the 2014 World Cup, and they had a big-screen TV in there and the World Cup game was on. And I was standing there with Linkin Park when Jermaine Jones scored that insane side-volley goal against Portugal—one of the greatest goals in US soccer history. And we all just, tears were falling, we were all hugging each other, it was full-blown football madness over this goal! I was there in Linkin Park's trailer watching it, and that's something that I'll never forget.

And then, you know, we went over the song and didn't have a lot of time to hang because they had to get through all the artists and get out there and do it. But I think the most special part of the day was after the show, behind the stage. I have a picture of myself and Chester and Mike just, like, holding each other. The thing about that photo was, I think they were aware of how intense the emotion and the anxiety and the pressure of all of it was [for me]. Their ability to make you feel like you've done a good job and that they were happy to have had the experience with you—it was overwhelming, and you could see it in the picture, where I'm just beaming. That moment, that photo, is going to be something that lives with me until I'm gone.

When [Yellowcard] broke up in 2017, when there was legitimately no thought or plan for us to ever be a band again, I had started doing Emo Night shows, which is basically just a fun party where people get to come and hang out with artists that they love, singing songs from 2000s Warped Tours in a small club, and it was a side hustle for me to help continue to make a living in music. I was flying to Phoenix on the day that Chester passed for an Emo Night show. I had a really early morning flight, I hadn't slept, so I went straight to the hotel to sleep, since I wouldn't have to be at the venue until probably 8:00 or 9:00 p.m. And when I woke up, I woke up to the news.

Chester and I weren't friends in the traditional sense—we didn't keep in touch, we didn't text each other, we didn't meet up when we were in town. But I was very surprised with how profoundly affected I was waking up to the news and was very concerned with how I was now supposed to go and do this fun party with fans on a day like that. So I went to the venue, and I made the decision—if I'm going to do the show tonight, and we're all going to be jumping around dancing and singing together, we need to make the show about celebrating his life and the impact that their music has had on all of us.

I was already going to play some acoustic songs, a couple of Yellow-card songs, at this show, and I learned "Shadow of the Day," which is not just one of my favorite Linkin Park songs, it's one of my favorite songs of all time, by any artist. I played "Shadow of the Day," and someone in the crowd filmed it on their phone, and it went up on YouTube. And you know, I've never had anything really go viral, but it blew up—hundreds of thousands of people saw this video of me playing the song.

So I'm on the phone with Mike and he says, "The band all saw your cover of 'Shadow of the Day,' and it was the first tribute we saw, of any of the tributes." He said they were doing a tribute show at the Hollywood Bowl in October, and they would like me to sing "Shadow of the Day." So of course I was beside myself, so honored and humbled.

I was told that I was going to be [the first special guest], and that didn't make it any easier. But it only took walking out onstage and seeing their faces and hearing their welcoming, positive energy, just radiating across the stage, to feel right at home. So I will never forget that experience, and there's no way to truly do justice to how full circle that moment was for my unique journey and connection to Linkin Park. It's so fascinating to me how my life intertwined with theirs and that I was included in this experience. It's one of the highlights, if not the highlight, of my musical career.

Mike is not centered in the video for his song "Place to Start." The camera is primarily focused on his right shoulder and the beam of sunlight pouring in from the window above it; the side of his face and the top of his T-shirt are visible, but only pieces, never the whole things. He's close—uncomfortably so. That's the point.

"Came so far, never thought it'd be done now / Stuck in a holding pattern, waiting to come down," he croons, pensive chords and unobtrusive beats buoying his wandering voice. There's a guitar neck standing next to him and a hi-hat cymbal in the background, indicating that the message is coming from Mike's home studio. "Did somebody else define me? Can I put the past behind me?" Mike continues. For a minute and a half, the shot doesn't move—it feels like a direct FaceTime with Mike, every fan on the receiving end of his questions and confessions, as the light desperately tries to enter his home.

Mike wasn't sleeping well in the weeks after Chester's death, so he'd get out of bed and wander into his studio to work in the dark. This was how "Looking for an Answer," the song he later performed at the tribute concert, originated. It was also how he returned to "Place to Start," after the song had been cast into the *One More Light* scrap heap a few months earlier. Mike had brought the bones of the track to the band as a demo, thinking the sparse production might work as an intro to the album, but the band never developed the song. During a weary day in those first few weeks, though, Mike "flipped on [my] phone and started recording 'Place to Start'—I sang it into the phone while it was playing." He liked how it looked—just his thoughts in his sanctuary, all artifice stripped away.

The lyrics were new, written in the wake of Chester's death, but he was intrigued by the notion that this song, which had begun before his friend passed away, could be a starting point for himself. Everything about "Place to Start" was deeply personal, but so was Mike's grief, pulsating through his mind and body. So he kept working on it.

As Linkin Park's future curled into a question mark, Mike made songs as a form of meditation, without a specific place or project to slot them in. "Looking for an Answer" would never be released—to date, Mike has performed the song only one time, at the tribute concert, a message to a friend frozen in a single moment. But the therapeutic effect of turning feelings into music extended beyond that one composition. Mike was now forty years old and recognized that his artistry could not remain stuck in his twenties and thirties. He needed to continue creating and continue healing—regardless of where he'd end up. He wrote songs to do both.

"The act of just sitting down and making things helped me process," Mike said. "It got me back in touch, I think, with why I started making music in the first place."

In January 2018, Mike unveiled the *Post Traumatic* EP, a surprise three-song project that started off with "Place to Start" and included accompanying homemade videos for each track. The music and visuals—more homemade recordings capturing Mike's complex feelings of loss and filmed with unpolished intimacy—were conceived as direct messages to fans, who were not only still mourning Chester but also coming to grips with the unknown future of Linkin Park.

After all, Mike had received plenty of messages himself: listeners were constantly reaching out on social media, asking him how he was feeling. "There were what seemed to be thousands of tributes," he recalled. "I felt like I had a little bit of a responsibility just to show up: I didn't want all of their effort or emotions to disappear into a black hole. I wanted them to know that I was here and listening."

Post Traumatic could have been limited to a three-song fan response, but song ideas kept flowing out of Mike, flecks of inspiration combed out of the heaviness of that year. He also felt like he had strengthened a lot as a writer as a result of the last two Linkin Park albums: *The Hunting Party* had included some outside songwriters, *One More Light* included a lot of them, and those sessions had been creative masterclasses that Mike could learn from and pull into his own process. That newfound expertise, combined with the ample emotional territory that he could mine, resulted in an album's worth of material. It was the fastest that Mike had ever made a full-length.

He knew that *Post Traumatic* should expand into a solo album—one released under his own name, too personal to exist under the Fort Minor banner—but Mike was "worried that my bandmates, some of my best friends, would feel abandoned." Rob's original percussion remained on "Place to Start," and Brad contributed to two of the eighteen tracks, but otherwise, *Post Traumatic* is as removed from the rest of Linkin Park as Mike's lone Fort Minor album was, but at a much more vulnerable time for the band.

When Mike explained the project and played some songs to the other four members, however, "they were more supportive than I thought they'd be," receptive to the honesty of the music and the organic nature of how it was made. Mike slept peacefully after talking to his bandmates—and woke up realizing that, in some sense, he was starting back at square one, having never before released an album as simply "Mike Shinoda."

Post Traumatic, which was released in June 2018, covers roughly nine months of Mike's life and is largely arranged in the order that the songs were written. The first half looks back with intimate specificity at the anger and despair he felt following Chester's passing: The outro of "Place to Start," for example, features voicemails of three people, including Dave, checking in on Mike following Chester's death. "Over Again" details the emotion Mike experienced during the Hollywood Bowl concert—the first verse was written on the day of the tribute show, and the second verse on the day after—with the hook meant to encapsulate that three-hour experience:

"Sometimes, you don't say goodbye once / You say goodbye over and over and over again."

Songs like "Watching As I Fall," "Nothing Makes Sense Anymore," and "Promises I Can't Keep" are as brutally candid as their titles suggest, and others scan as tear-stained journal entries even though the soundscapes are not forlorn but instead combine pop hooks reminiscent of *One More Light* with hip-hop, industrial, and dubstep production. Mike raps a fair amount but admitted ahead of the album release, "I didn't intend to make an album where I sang so much"; indeed, the bulk of *Post Traumatic* showcases the earnest warble that he exhibited in that "Place to Start" clip, stretched across every phase of loss. A decade earlier, Chester had encouraged Mike to sing lead on "In Between" from *Minutes to Midnight*, back when Mike's voice was mostly deployed for rapping and background vocals. In the years since, Mike had developed into a stronger, more emotive vocalist, and he used those tools to honor his professional partner.

Midway through *Post Traumatic*, the aptly titled synth-pop stomp "Crossing a Line" signals a change in perspective, as Mike begins to look forward. The second half of the album includes "Lift Off," a shit-talking rap battle featuring Machine Gun Kelly and Deftones' Chino Moreno; "Make It Up as I Go," a radio-ready collaboration with K.Flay that's been sped up from its *One More Light* demo; and "World's on Fire," a testament of gratitude to Mike's wife, Anna, and their children for keeping him grounded during an awful year.

Not every song is about Chester, and the album doesn't conclude with everything being okay for Mike. *Post Traumatic* is not a tribute album in the way that the Hollywood Bowl concert was a tribute concert; instead, it's a breathing document of Mike's tangle of feelings during a turbulent year. The album is compelling in its messiness, proud of its imperfections. After Chester's death, Mike realized that the five stages of grief—denial, anger, bargaining, depression, and acceptance—do not fit into neat, chronological compartments, and he wanted *Post Traumatic* to reflect that lack of tidy resolution.

"It started from a dark place," he said, "but it wasn't a straight line from there. And these songs are the same way."

––––––––––––

POST TRAUMATIC SCORED A TOP 20 debut on the *Billboard* 200, and as "Crossing a Line" and "Make It Up as I Go" received some rock and alternative airplay, Mike launched a solo tour that took him to theaters across North America, Asia, and Europe, backed by multi-instrumentalist music director Matt Harris and drummer Dan Mayo. The setlist included *Post Traumatic* songs as well as Linkin Park and Fort Minor tunes and was constantly shifting songs around—with a smaller band around him, the sets could afford to be a bit more spontaneous.

The first solo shows were tough for Mike to power through. "It wasn't that it was heavy or sad," he explained. "It was just emotionally more intense than what a normal set was like in my memory." But with time, they gradually got easier, and the atmosphere at the performances became increasingly hopeful. Mike shared stories of Chester from the stage, often memories of their times touring in the city in which he was performing, and those speeches later made their way onto YouTube for Linkin Park fans to enjoy. Each night, he took the time to thank the fans for their support—always, but especially over the past year.

As Mike's life and career began to feel closer to normal, the people around him found the strength to start moving on, too. Dave started cohosting a podcast, *Member Guest*, with professional golfer Brendan Steele, and they'd invite rock stars and PGA Tour winners on for free-flowing conversations. Meanwhile, Joe spent time overseas in 2019 touring China and Korea with a photo exhibit called *Carry On* that featured shots from Linkin Park's final shows with Chester and serving as a judge on a Korean reality TV show, the musical supergroup competition *Super Band*.

Joe also directed the 2018 music video for "Waste It on Me," a collaboration between a friend of Linkin Park, Steve Aoki, and BTS, a quickly rising K-pop group that would soon be headlining US stadiums. He appreciated the opportunity to work with young Korean artists, some of whom grew up listening to Linkin Park, on both *Super Band* and the video shoot. "Things are changing," Joe declared of Korean representation in American music, after many years of feeling like an outsider.

Although Linkin Park did not issue any new material featuring Chester's voice for years after his death, posthumous releases began to pop up outside the band's official sphere. In early 2019, Lamb of God guitarist Mark Morton released "Cross Off," a battering metal track with Chester on vocals that they had worked on three months before his passing and that Mike remembered Chester excitedly playing for him in his car.

And though the Grey Daze reunion that had been planned for 2017 turned into an afterthought in the wake of his death, Chester's former band announced a rerelease of their early music a few years later. *Amends*, which was issued in June 2020 and includes eleven songs from Grey Daze's first two albums, is fully remastered around Chester's original vocals and features a handful of special musical collaborators, turning what were once muddied grunge tracks into streamlined showcases of Chester's incomparable voice. In addition to Ryan Shuck, Korn's Brian "Head" Welch and James "Munky" Shaffer and Bush's Chris Traynor all contributed to *Amends*, with Jaime Bennington, Chester's eldest son, providing backing vocals on the somber ballad "Soul Song."

Naturally, the band asked for and received Talinda Bennington's blessing before pursuing the album in earnest. "The Grey Daze project is one of the ways we can continue to tell Chester's story and connect with his fans," Talinda wrote after it was announced in late 2019. For her part, Talinda had continued her activism in the years following Chester's passing, winning the 2020 Mental Health Ambassador Award from Didi Hirsch Mental Health Services that April for her work with 320 Changes Direction.

In March 2020, when the world shut down because of the coronavirus pandemic and the live industry came to a standstill, Mike, Dave, and Joe held a charity livestream viewing of a previously unseen 2001 Linkin Park concert in San Diego to raise money for touring crews and roadies. For forty-nine minutes, the trio of bandmates watched their younger selves bust through *Hybrid Theory* while sharing behind-the-scenes stories alongside the concert footage, like a retro director's commentary.

Dave reminisced about how Joe would get annoyed at Brad for jumping too boisterously around his DJ setup and messing with his gear, and Mike marveled during Chester's screaming on "Runaway." All three guys forgot the name of the demo "And One" as they watched themselves perform it—Dave asks, "Is this 'Carousel'?" which instantly became a meme in the fandom—and cringed at their turn-of-the-century styles, particularly Mike's purple-blue gelled hair and Chester's bleached-blond locks. "We were dyeing our own hair," Mike recalled fondly. "At this point in time, we had a platinum record, and we were on our second single, that did or was about to go to No. 1 at alternative rock—and we were, like, cutting each other's hair and putting Rite Aid garbage in our hair!" His face broke into a wide grin, and his body rocked to the side in laughter.

Fans loved the watch-along—as well as raising money for friends of the band in need, the video felt like an intimate check-in with pals during the COVID lockdown. As the pandemic stretched on, Mike harnessed that communication line for a different purpose: he began hosting interactive livestreams on Twitch, spending hours-long sessions producing instrumental songs in real time with fan participation, answering questions about Linkin Park and his career, and generally talking through quarantine thoughts and feelings.

Songs from the Twitch streams began to accumulate, with Mike starting tracks from scratch, letting fans pick genres and themes, and inviting musician friends to send loops as foundations. The tracks, which leaned toward spacey electronica, were "a product of the viewers' suggestions, my spur-of-the-moment ideas, and whatever inexplicable magic is floating in between," he explained. Each song wandered less over the course of these creations as Mike led the online community and identified the musical hooks in real time.

Mike bundled twelve songs in July 2020 as *Dropped Frames, Vol. 1*, the first of three full-lengths of free-ranging electronic music made with fans from around the world. These projects were independently funded and mostly instrumental: "Listen to them while you chill, while you work, while you paint, while you eat, while you play . . . wherever they fit into your life," Mike wrote. The *Dropped Frames* projects were created collaboratively, and without commercial aspirations, during an uncertain moment in the world. They were the sound of Mike letting the light directly into his home studio.

———————

As THE BAND MEMBERS EXPLORED new endeavors and side projects in the years following Chester's death, they'd be asked: So, what's going on with Linkin Park?

The answers often revolved around the guys staying in touch with each other—including members like Brad and Rob, who haven't been active on social media in recent years—but still uncertain of the makeup of the band's future. In 2020, for instance, Dave said that they had been "casually" writing new material before the pandemic, but the following year, Mike said that the guys don't have the "emotional and creative math" figured out for any sort of comeback. Hologram performances had become more commonplace in the decade since a fake 2Pac roamed the Coachella stage in 2012, but whenever they were asked about the idea of performing with a Chester hologram, the guys responded with a resounding "never." A stage return would obviously provoke consumer intrigue—Linkin Park had grossed a whopping $120 million in tickets over the course of their run, according to Boxscore—but for the band members, giving longtime fans false hope about a haphazard comeback seemed pointless.

"There's no tours, there's no music, there's no albums in the pipeline," Mike clarified in April 2022. "I say that because anytime the band says anything or does anything, everyone tries to start up the hype train, and we're like, 'No, no, no, no. Don't start up the hype train.' You're gonna disappoint yourself. Don't do that."

Time and again, they reiterated that there were no future plans while revisiting their past: the livestream watch-along of an old performance in early 2020 set the stage for *Hybrid Theory (20th Anniversary Edition)*, a comprehensive box set released that October. In addition to the original album and *Reanimation*, the set boasted B-sides, LPU rarities, three DVDs (including *Frat Party at the Pankake Festival*), and the highly sought-after demo "She Couldn't," a moody showcase of soft harmonies and programmed beats that had accidentally leaked online in 2009 but never been formally issued.

The box set was stuffed with goodies for hardcore listeners, while casual fans got to relive Linkin Park's diamond-selling debut in all its glory, thanks in part to Sirius XM's limited-run music channel, "Linkin Park Radio," and the band's press run reflecting on the staying power of *Hybrid Theory*. "It's a nice time to pause and think and focus on what it took to make that record, the impact it had, and the opportunity it allowed us to continue with our careers," Joe said. "For me, it's a testament to the camaraderie between all the guys in the band, to our friendship, to our work ethic, to the values in how we approached not just making music but the business of making music, and the way we interact with our fans."

Those fans responded to the rerelease with their wallets: *Hybrid Theory* reentered the *Billboard* 200 albums chart at No. 12 upon the release of the twentieth-anniversary edition, its highest ranking since 2002, and over sixty-six thousand box sets have been sold to date, according to Luminate. Yet the reality was, Linkin Park didn't need a box set to have their music live on into the late 2010s and early 2020s. In the five years following the band's final studio album, Linkin Park's legacy kept expanding as their songs kept getting reinterpreted, with new fans and artists molding different tracks into new shapes.

That's how a mash-up of Linkin Park's "Talking to Myself" and Twenty One Pilots' "Heavydirtysoul" earned over six million views; a splicing of "Heavy" and Evanescence's "My Immortal" earned rapturous YouTube comments like "I just couldn't stop crying"; and "Faint" crossed with Lady Gaga's "Just Dance" got tagged as "ridiculously fun" by *Kerrang!* A few years before former Bad Wolves frontman Tommy Vext issued a haunting, piano-led take on "Crawling" that made the blog rounds, the rap-rock group Fever 333 covered "In the End" for the Spotify Singles series, with singer Jason Aalon Butler enthusing, "I wish I could tell my fourteen-year-old self that one day I'd receive a DM from Mike Shinoda about him liking my music."

But those are just a few notable hard-rock Linkin Park cover versions. If you journey down a deep-enough YouTube wormhole, you'll discover an endless string of cross-genre song renditions, from K-pop group ATEEZ's operatic cover of "Numb" to a banjo-led bluegrass take on "What I've Done" by the Italian siblings Melodicka Bros to a jazzy string version of "In the End" by Postmodern Jukebox performer Robyn Adele Anderson.

There's a video of 266 musicians across thirty-five countries virtually performing "In the End" during the pandemic lockdown and another in which UK-based eleven-year-old Nandi Bushell goes berserk on the drums as she plays along to "Numb." Some of these clips predated Tik-Tok; others fit right in to its short-form virality—in 2023, for example, a trend took off on the platform that mashed up a sped-up version of "Lying from You" with rapper Project Pat's song "Take Da Charge," demonstrating that LP was doing well within the realms of Gen Z. And as artificial intelligence technology becomes more prevalent in popular music, AI versions of Chester "covering" other artists' songs are flooding YouTube—although new tech can't fully replicate the idiosyncrasies of his vocal approach, of course.

Perhaps the most fitting testament to the band's current reach is the number and variety of popular artists who have explicitly paid tribute to Linkin Park in recent years or cited the band as an important influence. Naturally, those have included major rock acts such as Bring Me the Horizon, whose frontman Oli Sykes has said that Linkin Park was the reason he wanted to be in a band in the first place; Of Mice & Men, whose singer Austin Carlile has pointed to *Hybrid Theory* as the first album he ever loved on his own terms; and Machine Gun Kelly, whose combination of rap and rock owes a lot to the Linkin Park CD he played on repeat in his youth. But that collection also includes more surprising nods, from, for example, The Weeknd, who shouted out Chester's impact during a 2021 Apple Music radio show, to Billie Eilish, who said that her favorite Linkin Park song is the *A Thousand Suns* deep cut "When They Come for Me"; even Rihanna called Chester "literally the most impressive talent I've ever seen live."

As Linkin Park's hiatus stretched past the five-year mark, their music was still being name-checked by superstars, performed by artists with followings large and small, made into memes, and mashed up with a litany of songs and styles. In the same way that Mike felt an obligation to respond to Linkin Park fans in the months after Chester's passing, listeners felt compelled to react to Linkin Park's music, paying homage to the songs and albums when it seemed like more of them would not be following. These gestures could be as tiny as a sped-up TikTok clip or as grand as a soul-burning cover, but the sentiment around the music was more or less the same. The band had shared pieces of themselves with the world for so many years, and now, in an act of reflection, the world was holding those pieces back up for them.

And those reflections will remain endless—there won't be a day when new remembrances and riffs on the band cease to be made. Linkin Park's body of work may be finite, but when refracted through the prism of a global fan base, its limitations do not exist.

CHAPTER 25

I t's early March 2023, the type of crisp, cloudless, low-fifties Monday in New York City that suggests spring will arrive sooner than expected. Mike got into town the previous night, and he's wearing a bomber jacket and camouflage pants while knocking out press hits at the Warner Records headquarters. He's got a packed schedule after a delayed flight to New York, but he's all smiles.

Rather improbably, Linkin Park has just scored its biggest hit in a decade.

"Lost," the high-powered anthem that was recorded during the sessions for *Meteora* and unearthed two decades later for the *Meteora (20th Anniversary Edition)*, exploded with enough force to astonish Linkin Park fans upon its February 2023 release. The song represented a never-heard-in-full demo with Chester's completed and fully mixed lead vocals—the most precious commodity imaginable for longtime listeners. A song that made it to the finish line had been stowed away and forgotten about, and now, it was here.

Five and a half years after Chester's passing, the experience of hearing his familiar voice sing an unfamiliar tune, delicately intone a verse before roaring through a chorus, wasn't just unexpected and satisfying—it was overwhelming. The reactions within the Linkin Park Discord Community, message boards, Reddit threads, and social platforms were steeped in years of aching nostalgia, missing Chester's voice and then feeling bowled over when it unexpectedly returned. Many fans captured their first-listen tears in YouTube reaction videos, with titles like "I was NOT Ready for Linkin Park's New Song 'Lost'" and "This Destroyed Me!"

But then, "Lost" transcended Linkin Park's fan base. The song debuted at No. 38 on the Hot 100 upon its release—the band's first Top 40 hit on the chart since 2012—and was subsequently promoted to rock radio as a new single. Programmers responded enthusiastically: "Lost" spent eight weeks at No. 1 on the Mainstream Rock chart, outlasting the No. 1 runs that year by singles from active bands like Foo Fighters and Metallica, and surpassed a staggering twenty weeks at No. 1 on Rock Airplay. Combine those radio hits with hundreds of millions of streams and countless fan remixes and reaction clips, and what could have been a gift to hardcore listeners as part of a box set (à la "She Couldn't," on the *Hybrid Theory (20th Anniversary Edition)* instead became one of the biggest rock hits of 2023.

"I felt like it would connect well with fans that were around back then," Mike said in March during his New York City trip. "I didn't expect it to, like, trend on TikTok!"

Mike was right to be surprised: songs like "Lost," posthumous singles released years after a band was last active, do not typically garner widespread listens outside of their respective fandoms. The closest analog to "Lost" is Nirvana's "You Know You're Right," a fan-favorite demo that was unveiled with a fully produced studio version in 2002 as part of a greatest-hits box set—but even that single didn't perform as well on the charts as "Lost"; it earned rock-radio play but peaked outside the Top 40 of the Hot 100.

Whereas TikTok trends have made it easier for old songs to be recontextualized as new hits, "Lost" was positioned as a new single from an old era. Mainstream curiosity about an unreleased Linkin Park song with Chester's lead vocals may have helped "Lost" score some piqued-interest listens in its first week of release, yet how does that explain its regular spins on rock radio in the weeks and months after it arrived?

Granted, it helped that "Lost" was created during one of the band's most commercially successful eras—*Meteora* already had three Top

40 singles on its track list, the most of any of the band's albums—and sounded closer to those hit singles than to a shrugged-off deep cut. "Lost" is a classic early-period Linkin Park anthem, with its soft-to-loud alchemy, electronic undertones and DJ scratches informing the hard-rock production, Mike's haunted midverse interjections, and outsized scream-along chorus.

Naturally, Chester's voice ties the song together, using the verses to examine the pieces of himself that will never be whole ("I'm trapped in yesterday / Where the pain is all I know") before unleashing hell in the hook ("I'm *LOST*! In these *memories*! / Living behind my *own illusion*!"). Brad said in February 2023, "When I heard it recently, for the first time in twenty years, I was really taken aback by the song, and particularly Chester's vocal performance. It's just so beautiful and raw and stunning."

The reason why "Lost" didn't make the *Meteora* track list—it was, in fact, the very last song to be cut from the twelve-song album—is because it sounded too similar to what would eventually become the album's biggest hit. "It had the same energy as 'Numb,'" Mike explained. "We were like, 'Oh, we can't have two "Numb"s on the album, let's save this for later.' And then I guess we left it on a hard drive and forgot about it!"

Over the years, fans spotted clues that "Lost" existed somewhere—a lyric sheet on a *Meteora* making-of DVD, a stray instrumental on an LPTV episode. But unlike "She Couldn't" from *Hybrid Theory*, which was leaked relatively intact years before its box-set release, "Lost" had been sitting dormant on that hard drive without ever seeing the light of day for two decades.

The quality of those archives are ultimately what compelled the band to revisit *Meteora*, after Mike was initially "not bullish" about releasing another twentieth-anniversary edition following the *Hybrid Theory* set in 2020. When Mike began sifting through outtakes from the *Meteora* sessions, however, he realized how much worthy material had been left on the cutting-room floor. "This is such a different animal than the *Hybrid Theory* one," Mike said ahead of the *Meteora* box set. "In the era of *Hybrid*

Theory, we were just kids in our bedrooms—we didn't save stuff, we weren't filming anything, video footage wasn't a thing. . . . We decided that we'd look into doing one for *Meteora*. And, immediately, we found *so much good stuff.*"

In addition to "Lost," the band stumbled on "Fighting Myself," which they remembered as an unfinished production but found vocal stems for in the summer of 2022; the final product sounds like a riveting sequel to "Papercut," with a tower of guitars surrounding Chester and Mike's interplay. "More the Victim" was originally released as the instrumental "Cumulus" on an LPU album but was fleshed out with slippery rap verses from Mike, a fire-breathing Chester hook, and plenty of slick Joe scratches. And the Mike-sung "Massive," the piano- and string-assisted "Healing Foot," and the sinister crunch of "A6" each nod toward the sonic evolution that Linkin Park was about to make on *Minutes to Midnight.*

For fans, the six unreleased demos represented a treasure trove from one of the band's most fruitful eras and were a source of comfort after many years without any new Linkin Park material. For the band members, the *Meteora* twentieth-anniversary set was an opportunity to revisit a huge project created during a formative period and spend some extra time with each other, over Zoom and in person.

Mike said putting together the *Hybrid Theory* box set just three years after Chester's passing felt "a little bittersweet," but going back to *Meteora* with his bandmates couldn't have been more enjoyable. After all, they were now longtime friends in their mid-forties reviewing long-forgotten songs and highly embarrassing clips from their mid-twenties. Mike let out a laugh when he remembered how Dave watched some of the behind-the-scenes footage with his family—and his kids mercilessly clowned on the band's hairstyles and outfits.

"It's a very feel-good nostalgia," Mike explained. "I think everybody had a different experience with unearthing this stuff, and for me, it felt like when you go into your attic and you find an old box of stuff from your childhood. Like, photographs you forgot you took, stuff that makes you go, 'Oh my God, this thing, I can't believe this thing still exists!' And it teleports you right back to that time."

So did hearing "Lost" throughout 2023: in the streaming era, when so much popular music can be played anytime on demand, encountering Chester's voice in an alternative-radio block or on a shuffled Spotify hits playlist felt like a chance reunion with an old friend. For a generation who had grown up being greeted by Chester when turning the dial or popping in a mixtape, "Lost" reopened a flood of stored-up memories. It wasn't just a newly released demo of a box set. It was a reminder of a bond that remained intact.

———————

ALTHOUGH MIKE HAD FLOWN OUT to New York one month before the release of the *Meteora* box set, he had actually traveled there on behalf of a different project. He was in town for the NYC premiere of *Scream VI*, the latest installment in the hit slasher series, since he contributed a pair of songs to its soundtrack—one of his own and another with a major pop star.

After touring behind *Post Traumatic* through 2019 and releasing the three *Dropped Frames* compilations at the start of the pandemic, Mike decided to take a break from releasing music with his vocals on it in the early 2020s and pivoted to being more of a studio collaborator. "I had been doing writing and production for other people for a while, maybe almost two years," Mike explained. "And a lot of those songs kind of went nowhere—sometimes because they maybe weren't that great, sometimes because the artist just wasn't feeling how they were fitting in with their material, or whatever. And I was getting pretty discouraged."

By the end of 2022, Mike had started messing around with some demos—"just for fun, just to get out of my head on it"—while he and the rest of Linkin Park were finishing up the *Meteora* twentieth-anniversary material. A producer for the *Scream* franchise gave him a ring to see if he'd be interested in working with Demi Lovato on a song for the upcoming film. Mike brought her his demos and played a few samples for the *Scream* producers; Demi liked one demo, and the *Scream* team liked another.

"They basically said, 'Is there any way you could do two songs for the movie?'" Mike recalled. And that's how he soundtracked the opening *and* closing credits for one of the highest-grossing horror movies of 2023.

"Still Alive," which Mike produced and cowrote with Demi and songwriter-musician Laura Veltz, is a guitar-heavy pop-punk song focused on fighting for survival (a common theme in every *Scream* plot, of course). The song wasn't inspired by the slasher franchise, though. Instead, the concept came from Mike's first conversation with Demi, a veteran pop virtuoso whose time in the public eye had been impacted by substance abuse and mental health issues.

"She said, 'I feel like I'm in a really good place where I want to be alive—to keep going, to treat my body well and take care of myself,'" recalled Mike. Just like he had done so many times before with Chester, Mike helped turn that conversation into the fulcrum of a musical collaboration.

On "Still Alive," Demi's vocal theatrics complement Mike's galloping percussion and electric snarl on what he described as a "badass empowerment song." The track contains some impressively visceral pop songwriting—"I'm still alive / I don't wanna just survive / Give me something to sink all my teeth in / Eat the devil and spit out my demons," Demi sings on the hook—and a driving arrangement from Mike that plays into the electro-rock sound that Demi had been diving deeper into at the time.

While "Still Alive" closes out *Scream VI*, the title credits flash into the sound of "In My Head," Mike's own song featuring rising Arizona singer-songwriter Kailee Morgue. Over stormy synths and tribal drums, Mike delivers an urgent pop track "about intrusive thoughts and paranoia and second-guessing," he said, and Kailee forms a call-and-response chorus, as if she's playing the role of Mike's innermost fears. "In My Head" is more somber thematically than "Still Alive" but sounds more freewheeling, with Mike feeding off of the frenetic pacing and knowing how to slam the gas on the pop harmonies.

By the time Mike issued "In My Head" in March 2023, it had been years since he had released a proper solo track. "One thing I like about this is the attitude—it's back to a more serious, darker aesthetic," he said. "I do want to make some more, maybe a little darker stuff. It just feels like what I'm into right now."

Although Mike didn't have a timetable for a solo follow-up to *Post Traumatic*, whatever trepidation he had about returning to the microphone seemed to have disappeared—and the years of futile studio work even carried a silver lining. "Since I have been working with so many different artists, writers, and producers in the last few years," Mike said, "I've picked up a bunch of [new] tools and perspectives."

Mike had released limited music prior to the pair of *Scream* songs. In 2021, he hopped on the single "Happy Endings" with Iann Dior and Upsahl and unveiled a six-minute "NFT mixtape" called *Ziggurats* later that year. In the time since, however, he's moved on to releasing songs under his own name while also producing for other artists. After working on songs with PVRIS and Grandson in 2023, Mike released a tenacious solo track, "Already Over," that boasted high-octane vocals, slashing guitars, and a hook primed to pummel alternative-radio blocks (the song was, in fact, the format's most-added new track during the week of its release in October 2023).

That recent work might crystallize a path to where a polymath like Mike is headed in the coming years. Linkin Park's musical architect has always been both a skilled studio whiz and a purposeful performer, able to bolster other voices while plainly expressing his own point of view. Some periods of Mike's life have been more prolific than others—but he's always creating, on some level, and he always will be.

"I feel reinvigorated," Mike reflected on that March day in New York City. "I feel like I'm a better writer than I was a few years ago, which is a good feeling."

FOLLOWING *METEORA (20TH ANNIVERSARY EDITION)*—WHICH helped the album return to the top 10 of the *Billboard* 200 chart upon its release—the specific future of Linkin Park remained unknown. Mike, Brad, Joe, Dave, and Rob were all in regular communication, but the path forward without Chester was still cloudy as the sixth anniversary of his death approached. Plus, all the members had families to think about, and the majority were still raising young children. The timetable of a return and the specifics of what it would look like were impossible to nail down, so the band could only offer refrains of *maybe, someday*, while reiterating that, deep down, the desire endured.

"The best answer I can give is I think that we will do something again at some point," Dave said. "I think we'll do, hopefully, new music. And I would love to play some shows." In a separate interview, Mike tried to navigate expectations by distinguishing between what was and was not realistic. "We're not touring right now," he asserted—but outside of that, "I don't think there's very much to say is off the table."

For Linkin Park fans, there will always be the hope of more—more unreleased material, more anniversary celebrations, more new music from the band, more in-person opportunities, more ways to honor Chester. No one, not even the members of Linkin Park themselves, knows precisely how much more there will be.

Yet when considering the band's future, Mike's words from "Waiting for the End" come to mind: "This is not the end, this is not the beginning / Just a voice, like a riot, rockin' every revision." Linkin Park's story is still being written and rewritten, a work in progress that did not end with Chester's passing in 2017. And the reason why it's ongoing is simple: Linkin Park is still everywhere.

The proof of how many people are still listening to the band is not just in its prevalence across modern music—it's in the numbers, too. Both *Hybrid Theory* and *Meteora* remain juggernauts to this day, still regularly appearing on the *Billboard* 200, charting alongside new albums more than two decades after their releases, having respectively earned 13.5 million and 8.5 million equivalent album units to date, according to Luminate. And the biggest hits from those albums, along with the rest of Linkin Park's catalog, still garner plenty of radio plays, with the band earning fifty-five thousand spins on terrestrial and satellite radio during an average month in 2023.

In an alt-rock radio ecosystem that allows for a few heritage bands to comfortably exist alongside new-school stars, Linkin Park are as omnipresent as bands like Nirvana, Pearl Jam, and Red Hot Chili Peppers—legends with deep catalogs of hits that rock fans of various ages still want to hear on repeat. They're also as enormous as the current stars. Many of the active rock headliners—think Foo Fighters, Paramore, and Fall Out Boy, all of whom have released new studio albums and toured arenas in the past two years—pull in between 20 million and 25 million monthly listeners on Spotify. Linkin Park haven't released an album or played a show since 2017, and despite that, their monthly listeners routinely hover around 34.2 million.

As the music industry shifted over the course of the guys' career, their mind-boggling sales and radio stats have translated to streaming achievements that are often just as staggering. *Hybrid Theory* recently crossed four billion total Spotify streams right around the time that the music video for "Numb" celebrated two billion YouTube views. And as the band has cracked seven-figure follower counts across social media—Instagram, 6.3 million; Twitter, 5.7 million; and TikTok, 1.1 million—their 57 million Facebook followers make them the most followed band on the platform. Put it this way: there are more people who follow Linkin Park on Facebook than people who live in Spain or Canada. However big you think Linkin Park are, they're *bigger*.

Eventually, those numbers will help signify a wider acknowledgment of the band's cultural impact, and the tide will turn on their critical standing in the modern rock canon. Linkin Park became enormous upon their debut and remain so today, but they were never a passing fad that happened to stick around. Instead, they rejected the rock trend that helped them explode and moved far beyond its contours in sound and significance. Any nu metal naysayer half-paying attention to Linkin Park's journey understands why their identity rose miles above that movement; any music fan who's at all plugged in to popular rock this century knows that the band released a plethora of stone-cold, singular hits. In 2025, Linkin Park will become eligible to be inducted into the Rock and Roll Hall of Fame. They may not make it in on the first ballot, but they deserve to—and hopefully, one day, they will be in.

Ultimately, though, these specific accolades don't matter. No plaque, trophy, or honorific could ever wholly define the legacy of a band so vital, whose songs throbbed with a guttural human emotion that could be latched on to like an instinct. The band's radically honest messages reached deep into the souls of their listeners at a time when mental health wasn't talked about enough and helped fans reckon with abstract concepts and specific issues. And often, Chester, the delicate scream of a generation, was the one delivering those messages.

In the years since Chester's passing, Linkin Park's music has not receded into the past, and its influence hasn't begun to flag. A thousand tiny moments in the recent life of the band are proof of that. It's Chester's name trending on Twitter on the fifth anniversary of his death in July 2022. It's the band getting nominated for an MTV Video Music Award in 2023 for "Lost," listed alongside some of the year's most high-profile rock tracks from Foo Fighters, Metallica, and Måneskin with a long-forgotten demo. It's the five-thousand-member "Art" channel in the LPU Discord, where fans share new Linkin Park drawings and tattoos. It's the next generation of music listeners—some of whom will casually check out the band's biggest hits, others of whom will tumble fully down the rabbit hole and become obsessed—discovering them every single day.

Mike is experiencing a little of that already as he watches his kids grow up and their friends find out what he does for a living. "They'll send my kids a message, like, 'Your dad is in Linkin Park? *Dude!*'" Mike said. "It's cool that they like it. The fact that it's still meaningful to anybody is . . . I mean, you know."

He didn't need to finish the thought. Linkin Park's music will be passed down, and to a bunch of kids from outside of Los Angeles (and one from Phoenix), that means everything.

It started with one show, one song, one album, one light. And now, it's become bigger than anyone could have ever imagined.

ACKNOWLEDGMENTS

This book wouldn't have been possible without Linkin Park fans around the world, and I mean that literally—the majority of my research was aided by tremendous fan archival efforts, including decades-old concert footage, tour data, elusive demos, and recording details you won't necessarily find in the liner notes. Thank you to anyone who offered a piece of this puzzle, and a special thanks to Linkinpedia and Linkin Park Live for the years of comprehensive documentation.

To Chester, Mike, Brad, Rob, Dave, and Joe: Thank you for everything. A special thanks to Laura Swanson for your help from day one, Ceri Roberts and the Warner Records team, and Ryan DeMarti and Trish Evangelista for offering so much support from Team Linkin Park.

Thank you to my agent, Anthony Mattero, for the years of support and for walking around Montclair in the rain with me one day as I explained this book idea. I could not have done this without your steadying force, and I am forever grateful. A huge thanks to Carrie Napolitano at Hachette for a wonderful editing experience and for the encouragement. And thank you to the whole Hachette team—especially Sean Moreau, Ashley Kiedrowski, and Lauren Rosenthal—for standing behind this book with such passion and kindness.

Thank you to everyone who helped me figure out how to write a nonfiction music book: Steven Hyden and Tom Breihan for answering some early questions and informing my perspective; Nadine Pena, Patrick Confrey, Maris Kreizman, Charlie Adelman, and Jamie Abzug for letting me pick your brains when I had no idea what I was doing; and Chris Payne for inspiring me to write a music book in the first place after writing a kick-ass one of your own. A special thanks to Andrew Unterberger for being the most thoughtful music editor that I could ever ask for—this book is better because of you.

An enormous shout-out to my entire *Billboard* team, past and present. A special thanks to Tye Comer, Bill Werde, Monica Damashek, Cortney Harding, Gail Mitchell, Jill Mapes, and Jess Letkemann for the early and continued support (and to Jess for going with me to Linkin Park at MSG!); Keith Caulfield, Joe Lynch, Katie Atkinson, Denise Schaefer, Erin Strecker, Trish Halpin, Laura Tucker, Gab Ginsberg, Erika Ramirez, Steven Horowitz, Benjamin Meadows-Ingram, Hilary Hughes, Jeff Benjamin, Bianca Gracie, Andrew Hampp, William Gruger, Craig Marks, Mike Bruno, Jayme Klock, and Ross Scarano for being my crew and helping me develop professionally; and Hannah Karp, Christine Werthman, Dana Droppo, Lyndsey Havens, Katie Bain, Rebecca Milzoff, Colin Stutz, Carl Lamarre, Neena Rouhani, Kristin Robinson, and Josh Glicksman for being incredibly encouraging as I worked on this book. If I didn't mention you by name, please know that I meant to do so. I couldn't have asked for a better career to this point and for better people with whom to share it.

Thanks to Ryan Shuck, Sonny Sandoval, Rob Swift, Skylar Grey, Amir Derakh, Travis Stever, and Ryan Key for sharing your stories with me and for strengthening this book with your interviews. You are all appreciated beyond words. Thanks to the folks at NAMI and Backline for all your incredible work to provide mental illness and mental health resources. I'm proud to partner with such important and exemplary organizations for this book.

To my guys—Jake, Pat, Nick, Chris, Darren, Dom, Dave, Leo—you are my brothers, and I'm grateful for all of you. To my sister Dara, who I'm proud of forever. Thank you to my family: Gary, Janette, Zach, Jared, Adrienne, Julian, Penelope, Gideon, Simon, Alan, Alicia, Zach, Sue, Peter, Matthew, Sarah, Nancy. You guys are my backbone. Thank you to Walter Bowne, Ed Brandhorst, Felicia Steele, Donna Shaw, Tony Klock, James Queally, Julie Miller, and all the teachers and editors who helped me along the way. Thank you to the *Rights to Ricky Sanchez* podcast for soundtracking many dog walks and helping me sort my thoughts while writing this book. Thank you to Murray for being the best dog on the entire planet.

To my parents, Beth and David: I am nowhere without you both. Thank you for always believing in me and for seeing me as a writer before I saw myself as one.

And to my wife Vanessa and our daughter Phoebe: thank you for filling my life with joy and purpose. You are my heart, and you are my home. I love you both forever.

REFERENCES

New interviews for the interludes sections have been condensed for clarity.
All sales statistics and data compiled in December 2023 and courtesy of Luminate.

CHAPTER 1

Blue, Jeff. *One Step Closer*. New York: Permuted Press, 2020.

Fresch, Will. "An Interview with Rob Bourdon." Linkin Park Times, March 2003. http://web.archive.org/web/20040807103427if_/http://lptimes.com/article /Crazewire_031203.html.

Lecaro, Lina. "Linkin Park's Rap 'N' Rock." *Los Angeles Times*, February 1, 2001. https://www.latimes.com/archives/la-xpm-2001-feb-01-ca-19532-story.html.

Morton, Luke. "The Secret History of Linkin Park's Hybrid Theory: In Their Own Words." *Kerrang!*, October 7, 2020. https://www.kerrang.com/the-secret-history -of-linkin-parks-hybrid-theory-in-their-own-words.

Moss, Corey, with Peter Wilkinson. "Linkin Park: In the Beginning." MTV, 2008. https://web.archive.org/web/20080930135447/http://www.mtv.com/bands/l /linkin_park/news_feature_mar_02/index.jhtml.

MYX Global. "MYX Headliner for November Mike Shinoda Reveals His First Job at a Produce Farm!" Facebook, November 1, 2019. https://www.facebook.com /MYXGlobal/videos/422523575078813/.

NME Blog. "Mike Shinoda, Linkin Park—Does Rock'n'Roll Kill Brain Cells?" *NME*, November 25, 2010. http://web.archive.org/web/20170814015946/http: //www.nme.com/blogs/nme-blogs/mike-shinoda-linkin-park-does-rocknroll -kill-brain-cells-781641.

Robb, Doug (@HoobaDoug). "I actually think that IS." X, August 12, 2022, 1:02 p.m., https://twitter.com/HoobaDoug/status/1558167038350221312.

Scraggs, Austin. "The Mellower Half of Linkin Park." Linkin Park Times, 2013; reprint, *Rolling Stone*, March 26, 2003. http://web.archive.org/web/20131019142856 /http://www.lptimes.com/article/RS_032603.html.

"UCLA Interview." Brad Delson Online (blog), September 2008. http://delsononline .blogspot.com/2008/09/ucla-interview.html.

CHAPTER 2

Booseman, Phil. "Dee Snider Doesn't Blame Grunge: 'Hair Metal Did It to Itself . . . It Wasn't Metal Anymore.'" MetalSucks, March 24, 2022. https://www .metalsucks.net/2022/03/24/dee-snider-doesnt-blame-grunge-hair-metal-did -it-to-itself-it-wasnt-metal-anymore/.

Hilburn, Robert. "Beyond the Grunge." *Los Angeles Times*, May 31, 1998. https://www .latimes.com/archives/la-xpm-1998-may-31-ca-54952-story.html.

Laing, Rob. "Eddie Vedder on the Legacy of Grunge: 'Girls, Girls, Girls and Mötley Crüe . . . I Hated It.'" MusicRadar, February 4, 2022. https://www.musicradar .com/news/eddie-vedder-grunge-pearl-jam-motley-crue.

94.9 the Rock Toronto. "Mike Shinoda on 'Post Traumatic,' Chester's Death, Performing with the Roots, Donald Trump + More." YouTube video, 23:16, June 26, 2018. https://www.youtube.com/watch?v=uZMsdPmKlXU.

Schuftan, Craig. *Entertain Us: The Rise and Fall of Alternative Rock in the Nineties.* Sydney, Australia: Harper360, 2015.

CHAPTER 3

Alex. "Club Tattoo's Chester Bennington Interview, Pt 1." Etnies, January 18, 2008. http://web.archive.org/web/20090106120537/http://etnies.com./blog/2008 /01/18/club-tattoos-chester-bennington-interview-pt-1/.

Bennington, Samantha. *Falling Love Notes: Memories of a Rock Star Wife.* Woodland Hills, CA: Around the Way Publishing, 2020.

Bryant, Tom. "Linkin Park, Kerrang! January 23, 2008." Tom-Bryant.com. http: //www.tom-bryant.com/linkin-park-kerrang—tom-bryant.html.

Buchanan, Brett. "Chester Bennington's Mother Emotionally Opens Up About First Time He Sang as Toddler." *Alternative Nation*, September 7, 2017. https://www.alternativenation.net/chester-bennington-mother-opens-up-first -time-sang-toddler/.

Doyle, Tomas. "'I Even Saw Some Fans Doing Heroin Outside One of Those Shows'—the Real Story Behind Linkin Park's Hybrid Theory." Louder, October 24, 2022. https://www.loudersound.com/features/the-real-story-behind -linkin-parks-hybrid-theory.

Fricke, David. "Linkin Park: David Fricke Talks to Chester Bennington About 'Hybrid Theory' Success." *Rolling Stone*, March 14, 2002. https://www .rollingstone.com/music/music-features/linkin-park-david-fricke-talks-to -chester-bennington-about-hybrid-theory-success-67820/4/.

Krause, Jonathan. "Grey Daze Story." Grey Daze. https://greydaze.clan.su/index/grey _daze_story_by_jonathan_krause/0-23.

Lestat. "A 'Sean Dowdell and His Friends?' to 'Grey Daze' Retrospective." Linkin Park Live, April 15, 2017. https://lplive.net/wiki/exclusives/sdahf-to-grey-daze -retrospective/.

Ragogna, Mike. "Conversations with Stone Temple Pilot's [*sic*] Chester Bennington, Gavin DeGraw and Boz Scaggs, Plus a Pillars and Tongues Exclusive." *Huff-Post*, October 28, 2013. https://www.huffpost.com/entry/conversations-with -stone_b_4168769.

Wiederhorn, Jon. "Linkin Park's Chester Bennington Gets Trapped in 'Saw 3D.'" Noisecreep, October 12, 2010. https://noisecreep.com/linkin-park-chester -bennington-saw-3d/.

CHAPTER 4

AndOne. "Grey Daze Story." Linkin Park Live, September 20, 2015. https://lplive
.net/wiki/exclusives/grey-daze-story/.

Bryant, Tom. "Linkin Park, Kerrang! January 23, 2008." Tom-Bryant.com. http:
//www.tom-bryant.com/linkin-park-kerrang—tom-bryant.html.

Christgau, Robert. "Nothing's Scary." Robert Christgau; reprint, *Village Voice*, October 13, 1998. https://www.robertchristgau.com/xg/rock/familyva-98.php.

Doyle, Tomas. "'I Even Saw Some of the Fans Doing Heroin Outside One of Those
Shows'—the Real Story Behind Linkin Park's Hybrid Theory." Louder, October 24, 2022. https://www.loudersound.com/features/the-real-story-behind
-linkin-parks-hybrid-theory.

Epstein, Dan. "Linkin Park's Chester Bennington: The Lost Interview." *Revolver*, July
20, 2018. https://www.revolvermag.com/music/linkin-parks-chester-bennington
-lost-interview.

Kaufman, Gil. "Korn, Limp Bizkit Hop on Family Values Tour Bandwagon." MTV,
July 9, 1998. https://www.mtv.com/news/63zgm0/korn-limp-bizkit-hop-on
-family-values-tour-bandwagon.

Linkin Park Live Archive. "LPLive Interview: Kyle Christner (2020.12.11)." YouTube
video, 56:59, July 4, 2021. https://www.youtube.com/watch?v=0N7tjGP7UDM.

LPL Staff. "Mike Q&A Summary 6/19/2020." Linkin Park Live, June 21, 2020.
https://lplive.net/forums/topic/14219-mike-qa-summary-6192020/.

94.9 the Rock Toronto. "Mike Shinoda on 'Post Traumatic', Chester's Death, Performing with the Roots, Donald Trump + More." YouTube video, 23:16, June
26, 2018. https://www.youtube.com/watch?v=uZMsdPmKlXU.

Wiederhorn, Jon. "25 Years Ago: Korn Take Nu Metal to the Masses with 'Follow
the Leader.'" Loudwire, August 18, 2023. https://loudwire.com/korn-follow-the
-leader-album-anniversary/.

CHAPTER 5

Chong, Elaine. "'Racism Wasn't a Feeling, It Was a Fact': Mike Shinoda on
His Family's WWII Incarceration." *Rolling Stone*, April 20, 2022. https:
//www.rollingstone.com/music/music-features/mike-shinoda-japanese-american
-internment-camps-1339017/.

CrypticRock. "Interview—Joe Hahn of Linkin Park Talks Filmmaking." Cryp-
tic Rock, May 27, 2015. https://crypticrock.com/interview-joe-hahn-of-linkin
-park-talks-filmmaking/.

"Curse-Free Music for the Young and the Restless." *Philippine Daily Inquirer*,
June 2, 2002. https://news.google.com/newspapers?id=B1s1AAAAIBAJ&sjid
=kiUMAAAAIBAJ&pg=703.

Derek (@dereklp). "No Cover Magazine // October 2000." X, October 14, 2020,
10:58 p.m. https://twitter.com/dereklp/status/1316604432696705025/photo/2.

Eun-byel, Im. "Linkin Park's Joe Hahn Talks Band, K-Pop, Future Plans." *Korea Herald*, April 25, 2019. https://www.koreaherald.com/view.php?ud =20190425000787.

Flynn, Katherine. "Back Story: A Different Tune with Linkin Park's Mike Shinoda." *Preservation Magazine* (National Trust for Historic Preservation), Spring 2016. https://savingplaces.org/stories/back-story-a-different-tune-mike-shinoda.

Fricke, David. "Linkin Park: David Fricke Talks to Chester Bennington About 'Hybrid Theory' Success." *Rolling Stone*, March 14, 2002. https://www.rollingstone.com /music/music-features/linkin-park-david-fricke-talks-to-chester-bennington -about-hybrid-theory-success-67820/2/.

Leivers, Dannii. "Linkin Park's Mike Shinoda: 'We Never Wanted to Be Part of Nu Metal.'" Louder, October 23, 2020. https://www.loudersound.com/features /linkin-park-mike-shinoda-interview-we-never-wanted-to-be-part-of-nu-metal.

Montgomery, James. "Two New Projects Let Fans Walk a Mile in Linkin Park's Shoes." MTV, November 8, 2004. https://www.mtv.com/news/0cuhzl/two-new -projects-let-fans-walk-a-mile-in-linkin-parks-shoes.

Price, Garret, dir. *Woodstock '99: Peace, Love, and Rage*. Documentary. Episode aired on HBO, 2021.

"The Roots of Rob's Beats (LPU 1, Issue 2)." Tumblr, July 17, 2012. https: //fyeahrobbourdon.tumblr.com/post/27427016621/the-roots-of-robs-beats -lpu-1-issue-2.

Scraggs, Austin. "The Mellower Half of Linkin Park." Linkin Park Times, 2013; reprint, *Rolling Stone*, March 26, 2003. http://web.archive.org/web /20131019142856/http://www.lptimes.com/article/RS_032603.html.

Spin Staff. "How to Succeed in Bizness . . . by Really, Really Trying: Our Limp Biz-kit Cover Story." *Spin*, December 27, 2020. https://www.spin.com/2020/12 /limp-bizkit-august-1999-cover-story/.

CHAPTER 6

Brooks, Hayden. "Mike Shinoda Opens Up About Mental Health in New 'Spit' Episode." iHeart, November 8, 2018. https://www.iheart.com/content/2018-11 -08-mike-shinoda-opens-up-about-mental-health-in-new-spit-episode/.

Leivers, Dannii. "Linkin Park's Mike Shinoda: 'We Never Wanted to Be Part of Nu Metal.'" Louder, October 23, 2020. https://www.loudersound.com/features /linkin-park-mike-shinoda-interview-we-never-wanted-to-be-part-of-nu-metal.

m_shinoda. "A.06 Was a Demo We T . . ." Reddit, August 12, 2015. https://www .reddit.com/r/IAmA/comments/3gqpvp/comment/cu0mei8/?utm_source =reddit&utm_medium=web2x&context=3.

MusicRadar. "Interview: Linkin Park's Mike Shinoda—'Chester's Voice Was Insane.'" MusicRadar, July 24, 2020. https://www.musicradar.com/news/interview -linkin-parks-mike-shinoda-chesters-voice-was-insane.

"One Step Closer" Linkin Park chat, September 4, 2003. http://web.archive.org /web/20030904144436/http://www.angelfire.com/rock2/1stepcloser /linkinpark.com_chat_010710.txt.

Shinoda Livestreams. "10.29.20—Choose Your Own Adventure." YouTube video, 1:58:47, November 4, 2020. https://www.youtube.com/watch?v=i0-4_N-OO_g.

"Shoutweb Interview 2000." Mike Shinoda Clan, March 4, 2016. https://web.archive .org/web/20160304203012/http://mikeshinodaclan.com/media/interviews /shoutweb-interview-2000/.

Tyrangiel, Josh. "Linkin Park Steps Out." *Time*, January 20, 2002. https://content .time.com/time/magazine/article/0,9171,195312-2,00.html.

CHAPTER 7

Carter, Emily. "Linkin Park Share Never-Before-Seen Footage from the Making of One Step Closer." *Kerrang!*, October 26, 2020. https://www.kerrang .com/linkin-park-share-never-before-seen-footage-from-the-making-of-one -step-closer.

Lipshutz, Jason. "The Story Behind Every Song on Linkin Park's 'Hybrid Theory': 20th Anniversary Track-by-Track." *Billboard*, October 5, 2020. https://www .billboard.com/music/rock/linkin-park-hybrid-theory-20th-anniversary-track -by-track-9460473/.

CHAPTER 8

Bodegon, Kara. "'It Was Inspired by Comic Books, Video Games, Anime I Grew Up With': Mike Shinoda on His Animated Video for 'World's on Fire'— Watch." Bandwagon, September 6, 2019. https://www.bandwagon.asia/articles /mike-shinoda-animated-music-video-worlds-on-fire-post-traumatic.

Hosken, Patrick. "How Linkin Park's 'Hybrid Theory' Design Helped Define the Band." MTV, October 9, 2020. https://www.mtv.com/news/cqxrrl/linkin-park -hybrid-theory-anniversary-artwork-frank-maddocks.

Lim, Cathy. "Getting Back to His Roots." *Rafu Shimpo—L.A. Japanese Daily News*, April 28, 2006. https://web.archive.org/web/20120314055559/http://www.rafu .com/mike_shinoda.html.

Linkin Park. "One Step Closer—Behind the Scenes—Linkin Park." YouTube video, 5:11, October 24, 2020. https://www.youtube.com/watch?v=CadM0JFWc3U.

Linkin Park Coalition. "Mike Shinoda at Anime Expo 2019." YouTube video, 10:23, July 6, 2019. https://www.youtube.com/watch?v=RreIdkwGaC8.

"LP Answers Your Questions." Linkin Park Central. https://www.angelfire.com/ca6 /linkinpark/lpanswers.html.

"Mike Shinoda: Illustration Alumni Story." ArtCenter College of Design. https: //www.artcenter.edu/about/alumni/alumni-stories/mike-shinoda.html.

MusicRadar. "Interview: Linkin Park's Mike Shinoda—'Chester's Voice Was Insane.'" MusicRadar, July 24, 2020. https://www.musicradar.com/news/interview -linkin-parks-mike-shinoda-chesters-voice-was-insane.

Phoenix LPLive220. "Linkin Park—New York, Roseland Ballroom 2000 (Full Show)." YouTube video, 27:05, November 24, 2019. https://www.youtube.com /watch?v=Qvm_jm9r-7I.

Qwerty95k. "Linkin Park—Roseland Ballroom, New York City 20.09.2000 (Full Show)." YouTube video, 34:07, August 27, 2017. https://www.youtube.com /watch?v=I5XuL3aYhBw.

Smith, Thomas. "Linkin Park's 'Hybrid Theory' Turns 15—the Story Behind Nu-Metal's 'Breakthrough Moment.'" *NME*, October 28, 2015. https://www .nme.com/blogs/nme-blogs/linkin-parks-hybrid-theory-turns-15-the-story -behind-nu-metals-breakthrough-moment-760711.

Witmer, Phil. "Beyond LinkinBall Z: The History of the Anime Music Video." *Vice*, July 13, 2016. https://www.vice.com/en/article/ryzyny/nie-tylko-linkinball-z -amatorskie-anime-w-teledyskach.

CHAPTER 9

DiMartino, Dave. "Parkin' with Linkin Park." Launch Music on Yahoo!, October 12, 2003. https://web.archive.org/web/20040217045653/http://launch.yahoo.com /read/feature.asp?contentID=212687.

Doyle, Tomas. "The Real Story Behind Linkin Park's Hybrid Theory." Louder, October 24, 2022. https://www.loudersound.com/features/the-real-story-behind -linkin-parks-hybrid-theory.

Griffiths, Neil. "Linkin Park's Early Success Sparked Rumours That They Were a 'Manufactured Boy Band.'" The Music, September 16, 2020. https: //themusic.com.au/news/mike-shinoda-linkin-park-boy-band-rumours-green -room-podcast-neil-griffiths/4TP59fT39vk/16-09-20.

"Linkin Park Text-Based Online Chat 11/30/2000." HOB.com, May 2, 2001. https://web.archive.org/web/20010502214435/http://hob.com/live /artistinterviews/001130linkinpark/.

"Metal-is.com Interview, Shut Up When I'm Talking to You." Mike Shinoda Clan, January 2001. https://web.archive.org/web/20110226001615 /http://mikeshinodaclan.com/media/interviews/metal-is-com-interview-shut -up-when-im-talking-to-you/.

Pappademas, Alex. "Revisit Our May 2003 Linkin Park Cover Story: How to Succeed in Rock n' Roll by Really, Really, Really Trying." *Spin*, July 20, 2017. https: //www.spin.com/2017/07/linkin-park-meteora-2003-profile/.

Sheffield, Rob. "Linkin Park's Compassionate Thrash." *Rolling Stone*, March 29, 2001. https://www.rollingstone.com/music/music-features/linkin-parks -compassionate-thrash-191959/.

"Transcript: LPU Chat with Chester." Linkin Park Association Forums, August 2, 2011. https://www.lpassociation.com/forum/threads/transcript-lpu-chat-with -chester.34537/?t=34537.

CHAPTER 10

Alleva, Dan. "Mike Shinoda Dismisses the Idea That Chester Bennington Hated 'In the End.'" Metal Injection, March 4, 2023. https://metalinjection.net/news /mike-shinoda-dismisses-the-idea-that-chester-bennington-hated-in-the-end.

Baltin, Steve. "Chester Bennington Opens Up About His Past Addictions." Noisecreep, July 16, 2009. https://noisecreep.com/chester-bennington-opens-up-about-his-past-addictions/.

Depeche Mode. "Linkin Park: Early Depeche Mode Influences." Facebook, May 19, 2017. https://www.facebook.com/depechemode/videos/10156109003515329/.

"In the End Genius Annotation." Genius. https://genius.com/annotations/3540271/standalone_embed.

"Linkin Park Text-Based Online Chat 11/30/2000." HOB.com, May 2, 2001. https://web.archive.org/web/20010502214435/http://hob.com/live/artistinterviews/001130linkinpark/.

"Linkin Park Web Interview." Mike Shinoda Clan, September 2000. https://web.archive.org/web/20110226001609/http://mikeshinodaclan.com/media/interviews/linkin-park-web-interview/.

m_shinoda. "I found the photos." Instagram post, October 10, 2020. https://www.instagram.com/p/CGK4LU1A-BW/.

Mike's posts. Lpproventheory.20m.com, July 7–December 8, 2002. http://lpproventheory.20m.com/studioreports.html.

Morton, Luke. "The Secret History of Linkin Park's Hybrid Theory: In Their Own Words." *Kerrang!*, October 7, 2020. https://www.kerrang.com/the-secret-history-of-linkin-parks-hybrid-theory-in-their-own-words.

Tyrangiel, Josh. "Linkin Park Steps Out." *Time*, January 20, 2002. https://content.time.com/time/magazine/article/0,9171,195312-2,00.html.

CHAPTER 11

Fresch, Will. "An Interview with Rob Bourdon." Linkin Park Times, March 2003. http://web.archive.org/web/20040807103427if_/http://lptimes.com/article/Crazewire_031203.html.

Howard Stern Show. "Mike Shinoda Opens Up About Losing Chester Bennington." YouTube video, 3:50, February 15, 2023. https://www.youtube.com/watch?v=bDNCQQvH8Oc.

Lamacq, Steve. "Evening Session Interview with Steve Lamacq—Uncut." Linkin Park Times, January 23, 2008; reprint, BBC Radio, June 13, 2001. https://web.archive.org/web/20080123122820/http://lptimes.com/article/BBC_061301.html.

Linkin Park. *Frat Party at the Pankake Festival*. DVD. Produced by Bill Berg-Hillinger, Joe Hahn, David May, and Angela Smith. Warner Reprise Video, Warner Bros. Records, November 20, 2001.

Linkin Park Live Archive. "Linkin Park—Wantagh, New York (2001.08.09; Gonna Meet a Rockstar)." YouTube video, 12:18, December 17, 2019. https://www.youtube.com/watch?v=Ay0y_x20sA4.

Linkinpedia. "Projekt Revolution 2002." Linkinpedia.com, last edited March 26, 2019. https://linkinpedia.com/index.php?title=Projekt_Revolution_2002.

Lipshutz, Jason. "Inside Linkin Park's 'Meteora' Return & How It Spawned the Year's Most Unlikely Rock Smash." *Billboard*, April 6, 2023. https://www.billboard .com/music/rock/linkin-park-meteora-feature-interviews-lost-1235298905/.

"Mike Shinoda on the Making of 'Meteora.'" Audacy.com, February 9, 2023. https: //www.audacy.com/podcast/audacy-interviews-9c131/episodes/mike-shinoda -on-the-making-of-meteora-bb848.

Pappademas, Alex. "Revisit Our May 2003 Linkin Park Cover Story: How to Succeed in Rock n' Roll by Really, Really, Really Trying." *Spin*, July 20, 2017. https: //www.spin.com/2017/07/linkin-park-meteora-2003-profile/.

CHAPTER 12

Baltin, Steve. "News: Linkin Park Ready Remix Album." *Rolling Stone*, February 22, 2002. http://web.archive.org/web/20020814214502/http://rollingstone.com/news /newsarticle.asp?nid=15468.

Davis, Darren. "Linkin Park's Bennington Praises Korn Singer's 'Damned' Lyrics." Launch—Your Yahoo! Music Experience, February 13, 2002. https://web .archive.org/web/20021116052333/http://launch.yahoo.com:80/read/news .asp?contentID=207702.

Holson, Laura M. "Young Band, Derailed Dream." *New York Times*, October 1, 2002. https://www.nytimes.com/2002/10/01/arts/young-band-derailed-dream .html?pagewanted=all.

Jenison, David. "X-Ecutioners Turn the Tables." E! Online, February 26, 2002. https://www.eonline.com/news/42918/x-ecutioners-turn-the-tables.

Linkin Park. "One Step Closer [Official Live on Late Night with Conan O'Brien]— Linkin Park." YouTube video, 2:52, January 16, 2021. https://www.youtube .com/watch?v=KVdwfjVSLnA.

Linkin Park Lives. "MTV Video Music Awards 2002 (Best Rock Video) Linkin Park." YouTube video, 1:59, January 14, 2020. https://www.youtube.com /watch?v=ocMGyIIxS6E.

Miss Mushrooms. "Rolling Stones [*sic*] Interview with Linkin Park April 2002 [Scribe]." Miss Mushrooms (blog), April 23, 2013. https://missmushrooms.wordpress .com/2013/04/23/rolling-stones-interview-with-linkin-park-april-2002-scribe/.

MTV UK. "Linkin Park | My Life on MTV | MTV Music." YouTube video, 5:14, June 11, 2021. https://www.youtube.com/watch?v=DM7d9-iBiHA.

Shinoda, Anna. "College, Sunset Strip, and Meeting Mike." Anna Shinoda, July 24, 2013. https://annashinoda.wordpress.com/2013/07/24/college-sunset-strip -and-meeting-mike/.

Swift, Rob. "The X-Ecutioners on MTV's TRL." YouTube video, 4:31, December 8, 2020. https://www.youtube.com/watch?v=GJTVQN6f894.

Tyrangiel, Josh. "Linkin Park Steps Out." *Time*, January 20, 2002. https://content .time.com/time/magazine/article/0,9171,195312-2,00.html.

Velez, Gonzalo. "LINKIN PARK—One Step Closer—Live MTV 2001," YouTube video, 3:24, August 3, 2020.

Wiederhorn, Jon. "Linkin Park Offer No Warning from Their Machine Shop." MTV, August 20, 2004. https://www.mtv.com/news/66jbmo/linkin-park -offer-no-warning-from-their-machine-shop.

CHAPTER 13

Quotations of the band members in this chapter that have never been published before derive from interviews I conducted with the guys for my feature story "Inside Linkin Park's 'Meteora' Return & How It Spawned the Year's Most Unlikely Rock Smash," in *Billboard* magazine, listed below.

"Breaking the Habit by Linkin Park." Songfacts. https://www.songfacts.com/facts /linkin-park/breaking-the-habit.

"A Chat with Linkin Park Bassist Phoenix." Linkin Park Times; reprint, *Manila Times*, June 3, 2004. http://web.archive.org/web/20040807062939if_/http: //lptimes.com/article/ManilaTimes_062104.html.

Easier to Run. "Linkin Park—Work in Progress (Full DVD) HD/60fps Meteora|20." YouTube video, 1:03:53, April 29, 2023. https://www.youtube.com /watch?v=pSHinG2n9hA.

"Linkin Park Are Saving the Best for Last." Linkin Park Times; reprint, MTVU.com, May 11, 2004. http://web.archive.org/web/20040807103347if_/http://lptimes .com/article/MTV_051104.html.

Linkinpedia. "Meteora." Linkinpedia.com. https://linkinpedia.com/index.php?title =Meteora.

Lipshutz, Jason. "Inside Linkin Park's 'Meteora' Return & How It Spawned the Year's Most Unlikely Rock Smash." *Billboard*, April 6, 2023. https://www.billboard .com/music/rock/linkin-park-meteora-feature-interviews-lost-1235298905/.

Molanphy, Chris. "Justin Timberlake and the AC/DC Rule." The Record, NPR, April 5, 2013. https://www.npr.org/sections/therecord/2013/04/04/176269938 /justin-timberlake-and-the-ac-dc-rule.

"Shoutweb Track by Track with Mike Shinoda." Mike Shinoda Clan, March 2023. mikeshinodaclan.com/media/interviews/shoutweb-track-by-track-with -mike-shinoda/.

CHAPTER 14

Casteel, Jay. "Mike Shinoda: The Mash-Up." BallerStatus, December 6, 2004. http: //web.archive.org/web/20041217172749/http://www.ballerstatus.net/beyond /read/id/49215265/.

"Jay-Z: The Fresh Air Interview." NPR, November 16, 2010. https://www.npr .org/2010/11/16/131334322/the-fresh-air-interview-jay-z-decoded.

Moss, Corey. "Grey Album Producer Danger Mouse Explains How He Did It." MTV, March 11, 2004. https://www.mtv.com/news/1krgx6/grey-album -producer-danger-mouse-explains-how-he-did-it.

Phoenix LPLive220. "Linkin Park Feat. Jay-Z—Collision Course: Live 2004 (Full DVD Special)." YouTube video, 45:02, April 8, 2020. https://www.youtube .com/watch?v=7PxHzl8piJY.

Pollack, Phyllis. "The Battle over the Double Black CD." CounterPunch, March 23, 2004. https://www.counterpunch.org/2004/03/23/the-battle-over-the -double-black-cd/.

Reid, Shaheem. "Remixers Turn Jay-Z's Black Album Grey, White and Brown." MTV, January 26, 2004. https://www.mtv.com/news/82lon1/remixers-turn -jay-zs-black-album-grey-white-and-brown.

Shih, Kevin. "Grammys LP and JZ." YouTube video, 1:28, February 10, 2006. https: //www.youtube.com/watch?v=lHbOu5kZnag.

Sorcinelli, Gino. "How 'The Grey Album' Re-Invented the Remix." Micro-Chop, August 25, 2019. https://medium.com/micro-chop/how-the-grey -album-re-invented-the-remix-740e7c9f2631.

305thODST. "Linkin Park—on the Record with FUSE." YouTube video, 14:58, August 9, 2011. https://www.youtube.com/watch?v=rU_zGY3PyLA.

Watkins (@GrouchyGreg). "Linkin Park: Walk This Way." AllHipHop, November 10, 2004. https://allhiphop.com/features/linkin-park-walk-this-way/.

Wiederhorn, Jon. "14 Years Ago: Linkin Park Team with Jay-Z on 'Collision Course.'" Loudwire, November 30, 2018. https://loudwire.com/linkin -park-jay-z-collision-course-album-anniversary/.

———. "Jay-Z and Linkin Park Show Danger Mouse How It's Done." MTV, October 4, 2004. https://www.mtv.com/news/6hj1hm/jay-z-and -linkin-park-show-danger-mouse-how-its-done.

CHAPTER 15

Arango, Tim. "Linkin Park Mulls Leaving the Firm." *New York Post*, June 17, 2006. https://web.archive.org/web/20060617200835/http://www.nypost.com /business/64027.htm.

Billboard Staff. "Linkin Park Wants out of Warner Bros. Contract." *Billboard*, May 2, 2005. https://www.billboard.com/music/music-news/linkin -park-wants-out-of-warner-bros-contract-1412993/.

Blabbermouth. "Linkin Park's Chester Bennington Recalls Days of Drug Abuse." Blabbermouth.net, December 8, 2016. https://blabbermouth.net/news/linkin -parks-chester-bennington-recalls-days-of-drug-abuse.

Brockwell, Jen. "Talinda Bennington." LinkinLady.net, May 10, 2013. https: //web.archive.org/web/20130510185010/http://www.linkinlady.net/2005/05 /talinda-bentley.html.

Flynn, Katherine. "Back Story: A Different Tune with Linkin Park's Mike Shinoda." *Preservation Magazine*, National Trust for Historic Preservation, Spring 2016. https://savingplaces.org/stories/back-story-a-different-tune-mike-shinoda.

Kreps, Daniel. "Linkin Park's Bennington Readies Side Project Dead by Sunrise." *Rolling Stone*, July 9, 2009. https://www.rollingstone.com/music/music-news /linkin-parks-bennington-readies-side-project-dead-by-sunrise-93322/.

Latest entries, Linkin Park Numb Journals. December 13, 2005. https://web.archive
.org/web/20051213200317/http://www.linkinpark.com/lpc/journalview
.php?id=12.

"A Letter from Anna Shinoda to the Members of Projekt Charity." LiveJournal,
Greenwheelfans. https://greenwheelfans.livejournal.com/20701.html.

Lim, Cathy. "Getting Back to His Roots." *Rafu Shimpo—L.A. Japanese Daily News*,
April 28, 2006. https://web.archive.org/web/20120314055559/http://www.rafu
.com/mike_shinoda.html.

"Linkin Park Will Stay with Warner Music." *New York Times*, December 28, 2005.
https://www.nytimes.com/2005/12/28/arts/music/linkin-park-will-stay-with
-warner-music.html?_r=0.

"Millions Gather for Live 8–Jul 2, 2005." CNN, July 3, 2005. https://www.cnn
.com/2005/SHOWBIZ/Music/07/02/live8.main/.

Moss, Corey. "Metal MC Shinoda, Mellow Singer Brook Reveal How They
Hooked Up." MTV, June 5, 2006. https://www.mtv.com/news/bx86cl/metal
-mc-shinoda-mellow-singer-brook-reveal-how-they-hooked-up.

"Our Story." Music for Relief. https://musicforrelief.org/our-story/.

"Profile: Mike Shinoda." Discover Nikkei, October 19, 2006. https://discovernikkei
.org/en/nikkeialbum/albums/546/slide/?page=9.

Qwerty95k. "Linkin Park—Rock Am Ring 2004 (Full Show)." YouTube video,
1:11:13, August 16, 2018. https://www.youtube.com/watch?v=sJy_PpcV478.

Ramirez, Carlos. "A Chat with Chester Bennington." Bullz-Eye.com, December 11, 2009. http://www.bullz-eye.com/music/interviews/2009/chester
_bennington.htm.

CHAPTER 16

"Kerrang Track by Track MTM Interview." Linkin Park Times, April 4, 2007. http:
//web.archive.org/web/20070506210215/http://lptimes.com/news2007/april
/news04042007.html.

Linkin Park. "The Making of Minutes to Midnight (Minutes to Midnight DVD)—
Linkin Park." YouTube video, 39:58, May 15, 2021. https://www.youtube.com
/watch?v=XazANPCQ4UI.

Montgomery, James. "Linkin Park Finish Apocalyptic Album, Revive Projekt Revolution Tour." MTV, March 6, 2007. https://www.mtv.com/news/ryxs56/linkin
-park-finish-apocalyptic-album-revive-projekt-revolution-tour.

Moss, Corey. "Linkin Park Say Nu-Metal Sound Is 'Completely Gone' on Next
LP." MTV, September 27, 2006. https://www.mtv.com/news/km2r20/linkin
-park-say-nu-metal-sound-is-completely-gone-on-next-lp.

———. "Rubin Turns to Linkin Park, Weezer After Winning Buckets of Grammys." MTV, February 13, 2007. https://www.mtv.com/news/0k2ec8/rubin
-turns-to-linkin-park-weezer-after-winning-buckets-of-grammys.

Shimazu, Harrison. "Mike Shinoda on Crafting Meteora, Songwriting, and the
Art of Vocal Production." Splice Blog, June 5, 2023. https://splice.com/blog
/mike-shinoda-interview-meteora-20th-anniversary/.

CHAPTER 17

Baltin, Steve. "Chester Bennington Opens Up About His Past Addictions." Noisecreep, July 16, 2009. https://noisecreep.com/chester-bennington-opens-up-about-his-past-addictions/.

Barbour, Rob, with Merlin Alderslade. "Chester Bennington Would Have Turned 47 Today. In 2017, in His Final Interview, He Gave Us These Touching Words About His Friend and Hero, Chris Cornell." Louder, March 20, 2023. https://www.loudersound.com/features/chester-bennington-would-have-turned-47-today-in-2017-in-his-final-interview-he-gave-us-these-touching-words-about-his-friend-and-hero-chris-cornell.

Dehcode Paradise. "Linkin Park Chester Bennington Last Full Interview." YouTube video, 42:59, July 30, 2017. https://www.youtube.com/watch?v=lmYQy-vzeBQ.

Hahninator. "Mike's Dead by Sunrise Update." Linkin Park Live, February 4, 2009. https://lplive.net/forums/topic/1014-mikes-dead-by-sunrise-update/.

Kelly, Amy. "Chester Bennington: 'Now I Can Write About Anything I Want.'" UltimateGuitar.com, 2009. https://www.ultimate-guitar.com/news/interviews/chester_bennington_now_i_can_write_about_anything_i_want.html.

Sherman, Maria. "The 7 Most Inspiring Things Gerard Way Has Ever Said." *Alternative Press*, June 15, 2017. https://www.altpress.com/my_chemical_romance_gerard_way_inspiring_quotes/.

"Shoutweb Track by Track with Mike Shinoda." Mike Shinoda Clan, March 2023. mikeshinodaclan.com/media/interviews/shoutweb-track-by-track-with-mike-shinoda/.

Simpson, Dave. "Chris Cornell: 'As a Performer, I'm Able to Do What I Want.'" *The Guardian*, March 13, 2009. https://www.theguardian.com/music/2009/mar/13/chris-cornell-interview-soundgarden-audioslave.

Stout, Gene. "As a Paris Restaurateur and Family Man, Life Is Now Good for Audioslave Rocker" *Seattle Post-Intelligencer*, April 20, 2006. https://www.seattlepi.com/ae/music/article/As-a-Paris-restaurateur-and-family-man-life-is-1201602.php.

TeamRock. "Thinking Out Loud: Chester Bennington on Drugs, Success and Going to the Shops." Louder, December 6, 2016. https://www.loudersound.com/features/chester-bennington-interview-linkin-park.

Walthall, Jessica. "The Evolution of the Mental Health Movement: NAMI: National Alliance on Mental Illness." National Alliance on Mental Health, June 1, 2020. https://www.nami.org/Blogs/NAMI-Blog/June-2020/The-Evolution-of-the-Mental-Health-Movement.

CHAPTER 18

Breihan, Tom. "Jay-Z Reps for Grizzly Bear." *Pitchfork*, August 31, 2009. https://pitchfork.com/news/36372-jay-z-reps-for-grizzly-bear/.

Erlewine, Stephen Thomas. "A Thousand Suns by Linkin Park Review." AllMusic. https://www.allmusic.com/album/a-thousand-suns-mw0002023497. Accessed January 26, 2024.

Gallo, Phil. "Linkin Park Use New Marketing Techniques to Connect with Fans." *Billboard*, June 15, 2012. https://www.billboard.com/music/music-news /linkin-park-use-new-marketing-techniques-to-connect-with-fans-1093535/.

Graff, Gary. "Linkin Park Hard at Work on Next Album." *Billboard*, May 22, 2009. https://www.billboard.com/music/music-news/linkin-park-hard-at-work-on -next-album-268559/.

Linkin Park. "Meeting of a Thousand Suns (A Thousand Suns DVD)—Linkin Park." YouTube video, 29:45, September 14, 2020. https://www.youtube.com /watch?v=t_lwT0lkO8Y.

"Linkin Park: Career Overview in Games." MetaCritic, September 28, 2010. https: //www.metacritic.com/person/linkin-park.

Lynch, Joe. "Linkin Park's Landmark 'Hybrid Theory': Looking Back on the (Not So Nice) Reviews It Got in 2000." *Billboard*, July 20, 2017. https://www.billboard .com/music/rock/linkin-park-hybrid-theory-reviews-7873850/.

Montgomery, James. "Linkin Park Bury 'A Thousand Suns' 'Concept Record' Talk." MTV, September 15, 2010. https://www.mtv.com/news/ecw82t/linkin -park-bury-a-thousand-suns-concept-record-talk.

———. "Linkin Park Say New Single 'The Catalyst' Is 'a Risk, but Worth It.'" MTV, August 12, 2010. https://www.mtv.com/news/160m9j/linkin -park-say-new-single-the-catalyst-is-a-risk-but-worth-it.

———. "Linkin Park's 'A Thousand Suns': 'Kid A,' All Grown Up?" MTV, August 31, 2010. https://www.mtv.com/news/sme6cs/linkin-parks-a-thousand-suns -kid-a-all-grown-up.

Recording Academy. "Arcade Fire Accepting the Grammy for Album of the Year at the 53rd Grammy Awards." YouTube video, 0:56, February 14, 2011. https: //www.youtube.com/watch?v=f5npCMAok-M.

Segall, Laurie. "Digital Music Sales Top Physical Sales." CNN Money, January 5, 2012. https://money.cnn.com/2012/01/05/technology/digital_music_sales/index .htm.

Shimazu, Harrison. "Mike Shinoda on Crafting Meteora, Songwriting, and the Art of Vocal Production." Splice Blog, June 5, 2023. https://splice.com/blog /mike-shinoda-interview-meteora-20th-anniversary/.

Shinoda Livestreams. "9.14.20—A Thousand Suns Style Track to Celebrate ATS Anniversary." YouTube video, 3:01:43, September 16, 2020. https://www .youtube.com/watch?v=Enh5qT3hBU0.

"A Thousand Suns by Linkin Park." MetaCritic. https://www.metacritic.com /music/a-thousand-suns/linkin-park/critic-reviews. Accessed December 6, 2023.

305thODST. "Linkin Park—on the Record with Fuse." YouTube video, 14:58, August 9, 2011. https://www.youtube.com/watch?v=rU_zGY3PyLA.

Trust, Gary. "Ten Years Ago, the Digital Download Era Began on the Hot 100." *Billboard*, February 12, 2015. https://www.billboard.com/pro /ten-years-ago-the-digital-download-era-began-on-the-hot-100/.

CHAPTER 19

Baltin, Steve. "Chester Bennington on Stone Temple Pilots: 'Gonna Make a Lot of Music Together.'" *Rolling Stone*, May 31, 2013. https://www.rollingstone.com/music/music-news/chester-bennington-on-stone-temple-pilots-gonna-make-a-lot-of-music-together-176759/.

———. "Linkin Park Planning Album for Early Next Year." *Rolling Stone*, July 26, 2011. https://www.rollingstone.com/music/music-news/linkin-park-planning-album-for-early-next-year-181873/.

———. "Linkin Park's Mike Shinoda on the Band's 'Personal' New Album." *Rolling Stone*, June 20, 2012. https://www.rollingstone.com/music/music-news/linkin-parks-mike-shinoda-on-the-bands-personal-new-album-176062/.

Coare, Sam. "The Sun Goes Down . . . Chester Bennington: 1976–2017." *Kerrang!*, August 2, 2017. https://www.kerrang.com/the-sun-goes-down-chester-bennington-1976-2017.

"Congratulations 'A Light That Never Comes' Unlocked." LP Recharge, September 20, 2013. https://web.archive.org/web/20130920112114/http://www.lprecharge.com/congratulations-a-light-that-never-comes-unlocked/.

"Conversations with Stone Temple Pilot's [*sic*] Chester Bennington, Gavin DeGraw and Boz Scaggs, Plus a Pillars and Tongues Exclusive." *HuffPost*, October 28, 2013. https://www.huffpost.com/entry/conversations-with-stone_b_4168769.

Gallo, Phil. "Linkin Park Use New Marketing Techniques to Connect with Fans." *Billboard*, June 15, 2012. https://www.billboard.com/music/music-news/linkin-park-use-new-marketing-techniques-to-connect-with-fans-1093535/.

Goodwyn, Tom. "Linkin Park: 'Our New Record Is Far More Personal.'" *NME*, April 20, 2012. https://www.nme.com/news/music/linkin-park-34-1277138.

Graff, Gary. "Linkin Park's Joe Hahn Makes Directorial Debut with 'Mall': Watch an Exclusive Clip." *Billboard*, September 9, 2014. https://www.billboard.com/music/music-news/linkin-park-joe-hahn-mall-exclusive-clip-6244112/.

Linkin Park. "Buried at Sea (Part 1 of 2) | LPTV #67 | Linkin Park." YouTube video, 6:52, April 26, 2012. https://www.youtube.com/watch?v=BwCjI4mWPFI&list=PLC8B88958B81AB3E1&index=72.

Linkin Park. "Buried at Sea (Part 2 of 2) | LPTV #68 | Linkin Park." YouTube video, 4:31, May 4, 2012. https://www.youtube.com/watch?v=innqyiqAITs.

Linkin Park. "Meeting of a Thousand Suns (A Thousand Suns DVD)—Linkin Park." YouTube video, 29:45, September 14, 2020. https://www.youtube.com/watch?v=t_lwT0lkO8Y.

"Listen to the New Linkin Park + Steve Aoki Track 'A Light That Never Comes.'" KROQ, September 16, 2013. https://web.archive.org/web/20130919000833/http://kroq.cbslocal.com/2013/09/16/listen-to-the-new-linkin-park-steve-aoki-track-a-light-that-never-comes/.

RevolverEdit. "Interview: Linkin Park Talk the Importance of Underground Music, Improving Their Live Show, and What Has Kept the Band from Breaking Up." *Revolver*, July 29, 2014. https://www.revolvermag.com/music

/interview-linkin-park-talk-importance-underground-music-improving-their -live-show-and-what-has.

"Rolling Stone Chat with Mike Shinoda and Mike Einziger Summary." Linkin Park Association Forums, May 2, 2012. https://www.lpassociation.com/forum/threads /rolling-stone-chat-with-mike-shinoda-and-mike-einziger-summary.36166/.

Shimazu, Harrison. "Mike Shinoda on Crafting Meteora, Songwriting, and the Art of Vocal Production." Splice Blog, June 5, 2023. https://splice.com/blog/mike -shinoda-interview-meteora-20th-anniversary.

CHAPTER 20

Bennington, Chester (@ChesterBe). "GATS was too rock." X, May 25, 2017, 10:05 a.m. https://twitter.com/ChesterBe/status/867773573993078784.

Dehcode Paradise. "Linkin Park Chester Bennington Last Full Interview." YouTube video, 42:59, July 30, 2017. https://www.youtube.com/watch?v=lmYQy-vzeBQ.

Grow, Kory. "Inside Linkin Park's Heavy New Album: 'We Need to Weed Out the Emo.'" *Rolling Stone*, April 10, 2014. https://www.rollingstone.com/music/music-news /inside-linkin-parks-heavy-new-album-we-need-to-weed-out-the-emo-247025/.

Imagine Dragons (@Imaginedragons). "Linkin Park has been and always will be." X, May 20, 2018, 9:04 p.m. https://twitter.com/Imaginedragons/status /998399076822634503.

"Linkin Park Live—2014.06.22 Ventura, California." Linkin Park Live. https: //lplive.net/shows/2014/20140622.

"Linkin Park Underground." Linkin Park Wiki. https://linkinpark.fandom.com /wiki/Linkin_Park_Underground. Accessed December 6, 2023.

Oswald, Derek. "Linkin Park Discuss the Hunting Party and Upcoming Carnivores Tour." AltWire, August 6, 2014. https://www.altwire.net/2014/08/06 /linkin-park-carnivores-press-conference/.

Qwerty95k. "Linkin Park—Ventura, CA | Vans Warped Tour 2014 (Full Show) HD." YouTube video, 35:58, November 3, 2021. https://www.youtube.com/watch?v =x7nMZLrZoxA.

RevolverEdit. "Interview: Linkin Park Talk the Importance of Underground Music, Improving Their Live Show, and What Has Kept the Band from Breaking Up." *Revolver*, July 29, 2014. https://www.revolvermag.com/music/interview-linkin -park-talk-importance-underground-music-improving-their-live-show-and -what-has.

Ringen, Jonathan. "Billboard Cover: Twenty One Pilots on Their Musical Bromance and Fleeting Fame—'It's Going to Go Away.'" *Billboard*, April 7, 2016. https://www.billboard.com/music/music-news/billboard-cover-twenty-one -pilots-on-friendship-fans-fame-7325416/.

r/LinkinPark. s.v., "Saved life." Reddit. https://www.reddit.com/r/LinkinPark/search /?q=saved+life&cId=cf995610-c851-44f5-8a68-c08ce6fdb943&type=link. Accessed December 6, 2023.

Rock Sound. "Mike Shinoda on Linkin Park's Surprise Warped Tour Performance—Warped Tour Memories." YouTube video, 4:00, July 28, 2018. https://www.youtube.com/watch?v=J8ycd18UCcQ.

Shinoda Livestreams. "5.11.20—Brand New Collaboration, Working on the Track Live Now. Pt 2." YouTube video, 1:59:57, May 11, 2020. https://www.youtube.com/watch?v=g_rt27gHAPo.

Tagat, Anurag. "Linkin Park Return to Heavy Roots on New Album." *Rolling Stone India*, June 17, 2014. https://rollingstoneindia.com/linkin-park-return-heavy-roots-new-album/.

CHAPTER 21

Baltin, Steve. "Linkin Park Talk 2016 Album at Charity Poker Tournament: 'We Have a Mountain of Material.'" *Billboard*, April 7, 2016. https://www.billboard.com/music/rock/linkin-park-2016-album-charity-poker-tournament-interview-7325484/.

Bennington, Chester. Annotation on "I Don't Like My Mind Right Now / Stacking Up Problems That Are So Unnecessary." Genius, February 16, 2017. https://genius.com/11369511.

Bennington, Chester (@ChesterBe). "For those who value my opinion." X, January 27, 2017, 12:40 a.m. https://twitter.com/ChesterBe/status/824884713265328128.

Christman, Ed. "U.S. On-Demand Streams Passed 618 Billion in 2017, Outpacing Sales Declines Again." *Billboard*, January 5, 2018. https://www.billboard.com/music/music-news/on-demand-streams-618-billion-2017-outpacing-sales-declines-8092882/.

Dehcode Paradise. "Linkin Park Chester Bennington Last Full Interview." YouTube video, 42:59, July 30, 2017. https://www.youtube.com/watch?v=lmYQy-vzeBQ.

Graff, Gary. "Linkin Park's Mike Shinoda Talks 'Heavy' New Single & Hooking Up with Kiiara." *Billboard*, February 16, 2017. https://www.billboard.com/music/rock/linkin-parks-mike-shinoda-talks-heavy-new-single-hooking-up-with-7694010/.

Grow, Kory. "Inside Linkin Park Singer Chester Bennington's Last Days." *Rolling Stone*, August 4, 2017. https://www.rollingstone.com/music/music-news/chester-benningtons-last-days-linkin-park-singers-mix-of-hope-heaviness-124862/.

Hickie, James. "The Story of Linkin Park's One More Light: 'The Most Important Thing to Do Is to Connect with the People You Love.'" *Kerrang!*, January 14, 2021. https://www.kerrang.com/linkin-park-the-story-behind-their-final-album-one-more-light.

"Into the Light: Linkin Park's Chester Bennington and Mike Shinoda on New Album One More Light." *Irish News*, April 19, 2017. https://www.irishnews.com/arts/2017/04/19/news/into-the-light-linkin-park-s-chester-bennington-and-mike-shinoda-on-new-album-one-more-light-1001642/.

"Kerrang! Magazine Interview with Linkin Park." Linkin Park Association Forums, March 1, 2017. https://www.lpassociation.com/forum/threads/kerrang-magazine-interview-with-linkin-park.42875/.

Linkin Park. "Chester Breaks His Ankle on the Hunting Party Tour | LPTV #123 | Linkin Park." YouTube video, 8:22, May 16, 2015. https://www.youtube.com /watch?v=7TM_-iOMlaE.

"Listen: Linkin Park's Chester—'If You Call Us Sell-Outs, I'll Punch You in Your F—-ing Mouth.'" Kerrang! Radio, May 19, 2017. https://planetradio .co.uk/kerrang/entertainment/music/listen-linkin-park-s-chester-call-us-sell -outs-ll-punch-f-ing-mouth/.

"One More Light by Linkin Park." MetaCritic. https://www.metacritic.com/music /one-more-light/linkin-park. Accessed January 18, 2024.

102.7KIISFM. "Chester Bennington Live with JoJo." YouTube video, 21:57, February 21, 2017. https://www.youtube.com/watch?v=jky8GTCIuYA.

"Producing Linkin Park's One More Light." Waves Audio, July 13, 2017. https: //www.waves.com/producing-linkin-park-one-more-light.

CHAPTER 22

Barbour, Rob, with Merlin Alderslade. "Chester Bennington Would Have Turned 47 Today. In 2017, in His Final Interview, He Gave Us These Touching Words About His Friend and Hero, Chris Cornell." Louder, March 20, 2023. https://www .loudersound.com/features/chester-bennington-would-have-turned-47-today-in -2017-in-his-final-interview-he-gave-us-these-touching-words-about-his-friend -and-hero-chris-cornell.

Bartleet, Larry. "Mike Shinoda Discusses Chester Bennington's Reaction to Chris Cornell's Suicide." NME, July 21, 2017. https://www.nme.com/news/music /chester-bennington-chris-cornells-grief-2113797.

Bennington, Chester (@ChesterBe). "With all of my love @chriscornell." X, May 18, 2017, 9:28 a.m. https://twitter.com/ChesterBe/status/865227703091208192.

Bennington, Talinda (@TalindaB). "One of Chester's greatest gifts." X, December 10, 2019, 6:13 p.m. https://twitter.com/TalindaB/status/1204569826724737024.

Blistein, Jon. "Chester Bennington Laid to Rest as Fans Organize Memorials." Rolling Stone, August 1, 2017. https://www.rollingstone.com/music/music-news /chester-bennington-laid-to-rest-as-fans-organize-memorials-253516/.

Caulfield, Keith. "Linkin Park Streams Increase 730% in Wake of Chester Bennington's Death." Billboard, July 22, 2017. https://www.billboard.com/pro /linkin-park-streams-increase-chester-bennington-death/.

"Chester Bennington: Musicians, Famous Fans React to Linkin Park Singer's Death." Rolling Stone, July 20, 2017. https://www.rollingstone.com/music/music -news/chester-bennington-musicians-famous-fans-react-to-linkin-park-singers -death-201061/.

Dehcode Paradise. "Linkin Park Chester Bennington Last Full Interview." YouTube video, 42:59, July 30, 2017. https://www.youtube.com/watch?v=lmYQy-vzeBQ.

Farrell, David Phoenix (@phoenixlp). "Heartbroken." X, July 20, 2017, 2:09 p.m. https://twitter.com/phoenixlp/status/888128773492678657.

———. Home page. X. https://twitter.com/phoenixlp. Accessed December 6, 2023.

Gilmore, Joe. "Widow Says Chester Bennington Was 'Full of Life' in Weeks Before Death." KTAR News, February 7, 2018. https://ktar.com/story/1937081/benningtons-widow-speaks-husbands/.

Graff, Gary. "Linkin Park's Brad Delson 'Super Grateful' for Polarizing New Album's No. 1 Debut." *Billboard*, June 12, 2017. https://www.billboard.com/music/rock/linkin-park-brad-delson-one-more-light-debut-interview-7825898/.

Grow, Kory. "Chester Bennington's Autopsy Report Released." *Rolling Stone*, December 5, 2017. https://www.rollingstone.com/music/music-news/chester-benningtons-autopsy-report-released-128514/.

———. "Inside Linkin Park Singer Chester Bennington's Last Days." *Rolling Stone*, August 4, 2017. https://www.rollingstone.com/music/music-news/chester-benningtons-last-days-linkin-park-singers-mix-of-hope-heaviness-124862/.

———. "Linkin Park's Mike Shinoda Opens Up About Life After Chester Bennington." *Rolling Stone*, June 15, 2018. https://www.rollingstone.com/music/music-features/linkin-parks-mike-shinoda-opens-up-about-life-after-chester-bennington-628689/.

Linkin Park (@Linkinpark). "#OneMoreLight Live." X, November 15, 2017, 10:05 a.m. https://twitter.com/linkinpark/status/930844235816767488/photo/1.

"Meet Sean Dowdell of Club Tattoo." VoyagePhoenix, December 20, 2017. http://voyagephoenix.com/interview/meet-sean-dowdell-club-tattoo-scottsdale-north-scottsdale-mesa-tempe-also-2-locations-las-vegas/.

Monty's Vault. "Linkin Park—Chesters Last Show (Full Concert) Birmingham 2017." YouTube video, 1:48:37, July 26, 2017. https://www.youtube.com/watch?v=LurMLRvd6dI.

The Mountain Goats (@mountain_goats). "Linkin Park meant a lot." X, July 20, 2017, 1:52 p.m. https://twitter.com/mountain_goats/status/888124536041820165.

Mrjoehahn. "Always shining." Instagram, July 21, 2017. https://www.instagram.com/p/BW04iNpBmL9/.

———. "Dear Chester." Instagram, July 24, 2017. https://www.instagram.com/p/BW75xh6hcO6/.

o0rapture0o. "Linkin Park—Papercut (Live—Chester Falls!)." YouTube video, 3:47, October 16, 2007. https://www.youtube.com/watch?v=k6jfKkqlY6U.

r/LinkinPark. s.v., "Thank you Chester." Reddit, https://www.reddit.com/r/LinkinPark/search/?q=thank+you+chester&type=link&cId=627ad38f-e5b9-4103-80bb-5b28d0ff717d&iId=214b7b0f-cdd4-442c-bcb6-e6d87efaad21. Accessed December 6, 2023.

Shinoda, Mike (@Mikeshinoda). "Shocked and heartbroken, but it's true. An official statement will come out as soon as we have one." X, July 20, 2017, 1:03 p.m. https://twitter.com/mikeshinoda/status/888112045190561793.

Van Luling, Todd. "Blink-182 and Linkin Park Just Combined to Become Blinkin Park." *HuffPost*, May 4, 2017. https://www.huffpost.com/entry/blink-182-linkin-park_n_590b58c4e4b0104c734c9ceb.

CHAPTER 23

Cagle, Jess. "Mariah Carey: My Battle with Bipolar Disorder." *People*, April 11, 2018. https://people.com/music/mariah-carey-bipolar-disorder-diagnosis-exclusive/.

Chan, Anna. "Musicians Who Have Opened Up About Their Mental Health Struggles." *Billboard*, October 9, 2023. https://www.billboard.com/lists /stars-mental-health-issues-struggles/michelle-williams-mental-health/.

Graff, Gary. "Linkin Park's Brad Delson 'Super Grateful' for Polarizing New Album's No. 1 Debut." *Billboard*, June 12, 2017. https://www.billboard.com/music/rock /linkin-park-brad-delson-one-more-light-debut-interview-7825898/.

———. "Mike Shinoda Talks His 'Therapeutic' Solo Album & the Future of Linkin Park." *Billboard*, June 13, 2018. https://www.billboard.com/music/rock /mike-shinoda-post-traumatic-interview-8460533/.

Grow, Kory. "Linkin Park's Mike Shinoda Opens Up About Life After Chester Bennington." *Rolling Stone*, June 15, 2018. https://www.rollingstone.com/music /music-features/linkin-parks-mike-shinoda-opens-up-about-life-after-chester -bennington-628689/.

Linkin Park. "Linkin Park & Friends Celebrate Life in Honor of Chester Bennington—[Live from the Hollywood Bowl]." YouTube vide, 3:00:07, October 27, 2017. https://www.youtube.com/watch?v=9VoLHdADma8.

"Mike Shinoda Featured in Kerrang! Magazine: Interview About Chester, Grief, New Music and Art." Linkin Park Association Forums, March 21, 2018. https://www .lpassociation.com/forum/threads/mike-shinoda-featured-in-kerrang-magazine -interview-about-chester-grief-new-music-and-art.44321/.

Newman, Melinda. "Linkin Park Links Its Music for Relief Charity with Entertainment Industry Foundation: Exclusive." *Billboard*, March 21, 2018. https://www.billboard.com/music/music-news/linkin-park-music-for-relief -fund-entertainment-industry-foundation-8256072/.

"One More Light." Music for Relief. https://musicforrelief.org/one-more-light-fund/.

Shinoda, Mike (@mikeshinoda). "I have every intention." X, January 25, 2018, 11:54 a.m. https://twitter.com/mikeshinoda/status/956601196290064384.

Shinoda, Mike, with Ilana Kaplan. "Linkin Park's Mike Shinoda on Life After Chester Bennington, in His Own Words." *Vulture*, March 29, 2018. https://www.vulture .com/2018/03/linkin-park-mike-shinoda-interview-chester-bennington-death .html.

SiriusXM Entertainment. "Bassist Dave 'Phoenix' Pharrell Talks Future of Linkin Park." Soundcloud, December 11, 2018. https://soundcloud.com /siriusxmentertainment/bassist-dave-phoenix-pharrell-talks-future-of-linkin -park.

Stubblebine, Allison. "Linkin Park Announce 'One More Light' Live Album, Dedicate It to Late Frontman Chester Bennington in Heartbreaking Tweet." *Billboard*, November 15, 2017. https://www.billboard.com/music/rock/linkin-park -chester-bennington-one-more-light-live-album-8038404/.

"320 Changes Direction." Give an Hour. https://giveanhour.org/wellnessambassador /initiatives/320-changes-direction/.

CHAPTER 24

Badgalriri. "Literally the most impressive talent." Instagram, July 20, 2017. https: //www.instagram.com/p/BWx1hCWDYZX/?utm_source=ig_embed&ig _rid=6918e99b-1a8b-475b-b774-3f8906e18a17.

Baltin, Steve. "Linkin Park's Mike Shinoda on His Solo Career and Being a 'Debut Artist' Again." *Variety*, May 14, 2018. https://variety.com/2018/music/news /linkin-parks-mike-shinoda-on-his-solo-album-and-concerts-and-being -debut-artist-again-1202809352/.

Bennington, Talinda (@TalindaB). "One of Chester's greatest gifts." X, December 10, 2019, 6:13 p.m. https://twitter.com/TalindaB/status/1204569826724737024.

Carter, Emily. "Fever 333 Share Awesome Cover of Linkin Park's In the End." *Kerrang!*, October 28, 2020. https://www.kerrang.com/fever-333-share -awesome-cover-of-linkin-parks-in-the-end.

———. "Mike Shinoda: There's No New Linkin Park Album in the Pipeline." *Kerrang!*, April 25, 2022. https://www.kerrang.com/mike-shinoda -theres-no-new-linkin-park-album-in-the-pipeline.

———. "Mike Shinoda on a Linkin Park Live Return: 'Now Is Not the Time.'" *Kerrang!*, October 28, 2021. https://www.kerrang.com/mike-shinoda -on-a-linkin-park-live-return-now-is-not-the-time.

"Chester Bennington's First Band Enlist His Son to Re-Record Classic Songs" *Kerrang!*, February 12, 2019. https://www.kerrang.com/chester-benningtons -first-band-enlist-his-to-re-record-classic-songs.

Dowd, Rachael. "Here's How Mike Shinoda Created His New Album Entirely on Twitch." *Alternative Press*, June 30, 2020. https://www.altpress.com/mike -shinoda-twitch-dropped-frames-vol-1-album/.

Eun-byel, Im. "[Herald Interview] Linkin Park's Joe Hahn Talks Band, K-Pop, Future Plans." *Korea Herald*, April 25, 2019. http://www.koreaherald.com/view .php?ud=20190425000787.

———. "Linkin Park's Joe Hahn Shares Epiphany Through Photo Exhibition in Korea." *Korea Herald*, July 19, 2019. https://www.koreaherald.com/view .php?ud=20190719000538.

Graff, Gary. "Mike Shinoda Talks His 'Therapeutic' Solo Album & the Future of Linkin Park." *Billboard*, June 13, 2018. https://www.billboard.com/music/rock /mike-shinoda-post-traumatic-interview-8460533/.

Grave Danger. "'Heavy Immortal' (Evanescence vs. Linkin Park Ft. Kiiara) [Grave Danger Mashup]." YouTube video, 4:46, November 24, 2019. https://www .youtube.com/watch?v=mFRPzXnsoqY.

Grow, Kory. "Linkin Park's Mike Shinoda Opens Up About Life After Chester Bennington." *Rolling Stone*, June 15, 2018. https://www.rollingstone.com/music /music-features/linkin-parks-mike-shinoda-opens-up-about-life-after-chester -bennington-628689/.

Kill_mR_DJ mashups. "Marshmello vs Linkin Park vs Twenty Øne Piløts—Talking to Wolves (Kill_mR_DJ Mashup)." YouTube video, 4:30, December 1, 2017. https://www.youtube.com/watch?v=z3HtoCfkZyQ.

Linkin Park. "Linkin Park Reacts to a Linkin Park Show from 2001." YouTube video, 49:44, March 24, 2020. https://www.youtube.com/watch?v=G3mk142cZjI.

"Linkin Park Have Been Working on New Music." Kerrang!, April 28, 2020. https://www.kerrang.com/linkin-park-have-been-working-on-new-music.

"Linkin Park's Joe Hahn Will Judge a Korean Reality TV Show." Kerrang!, April 16, 2019. https://www.kerrang.com/linkin-parks-joe-hahn-will-judge-a-korean-reality-tv-show.

Lipshutz, Jason. "The Story Behind Every Song on Linkin Park's 'Hybrid Theory': 20th Anniversary Track-by-Track." Billboard, October 5, 2020. https://www.billboard.com/music/rock/linkin-park-hybrid-theory-20th-anniversary-track-by-track-9460473/.

LPL Staff. "Review: Mike Shinoda's Post Traumatic Tour." Linkin Park Live, November 5, 2018. https://lplive.net/forums/topic/13588-review-mike-shinodas-post-traumatic-tour/.

"Mike Shinoda Featured in Kerrang! Magazine: Interview About Chester, Grief, New Music and Art." Linkin Park Association Forums, March 21, 2018. https://www.lpassociation.com/forum/threads/mike-shinoda-featured-in-kerrang-magazine-interview-about-chester-grief-new-music-and-art.44321/.

"Mike Shinoda Praises Mark Morton for Chester Bennington Collaboration." Kerrang!, January 14, 2019. https://www.kerrang.com/mike-shinoda-praises-mark-morton-for-chester-bennington-collaboration.

Rhine Fan Account (@LPRhinestone). "Billie's favorite Linkin Park song." X, June 29, 2022, 10:24 p.m. https://twitter.com/LPrhinestone/status/1542363301711167488?lang=en.

Shinoda, Mike, with Ilana Kaplan. "Linkin Park's Mike Shinoda on Life After Chester Bennington, in His Own Words." Vulture, March 29, 2018. https://www.vulture.com/2018/03/linkin-park-mike-shinoda-interview-chester-bennington-death.html.

Shinoda, Mike. Annotation on "They'll Tell You I Don't Care Anymore / and I Hope You'll Know That's a Lie." Genius, March 29, 2018. https://genius.com/14197212.

———. "Dropped Frames Volume 1 /// Available July 10th." Facebook, June 30, 2020. https://www.facebook.com/mikeshinoda/videos/300283931148039.

———. "Place to Start (Official Video)—Mike Shinoda." YouTube video, 2:12, January 25, 2018. https://www.youtube.com/watch?v=6tEQoF_8Z7s.

"This Mash-up of Linkin Park and Lady Gaga Is a Ridiculously Good Time." Kerrang!, October 8, 2020. https://www.kerrang.com/this-mash-up-of-linkin-parks-faint-and-lady-gagas-just-dance-is-a-ridiculously-good-time.

Trapp, Philip. "The Weeknd Admits His Deftones Influence, Honors Chester Bennington." Loudwire, August 19, 2021. https://loudwire.com/the-weeknd-deftones-chester-bennington-linkin-park/.

Travers, Paul. "10 Bands Who Wouldn't Be Here Without Linkin Park." *Kerrang!*, August 20, 2020. https://www.kerrang.com/10-bands-who-wouldnt -be-here-without-linkin-park.

CHAPTER 25

Blabbermouth. "Linkin Park Bassist on Band's Future: 'I Think That We Will Do Something Again at Some Point.'" Blabbermouth.net, April 7, 2023. https: //blabbermouth.net/news/linkin-park-bassist-on-bands-future-i-think-that-we -will-do-something-again-at-some-point.

Carter, Emily. "Fans Pay Tribute to Chester Bennington on the Fifth Anniversary of His Death." *Kerrang!*, July 20, 2022. https://www.kerrang.com/linkin-park -fans-pay-tribute-to-chester-bennington-on-the-fifth-anniversary-of-his-death.

Jenkins, Craig. "'We Were Obsessed.'" Vulture, April 3, 2023. https://www.vulture .com/2023/04/mike-shinoda-linkin-park-meteora.html.

"Linkin Park—Lost." Genius, February 10, 2023. https://genius.com/Linkin-park -lost-lyrics.

Lipshutz, Jason. "Inside Linkin Park's 'Meteora' Return & How It Spawned the Year's Most Unlikely Rock Smash." *Billboard*, April 6, 2023. https://www.billboard .com/music/rock/linkin-park-meteora-feature-interviews-lost-1235298905/.

rd1994. "Brads Notes on the Lost Demos." r/LinkinPark, Reddit, April 15, 2023. https://www.reddit.com/r/LinkinPark/comments/12n1qaq/brads_notes _on_the_lost_demos/?rdt=63817.

Ross, Alex Robert. "Mike Shinoda Returns to Linkin Park's Endless Winter." Fader, February 16, 2023. https://www.thefader.com/2023/02/16/mike -shinoda-returns-to-linkin-parks-endless-winter.

Shutler, Ali. "Mike Shinoda Suggests That New Linkin Park Music Is Possible." *NME*, February 12, 2023. https://www.nme.com/news/music/mike -shinoda-suggests-that-new-linkin-park-music-is-possible-3396978.

INDEX